Meeting the Middle East

Travels in Arabia

By Jason Smart

Text and Photographs Copyright © 2015 Jason Smart

All Rights Reserved. No part of this book may be reproduced or transmitted in any form or by any means, electronic or mechanical, including photocopying, recording, or any information storage and retrieval system, without prior written permission of the Author.

First English edition published in 2015 by Smart Travel Publishing

Cover design by Ace Graphics

ASIN: B00VTO4EGM
ISBN-13: 978-1511639736
ISBN-10: 1511639733

Smart, Jason J
Meeting the Middle East: Travels in Arabia

For Hayley

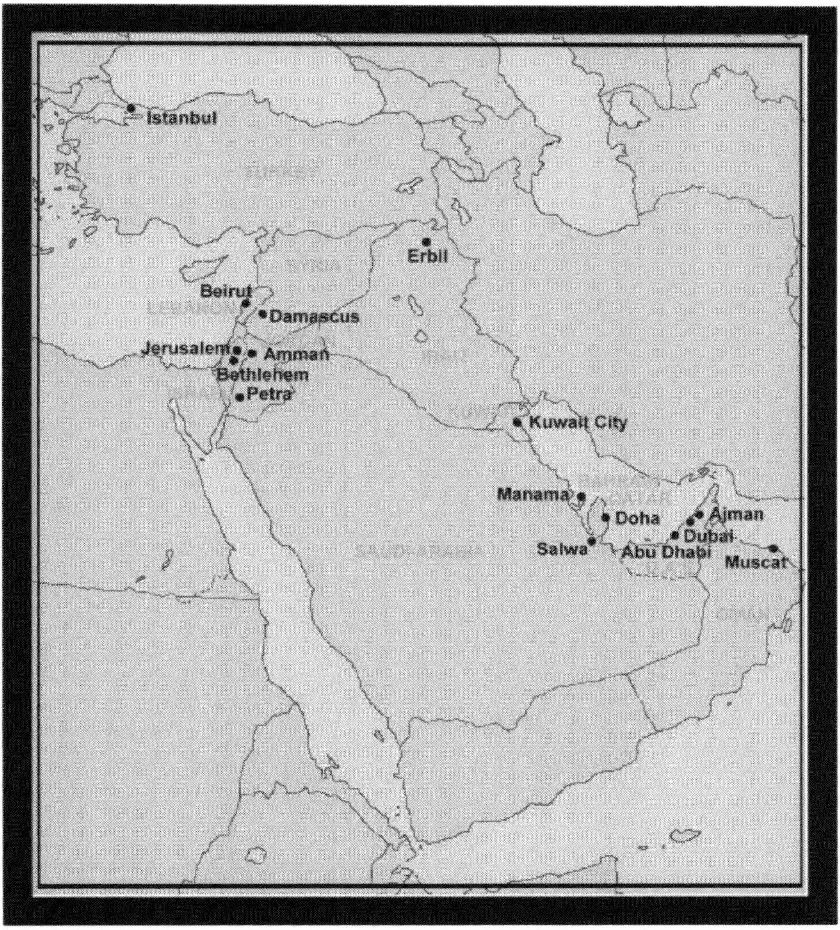
Istanbul
TURKEY
Erbil
SYRIA
Beirut
LEBANON
Damascus
JORDAN
Jerusalem
Amman
Bethlehem
IRAQ
Petra
Kuwait City
BAHRAIN
Manama
QATAR
Doha
Ajman
Dubai
Salwa
Abu Dhabi
SAUDI ARABIA
U.A.E.
Muscat
OMAN

Contents

Prologue 1

Chapter 1. The Glitz of Qatar 7

Chapter 2. A Transit through the Kingdom of Saudi Arabia 23

Chapter 3. Abu Dhabi: Capital of the Emirates 35

Chapter 4. Sightseeing in Qatar 49

Chapter 5. Dubai: Arabia made Easy 69

Chapter 6. Muscat, Oman – the quieter side of the Gulf 87

Chapter 7. The smallest state in Arabia: Bahrain 101

Chapter 8. Beirut and Byblos 115

Chapter 9. Istanbul: Where East meets West 131

Chapter 10. Onward to Jordan 145

Chapter 11. The Road to Damascus 161

Chapter 12. Petra and the Dead Sea 175

Chapter 13. Kuwait City 191

Chapter 14. A Day trip to Jerusalem 205

Chapter 15. Palestine and the Bible 225

Chapter 16. Iraqi Kurdistan 239

Chapter 17. Ending in Ajman 259

Prologue

The white Land Cruiser approached the rear of our saloon car, flashing its lights. I was overtaking a small bus filled with low-paid immigrant workers. The men were heading back to their work camp after completing their latest twelve hours of on one of the highway developments going on all across Qatar. Outside, a flat expanse of brown sand and marching electricity pylons filled the view: a typical scene outside the major towns. In the distance, a red sun was rapidly disappearing over the horizon.

Flash! Flash! Flash! The Land Cruiser was almost upon me, but I was still passing the bus in the second lane, my foot pressed flat down on the accelerator. A few workers wearily gazed at me, blankness in their eyes, tiredness on their faces.

FLASH! FLASH! FLASH! The silver grille of the 4x4 filled my rear-view mirror.

"There's another idiot behind me," I said to my wife. "He's up against my bumper." Angela turned round and shook her head. Both of us were used to this type of behaviour from aggressive Qatari drivers. I edged past the bus then decided to stage a small protest. I carried on for a few moments in the fast lane, relishing the fact I was annoying the man behind. He moved within a centimetre of our car, flashing more furiously than ever, but I hung on until I was ready. Two seconds more and I indicated I was going to move. The Arab driver was immediately upon me. The problem was that he miscalculated his overtaking manoeuvre and clipped my left bumper.

Two things happened.

First, the engine stalled and, second, the impact sent us careening onto the rough patch of highway that served as a rudimentary hard shoulder. Instinctively, I braked and came to a standstill, the inertia and silence inside the car almost unreal. Angela looked shell-shocked, gripping the side of her seat. The bus passed; every passenger staring. I released my grip on the steering wheel and glanced in the rear view mirror. Behind me, also at a standstill, was the white Land Cruiser.

2

"*What the hell was he playing at?*" I said to my wife. I was furious! Before Angela could stop me, I climbed into the heat of the Middle East, a temperature that could sap the strength of the unwary in minutes. The Land Cruiser was twenty metres away, and the driver, a man in his thirties wearing a white *thawb,* the long, ankle-length garment favoured by men in Arabia, was already emerging from the door. Dust was eddying around his car's headlights.

"Salaam alaikum," he said politely, *peace be upon you*, the standard greeting across the Arabic world. He didn't seem bothered or upset that he'd just rammed me off the road. His expression was neutral, perhaps even friendly, and, despite my bubbling anger, I noticed he was impeccably turned out: a gold pen in his top pocket, manicured black stubble on his angular face, expensive sandals on his feet and a white headdress clipped into place with a sturdy black band.

I didn't reply to the man's greeting. "You were *that* far from my bumper," I said sharply. I shook my head and tutted. Any accident, no matter how small or trivial, was a police matter in Qatar. Without an official piece of paper saying that the police had attended a bump, then no one would repair any damage. But at least the man had stopped, I reasoned. He could've easily driven off.

I looked at my rear bumper and mercifully saw no damage, not even a scratch in the paintwork. The Arab man inspected his car; it seemed damage-free, too. And that was when I noticed the hooded falcon inside his car. It was sitting in the central compartment between the front seats. I opened my mouth and then closed it.

"How is car?" the man asked, gesturing to my bumper.

"It's fine," I said.

"Good. So there is no problem."

"No problem? You just rammed me off the road!"

"But everything okay. No problem." He turned to leave.

I laughed despite myself. It seemed such an absurd situation to be in: a Qatari man transporting a hooded falcon across the desert while ramming cars off the road. I said, "We need to call the police."

The Arab man turned. "Why? No damage! Everything okay. Police waste our time."

He had a point. The police would take ages to arrive, and, when they did, there would be a lot of form filling and interviews. Then we'd have to contact our insurance companies – all for a collision that had caused no damage. Did I really want to sit in the desert for an hour if there was no need?

I nodded at the man. He nodded his head in return and we both walked to our vehicles.

3

"What did he say?" Angela asked.

"Nothing much. There was no damage, though. There wasn't much to say."

"Did he apologise?"

"Not really. He acted as if he did this sort of thing all the time."

I turned the ignition key and heard only the empty click of the starter motor. I tried it again, with the same result. The jolt from the Land Cruiser had probably knocked it out of commission. I tried it for a third time. Nothing. Maybe the Arab man had some jump leads we could use, and I glanced in the rear-view mirror. He was still there, speaking into his phone. I jumped out and ran to his car.

"My engine is not working." I said, miming me turning the ignition key and nothing happening.

The man in white nodded. "No problem. I push."

I nodded, fair enough. Maybe a jump-start would do the trick, especially since our car had manual transmission, though I couldn't imagine how he would push it; especially along a flat piece of rough terrain, but that was his problem, not mine. I rushed back to my car, engaged second gear and pushed in the clutch pedal. I informed Angela of our plan.

"He's going to push it? Are you sure?"

"That's what he said."

I looked in the mirror and saw the Land Cruiser rolling up behind me, bumper to bumper. So that was his plan – to push me with his car! He was waiting for me to give the signal. When I did, he gently made contact with the rear of our car and then let rip. A second later, he propelled us at speed along the sandy verge, crunching and jolting, until we reached sufficient speed for me to lift the clutch. I did so, gunning the accelerator at the same time, relieved when the engine caught and powered into life. I stuck my thumb in the mirror and the Land Cruiser slowed, allowing us to move under our own power. I drove for a few more seconds, waiting for the engine to conk out, but when it didn't, I swung onto the highway, relishing the smooth surface again. The Land Cruiser moved onto the highway too, pulling parallel to me. The man who had barged me off the highway was grinning. When I gave another thumbs-up, he waved and then tore off, no doubt to flash his lights at someone else further along. But I couldn't help but be impressed: the Qatari man had been calm, poised and polite throughout – a true gentleman, in fact.

Part 1

Qatar – Saudi Arabia – Abu Dhabi – Qatar

Chapter 1. The Glitz of Qatar

FCO travel advice: Most visits are trouble free. There is an underlying threat of terrorism. Road discipline in very poor; speeds are high. Qatar has a very high fatality rate for road accidents. Minor expressions of 'road rage' like rude gestures can attract significant penalties.

Even after three years of living and working in Qatar, the richest country in the world, the neon and glitz of Doha, its capital, could still make us gawp in amazement. A metallic whirlwind, a golden pyramid, a huge sphere and even a sleek torpedo were just some of the shapes on offer. At night, the skyscrapers of West Bay shone with blue, red and yellow neon, making it seem as if we were driving through a futuristic city in *Bladerunner*. Doha had one of the best skylines in the world.

The traffic was bad, though. If we weren't queued at traffic lights, or caught up in yet another roadwork-induced traffic snarl, motorists would be snapping at our bumper, weaving around and ignoring any form of basic lane discipline. No wonder Qatar has one of the world's worst safety records. In fact, being involved in a traffic accident is the most likely way to die in Qatar.

The worst drivers are young Qatari men. With no way of venting their flowing testosterone, young Qataris drive like true maniacs. Late at night, when the traffic is least busy, they tear along the highways, racing each other, performing mad stunts and leaving stupendous black skid marks on the road as they battle for supremacy. Many Qatari youths have powerful cars which, when coupled with a police system that does little to enforce traffic laws, sometimes ends in disaster. One of the worst accidents Angela and I read about involved an eighteen-year-old Qatari man driving his Land Cruiser at speed. For whatever reason, he smashed into the back of a parked car. A married Filipino couple, their one-year-old baby and two of their friends were inside the stationary car. The

Land Cruiser hit their car with such force that it rocketed forward, flipped sideways on the pavement and then burst into flames. All five people died at the scene. As for the Qatari youth, he was badly injured but alive, and when police looked into his driving record, they found he had no driving licence, no car insurance, and, in the thirteen months prior to the accident, had managed to rack up forty-four traffic volitions.

When Angela and I first arrived in Qatar, we had been understandably nervous about driving. Within a few days, we had seen the aftermath of a collision between a Land Cruiser and a Nepalese pedestrian. The poor man was lying dead at the side of the road, bent at an unnatural angle and surrounded by a group of his workmates. The police were interviewing the driver of the Land Cruiser, a local man, nearby.

A few weeks later, we passed the wreckage of a truck and a car. Inside the crumpled Mitsubishi Lancer was a woman slumped across the steering wheel. We couldn't tell whether she was dead or alive, but the blood pooling underneath the car was not a good sign. So the first time I sat behind the wheel in Qatar was a nerve-racking ordeal, made worse because I was driving on the right-hand side instead of the UK left. Despite this, I quickly grew to enjoy the high-octane journeys we took around Doha, especially since petrol was only one riyal (17p) a litre and U-turns, a manoeuvre banned in much of the developed world, were allowed. I grew accustomed to cars reversing along hard shoulders, or stopping on roundabouts for no reason, or racing past me at over 200km/hour, or flashing me incessantly with their lights or, best of all, blasting me with their horn if I delayed moving off from the green light for even half a nanosecond. In fact, after about six months, I became as bad as the rest of them.

2

Aside from its roads, Qatar is one of the safest countries in the world for Westerners to go about their business. Day or night, a person can walk down any street or alleyway and not fall foul of a dreadful deed. The murder rate in Qatar is enviably low but that's not to say the Qatari criminal justice system isn't busy: quite the opposite, in fact. The prisons are full to bursting, mainly with inmates from India, Nepal, the Philippines and Pakistan, incarcerated for petty crimes that wouldn't even warrant a caution in most other countries. One particularly memorable headline in the *Gulf Times* read: *Nepali Man Gets 1-Year Jail for Stealing Onions.* According to the article, the police managed to recover the onions.

Another story, typical of the type, involved a Filipino maid and a Bangladeshi driver. Their Arab employer caught them having 'illicit' relations in his house. According to the article, the man of the house returned home and noticed some strange shoes outside the maid's bedroom. Suspicious, he barged into her room, only to find the maid alone and fully clothed. Unfortunately, he also noticed the quivering (and equally fully clothed) Bangladeshi man hiding under the bed. The police came and arrested them, and the pair were jailed for a year, facing deportation as soon as their sentences ended. It was the standard punishment for virtually everything in Qatar.

Most Qatari families, and indeed many high-earning expats, have live-in maids. They are usually women from South East Asia or East Africa, flown in to do the housework and to look after the family's children. The vast majority of families treat their maids well, but enough stories of ill treatment filter through that when one absconds, it is not such a surprise. In Qatar, and much of the Gulf, leaving a job is not as simple as it sounds. Employing families sponsor all their maids and usually take possession of their passport on arrival. This effectively bars them from getting another job or leaving the country. The Qatari authorities claim this is to stop workers from stealing from their employers and then leaving the country. Amnesty International says it is a form of modern-day slavery. Whatever the viewpoint, a maid running away from a sponsoring family is a big deal.

When the family realise that their maid has absconded, they will call the police, who in turn will arrest and fine the maid. Because she has no income to pay the fine, the Qatari courts will detain her in a women's prison, populated by women in similar predicaments. Some will be there for absconding; others will be there for having illicit relations and a few will be in prison for having a baby out of wedlock. After one year, they will all be deported back to their home countries, where queues of other women will be waiting to replace them.

Go to any shopping mall in Doha, and trailing after rich families, pushing prams or carrying infants, are maids. Usually, they are dressed in 'maid' clothing: loose-fitting robes that resemble pyjamas. Angela couldn't stand the maid clothes, feeling they were demeaning to the women wearing them. But not all employing families treated their maids this way. One evening, Angela and I were celebrating her birthday in one of Doha's expensive restaurants when a Qatari woman wearing an *abaya*, a full-length black robe and head covering, strolled in with her two young children. Behind them was a Filipino maid. Instead of wearing pyjamas, she was in her own clothes. All four sat at the next table to ours. The maid was chatting away freely with the Qatari woman, laughing and joking, helping to cut the kids' food up before enjoying her own meal. All four clearly enjoyed each other's company. It was a lovely thing to see.

Another lovely thing about Qatar is the weather, at least between November and March. From April to October, it is unbearable: an oven-like heat that saps strength and makes standing outside for more than a few minutes a cause for concern. Once, in an attempt to investigate just how hot it was, we removed a chunk of chocolate from the fridge, donned our hats and stood outside. In less than a minute, the chocolate was running across Angela's hand, dripping to the ground. It really was *that* hot.

The best way to describe the heat is to imagine standing a few feet away from a raging bonfire. The heat that hits your face, sizzles your hair and burns your lungs is the same heat of a Qatari summer.

At least with a bonfire you can turn around or walk away. This perpetual heat does have one advantage: during the summer, wet clothes dry on the line in minutes. But whatever the month, the one thing that Qatar can virtually guarantee is waking up to sunshine streaming through the curtains.

3

Our curtains belonged to our apartment in Al Khor, a coastal town fifty kilometres north of Doha. It had originally been a fishing village but quickly turned into a service settlement for Ras Laffan Industrial City, Qatar's main centre for the production of liquefied natural gas – the source of almost all the country's income. At night, the gas flares of Ras Laffan hover on the horizon like ethereal orange ghosts. Despite being Qatar's second city, Al Khor only has a population of around 30,000. It has no skyscrapers, its taxi service is scant and unreliable, but it does have a long strip of shops (mostly general stores, hardware shops and shawarma cafes), together with a small food quarter known as Cholesterol Corner due to McDonald's, Hardee's and KFC all being next door to each other. It also has a lively fish market and a plush hotel that hardly anyone stays in because it doesn't serve alcohol.

One of the largest constructions in Al Khor is its football stadium. Lit by floodlights at night and capable of holding 20,000 people, it is home to the local team, Al Khor, a team playing in the top tier of Qatari football, the Qatari Stars League. One day, Angela and I went to support them, and, after paying the ridiculously cheap ten-riyal (£1.80) entrance fee, we entered the stadium to find thousands of empty seats, with perhaps only two hundred spectators. They were mostly young Qatari supporters under the direction of one fanatical fan with a drum. At his command, the Al Khor supporters offered a barrage of chanting, drumming and jolly Arabic singing, which did not let up until half time. When a man came around selling soft drinks from an ice cooler, Angela and I took our leave, glad we'd supported our local team, even if it was for only forty-five minutes.

4

Angela and I were driving in Doha when Qatar won the World Cup bid, an event that finally brought Qatar onto the world stage. We knew they had won because of the mass beeping and headlight flashing from the Land Cruisers, Hummers and Lexuses. This quickly turned into a mass celebration of gridlock and jubilant honking. Thirty minutes later, the traffic in the city centre was at a standstill and we were stuck in the middle, watching Qatari motorists waving flags (and in some cases, swords) or dancing along in the streets. Later, we heard that someone had brought their pet cheetah along for the fun too.

"You won't believe this," said a friend of ours a few days later. He worked as a construction site manager in Doha. "I've just finished working on a winter palace for a rich Qatari. You should see it: state of the art bedrooms, sweeping staircases and an Olympic-sized pool – the works. But the best thing is a running track for his pet leopards! Can you believe that! A racing track for leopards!"

The thing is, I could believe it. Qataris literally dripped with money, and exotic pets were just some of the trophies they bought. Another friend of ours, a teacher in Doha, told us a similar story. A Qatari boy in his class had just returned from a family holiday in South Africa. The six-year-old boy said he had shot and killed fifty rabbits. When our friend queried this, the boy was adamant. At hometime, the teacher questioned the boy's maid, who verified the story. She said that the whole family had driven to a farm in the African countryside where a large truck filled with hundreds of rabbits arrived. A man released the animals into a walled enclosure about the size of a tennis court, and then passed the children automatic weapons. By the time the carnage was over, about five hundred rabbits were dead: a horrific event to think about for most Westerners.

The Qatari authorities, on the other hand, tolerated a certain type of Western behaviour that many Muslims found abhorrent. Almost all of the top-end hotels in Doha served booze. Smoke-filled bars, such as the Irish Harp, the Rose & Thistle and the Sports Bar ran their happy hours between 5pm and 7pm, and that was when the bars were bursting with expats, quaffing pints of lager and glasses of wine for six pounds instead of the usual twelve. If a person didn't want to drink in one of the bars, then they could always drink at home, provided they had an alcohol licence. To obtain this important credit card-sized piece of plastic, an expat had to see an official at the Qatar Distribution Centre (known locally as the Booze Souq) to prove that they were not a Muslim and that they earned above the minimum threshold. After paying a 1000-riyal deposit (£180), the QDC's management issued them with a card that allowed entry into the only alcohol store in Qatar.

The first time Angela and I visited the Qatar Distribution Centre was a surreal experience. Inside its doors, people were pushing huge trolleys full of beer, wine, whisky and everything else that planes could fly into the country. Men and women were manhandling crates of beer and bumper packs of vodka onto their supersized trolleys. But as well as booze and a few expensive cigars, the booze souq sold something else: tucked in one part was a recent addition – a walk-in fridge filled with the most taboo foodstuff in Islam: pork; sausages, packs of bacon and joints of ham filled the cold shelves. On the fridge's first day of opening, there was almost a riot to get in.

5

The rate of construction going on all over Qatar was phenomenal. Gigantic building sites, forests of cranes and legions of construction workers, all scurrying over the shells of tomorrow's skyscrapers and stadiums, littered Doha and its suburbs. Even Al Khor was in the middle of a building boom, with shops and stores springing up hither and thither. Most would end up selling the same things: general household goods.

In these shops, platoons of low-paid, predominantly male, workers would loiter in the aisles, sit at the tills or mostly just wait for customers to enter their Logic Hyper Marts. These men were mainly Bangladeshis and Nepalese, earning around 900 riyals per month (£160), most of which they sent home to their families. They would do all the menial jobs that no one else wanted to do in Qatar: cleaning, gardening, labouring, supermarket bag packing, lorry driving and tea making. They worked six days a week, and on their day off, Friday, they formed themselves into cricket teams, or more likely, wandered around the shops of Al Khor strip.

Around sunset, hundreds of men, often in their best clothes, would gather around the grocery and hardware stores, shaking hands, topping up their mobile phones or wiring money to their families back home. Mostly, though, they just hung out with one another. Despite the high concentration of men, not once did we feel threatened. Yes, Angela was stared at a lot, as was every other western woman, but most of the time the ex-pat workers were deferential to us. In fact, it sometimes saddened us the way they would part to let us through, as if they believed us to be more important than them.

One time, Angela and I spotted a group of men crowding around something in one of the stores. Some were grinning; others were wide-eyed and transfixed. When they left, we walked over to find out what it was. It turned out to be a box of women's underwear; the men had been staring at the scantily clad model on the front.

Another funny story involved a female colleague of ours who had ventured into Al Khor one Friday evening to buy a few groceries. As she wandered the aisles, she felt the usual stares and ogles, but ignored them, used to such behaviour. As she rounded one aisle, though, she caught sight of a whole gang of men openly gawping at her chest. She finally cracked.

"Do you want to take a photo?" she snarled, hoping to shame them, but it had the opposite effect, for the men frantically pulled out their mobile phones to take a picture. Before they could do so, she turned tail and fled.

Shopping in Doha is an altogether different experience. The malls are huge, plush and full of every Western brand name you can think of. Wandering into Villaggio Mall for the first time is an experience most expats will remember, mainly because of the canal running through the centre (complete with electric-powered gondolas and men in striped shirts). But apart from the Venetian-style buildings painted onto its vast walls, Villaggio is the same as every other Doha shopping mall. All of them have a large French-owned Carrefour supermarket in the middle (which sometimes sells locally sourced camel meat), with an endless parade of clothes, gadget and jewellery shops spreading around it on the various floors. Groups of Qatari men will be sitting outside Starbucks (their preferred brand of Western coffee) smoking cigarettes despite the signs telling them not to. Bored-looking Nepalese security guards will be wandering around, looking out for stray low-paid workers.

Qatar's malls do not like South East Asian construction workers entering their establishments. The men might be tempted to steal things or, at the very least, put off the regular shoppers, especially the women, by staring at them. So they came up with a rule whereby only men accompanied by women or children could gain entry. They called their malls *family-only zones.* Almost all the low-paid workers have left their wives and children back home, and so this effectively barred them from entering. Teams of security guards patrol the main entrances, seeking out men in overalls, citing the family-only rule if any of the men tried to walk through the door. None of them ever stopped me, though, not even when I was by myself. It made a mockery of the system.

Angela and I did our weekly shopping in a mall called Landmark. The busiest section was its food court: a busy tangle of KFCs, Dunkin Donuts, Pizza Huts and McDonald's. The clientele was usually fifty percent Filipino, thirty percent Western, the rest Arabs. Troops of Nepalese and Bangladeshi workers armed with mops and buckets cleared away the mess, throwing away food that they would never be able to afford themselves. More workers hung around by the supermarket checkouts. These trolleyboys, as they were known, packed bags for people too lazy to do it themselves. But at least they were working in an air-conditioned environment, as opposed to the heat outside. In the overflowing car park, an army of car washers toiled for their daily pittance. I once said to Angela that if all these low-paid workers suddenly went on strike (which they never would, because it is illegal to strike in Qatar) or decided to go home (which they would also not do because their families depend on the money they send), then the country would grind to a sudden and dramatic halt. Neither of us could imagine a Qatari flipping burgers, digging a road or, God forbid, cleaning a toilet.

6

One thing that cannot be denied about Qataris, however, is their hospitality. One day, Angela and I were having lunch with an artist friend of ours called Claire. She asked whether we wanted to visit a farm with her. She was selling a few of her paintings to the farm owner, a Qatari man called Salman. We agreed, and later that evening, the three of us all piled into her car and drove across a dark desert until we found a rough track that led to his farm.

It was not a farm as such, more of a palace. When we knocked on the grand door, a Nepalese man answered. He seemed surprised to be receiving visitors at such an hour. The man of the house soon appeared behind him: a large middle-aged gent in a white thawb and headscarf. "Come in, Claire! Come in, my friends!"

Salman led us to a large rectangular room lined with cushioned seats around each edge. Another man in a white thawb was sitting on one of the cushions next to an *oud*, a pear-shaped stringed instrument that resembled a lute. Salman introduced him as Ahmed, his younger brother. When we sat down, Salman asked us what we wanted to drink.

I opted for some water, as did everyone else, and then Claire showed off her paintings. Both Salman and Ahmed regarded them and, after some negotiation, Salman bought all three. Then he picked up some small drums and said something to his brother in Arabic. Ahmed nodded and picked up the oud and manoeuvred a microphone in front of his face. Then the men started to play for us. For the next ten minutes, we listened to a recital of authentic Bedouin music complete with singing, oud plucking and wild percussion. When it finished, Claire, Angela and I clapped heartily.

Salman laid his drums on the floor. "Come," he said. "I want to show you something."

We followed him into a large adjoining room split in half by a huge glass wall. It was too dark behind the glass to see what was there. When Salman switched on the lights, we saw it was a mock-up of a desert scene: large boulders, spiky plants, gangly trees and lots of sand. There were animals too: rabbits hopping like mad, mouse-like creatures scurrying for cover, and hundreds of small birds flying around like confetti. Salman ushered his Nepalese manservant to find the key so we could go in.

I was more worried about the birds than anything else. I didn't want them leaving mess on my head or shoulders, but they kept well clear, as did all the other creatures which were darting off in all directions. Salman saw me looking at a rabbit that had stopped near a stunted tree. "You like the rabbit?" he asked above the din of furiously chirping birds. "If you catch, you can keep!"

Back in the rectangular room, it was time for another musical recital, the song sounding the same as the last one. When it ended, we made our excuses to leave.

"No! You must stay," said Salman. "We have a feast coming!"

And he was right. Fifteen minutes later, a large delivery truck arrived filled with hot food – shawarma, falafel, whole chickens and hummus – all offloaded by a team of Nepalese men. By the time we'd eaten our fill, and listened to a few more ditties, I realised I had really enjoyed myself. Salman had been a great host.

We left the farm behind and entered the darkness of Arabia. Just another average evening on a Qatari farm.

7

The visit to the farm, perhaps more than any other, showed us just how warm and inviting the people of the Middle East were. Many people who live in the West are of the belief that the Middle East is full of Muslim extremists who hate every Westerner with undisguised fury. From bullet-ridden streets in Damascus to car bombings in Baghdad's side streets, the Middle East, they believe, is a region to avoid and fear. Seemingly every day, there are stories of kidnappings in Yemen or of Islamic fundamentalists ranting into microphones. And from this dark cloud of chaos, an even darker entity has arisen: Islamic State. They, above all others in the turbulent world of Arabia, have created the most violent and primitive version of the Middle East known to man, where the wrong sort of Muslim is crucified, where a young woman is stoned to death for having a boyfriend, and extremists wearing black hoods stand behind cowering Westerners. When gory videos of public crucifixions and Westerners being beheaded started appearing on the Internet in 2014, the world reaction to Islamic State was of horror.

But the Middle East is a vast landmass, made up of many peoples and nations, all with different histories and customs. To classify the whole region as the home of terrorists would be wholly erroneous. Oman, for example, has not been associated with any terrorist activities for a long while. It shuns the idea that any of its subjects are even interested in terror. Living in Qatar brings a sense of realism to expats. We live among Muslims, we hear the call to prayer every day and we see that Muslims are the same as us – raising their families, watching the same movies at the cinema and enjoying days out by the ocean. The Middle East we know is a region to enjoy and it was somewhere I was keen to explore further.

"Where would we go, though?" asked Angela when I mooted the idea of travelling around the region. "We've already been to Dubai."

"But that was just to go shopping and sit by the pool. This time we should see things properly."

Angela considered this. "I quite fancy Jordan. Petra is supposed to be amazing. Beirut's meant to be good too. But I'm not going to Iraq or Yemen."

She was right. There *were* certain countries in the Middle East that were no-go areas. Take Iran. *'The FCO advise against all but essential travel to Iran,'* the UK Foreign Office website stated. *'British travellers face greater risks than nationals of many other countries due to high levels of suspicion about the UK.'* Even Lebanon had some worrying information, saying there was *'a high risk of attacks by Islamist extremist groups, which could be indiscriminate and affect places visited by foreigners.'*

The advice for Yemen was stronger. *'We advise against all travel to Yemen and strongly urge British nationals to leave. There is a very high threat of kidnap from armed tribes, criminals and terrorists.'*

Perhaps unsurprisingly, Syria offered the starkest warning. *'British nationals in Syria should leave now by any practical means. Full scale military operations involving the use of small arms, tanks, artillery and aircraft are ongoing.'*

"The U.A.E. and Oman are okay," I said to my wife, "and so are Jordan and Turkey. Kuwait is also fine. Besides, the warnings are relative; someone could shoot us in London, or stab us in New York. The only countries the Foreign Office says we shouldn't visit are Syria and Yemen."

"What about Iraq?"

"Most of it's off-limits, but there's a part in the north called Kurdistan which is fine. But I think we should leave Iraq for the time being – work our way up to it gradually. First stop should be Abu

Dhabi. It's safe and easy and we both want to go there anyway. I've been checking it out; we can drive to it. No airports to deal with. Just get in our car, drive through Saudi Arabia, and arrive in Abu Dhabi seven hours later. I was speaking to someone at work who knows an agent in Doha who can organise Saudi transit visas for us."

Angela pondered my proposal for a moment. "Saudi? I'll have to cover up."

"Only for a short while."

"I'll have to walk behind you."

"You should do that anyway. But I don't think we'll be getting out of the car much."

Angela looked outside at the developing sandstorm. Sandstorms were common in Qatar. Whenever a fierce one whipped up, sand particles invaded our apartment, getting in through minuscule window edges and tiny cracks under the door.

I pressed on. "Abu Dhabi is supposed to be beautiful. It has a massive white mosque and a long corniche. It'll be a good place to start."

"Let's do it."

And so my grand plan turned from a seed into the start of something. For the next few weeks, I tweaked routes, investigated flight and hotels, and ended up with a prototype itinerary. We would split the trip into three sections. Part one would be the shortest: a drive through Saudi Arabia to Abu Dhabi and back. We would spend only two nights away from home. Part two would be longer, involving a lot of flights and different hotels. We would start in Dubai, and then fly onto Oman, Bahrain, Lebanon, Turkey and finally Jordan. I was particularly looking forward to Jordan because of the Dead Sea, somewhere I'd wanted to go since I was a child. After arriving back in Qatar, I would prepare for part three of the adventure: a solo jaunt starting in Kuwait. From there I'd fly back to Jordan so I could travel overland to Israel. Then I'd head to Kurdistan in Iraq. My adventure would end in the U.A.E., in the tiny Emirate of Ajman. But first things first, I had to deal with the immediate task at hand – securing transit visas for a passage through the Kingdom of Saudi Arabia.

Top row: The sleepy town of Al Khor; The Venetian-themed Villaggio shopping mall
Middle Row: West Bay in Doha, as seen from the air; A dhow sets sail across the Arabian Gulf
Bottom Row: Panorama of Doha, looking along the corniche; The skyline of Doha

Chapter 2. A Transit through the Kingdom of Saudi Arabia

FCO travel advice: Public demonstrations are illegal in Saudi Arabia. Follow local media and be alert to developments, which may trigger public disturbances. Standards of driving are poor and there are a high number of serious accidents.

The only overland journey between Qatar and the United Arab Emirates goes through the Kingdom of Saudi Arabia. That was why most people took the plane, especially since the flight lasted less than one hour and, in Middle Eastern terms, was relatively cheap. But Angela and I wanted to drive, largely *because* of the transit through Saudi Arabia. It would be our only chance to see a little bit of this elusive country.

After getting directions to a small office in a Doha backstreet (which also doubled up as a tailor's shop), Angela and I handed over our passports, forms and visa fees to a moustachioed Indian man. We gave him a little extra to cover his costs. The man told us to return in three days, wobbling his head slightly.

"And you will definitely be able to get the Saudi transit visas?" I asked.

"Yes. No problem! I promise one thousand percent, sir!" He wobbled some more.

He was good to his word. When we returned three days later, the same man recognised us as we walked through the door. "Ah, Mister Jason and his wife, Angela. I have your visas!" He rummaged in a wooden drawer and produced our passports. I flicked through until I arrived at the full-page transit visa for Saudi Arabia. It had a grainy black and white photo of me on the left, and underneath that, it stated the visa was valid for one round trip, lasting a single day in each direction. If, for whatever reason, our transit took longer than one day, then we could expect serious repercussions: at a minimum, a fine of $750 for every extra day we took. Not that we planned to linger in Saudi Arabia. Angela's visa was also good to go too, and so we thanked the man, left his tailor's shop and whooped for joy. We had vaulted the trickiest hurdle with ease.

2

"All set?" I said to Angela as we climbed into our car in Al Khor.

"I think so."

As usual, the heat inside the vehicle hit us like an oven – an all-pervading scorch that attacked the lungs and assaulted our pores within a second. Absently, I touched the metal part of the seatbelt and emitted a screech of pain. Even the steering wheel was impossible to touch, and so the only thing both of us could do was flop in our seats and wait for the air conditioning to kick in.

"Got your veil to cover your head?"

Angela nodded. "Yes. Look." She showed me her green silk scarf, which she planned to fashion into a veil for the border crossing.

The journey from Al Khor took us along a wide eight-lane stretch of highway known locally as the North Road because it led from Doha to the northern tip of Qatar, the location of the proposed bridge that would one day connect Qatar with the island nation of Bahrain. Harsh scrub and desert flanked the road, with the occasional farmhouse, electricity pylon or sand-coloured villa to break the monotony. The sky was a dirty cream colour, almost the same as the desert that surrounded us.

As we approached the outskirts of Doha, we came to the first of an endless set of traffic lights and joined the huge jam caused by them. Unlike the UK (and most other countries in the Western world), traffic lights in Qatar stayed on red (and green) for an insane length of time. The minutes passed ludicrously slowly as more traffic joined from behind. And still the lights stayed resolutely red.

"This is ridiculous," I said for the millionth time. "Look at how many cars there are." At least two hundred by my reckoning. I'd read somewhere that three hundred new cars joined the scrum of

Qatar's roads every single day. *Three hundred a day!* That was close to ten thousand cars a month! The streets of the capital simply couldn't cope.

"Go!" said Angela. Already scores of cars were beeping furiously that I was delaying their movement. And so it continued until we hit the next set of lights, and the ones after that.

Eventually we turned onto a long stretch of highway called Salwa Road, a perpetually gridlocked strip of tarmac lined with car dealerships and furniture stores. We passed them, wondering when the whole road system would finally give up its movement for good. It didn't seem far away.

One hour and twenty minutes after setting off from Al Khor, we cleared the city limits of Doha and hit the open highway. A large blue sign told us the only thing of note ahead was the Kingdom of Saudi Arabia.

3

The Qatari border was empty of traffic. We rolled up to the immigration booth and handed our passports and vehicle registration documents over to the black-veiled woman sitting behind the partition. She took them and started to check whether we had valid exit permits.

Exit permits are a fact of life in Qatar. If any expat worker wishes to leave the country (even for one day) then they have to apply for an exit permit. For Angela and me, this simply amounted to informing a woman in Human Resources that we were about to leave the country. A day later, she would hand us a slip of paper written in Arabic – the exit permit – and we were good to go. It was an annoyance but not a major one. The main problem was remembering to ask for the exit permits in the first place, which, thankfully, we always did. Other colleagues were not so lucky. On more than one occasion, some had turned up at the airport only to find they had forgotten to arrange exit permits. Immigration refused to let them leave and they had no choice but to miss their flight and return home.

Our exit permits were fine and so we cleared the Qatari border in less than two minutes. We then drove through the short stretch of No Man's Land between Qatar and Saudi Arabia, and noticed that, at the half way stage, the sleek black Qatari highway turned into an old grey road. Soon after, we arrived at the Saudi border.

A few trucks, a large skip and a set of immigration huts made up the border. A few lorry drivers were standing near their vehicles, chatting and smoking cigarettes. Others had gathered around one of the huts. Apart from the HGVs, the only other traffic was a white Land Cruiser in front. It had overtaken us in No Man's Land. While Angela put on her head covering, I trundled up behind the Land Cruiser, passing underneath a large green sign written in both English and Arabic: *Saudi Customs* it proclaimed.

"Is this okay?" asked Angela. I studied her scarf, searching out any stray hair that might have escaped the covering. It looked fine to me. When the Land Cruiser moved off, we moved forward to the booth. It was our turn at Saudi immigration.

4

With my car window wide open, the heat of Arabia percolated around our heads. The man in the green uniform and shades took our passports with a muted nod. He looked about thirty, and sported expensive sunglasses and designer stubble. He probed my passport, this way and that, turning from our Qatari residents' permit sticker to the Saudi transit visa. He shook his head and grunted at me in Arabic.

I shrugged. "I'm sorry, I only speak English."

The man ignored me and picked Angela's passport up. Her folded up exit permit fell out, which the immigration official opened and read. He shook his head and closed both passports. Then he shook his finger at us. This time, he addressed us in broken English. "No Firg-eerz, eh?"

"Sorry?" I said.

"No Firg-eerz! You get firg-eerz!"

I looked at the man blankly. In return, he exhaled heavily. Then his eyes lit up. He held up one hand, with his digits outstretched. "Firg-eerz skhaan!"

Scan! Ah, he needed us to get our fingers scanned. I'd read about this, but in our haste to get through the border, I'd forgotten all about it. The guard handed our passports back and pointed somewhere behind him.

We reversed and parked the car, noticing the fingerprint booth – a sand-coloured hut – at one end of the border complex. A small bunch of bored-looking truck drivers were hanging around the two hatches. When they saw us approach, they all moved out of the way, apparently not in any rush to clear customs themselves. At the hatch, I laid my fingers and then my thumbs on the scanner, while Angela did the same at the adjacent booth. The man in charge of my scanner pressed a button, printed something out, and then gave the slip of paper an official stamp. After he'd checked my passport, he told me I was done. I moved across to Angela's hatch.

The man was pressing his sweaty palm onto the back of Angela's hand to secure a better purchase for his scanner. A few of the truck drivers started to watch and so did I. The man clicked on his computer, but the scanner failed to work its magic, so he sprayed Angela's fingers with something, and then rubbed it in like a professional hand masseur. Finally, he pressed her hand back down on the scanning machine.

"No good!" he said after looking at his computer screen. Angela glanced at me and rolled her eyes. The man reached out his hairy hand once more to cajole Angela's fingers into position. He either had a faulty machine or else possessed an unnatural fetish for fingers, but finally he got it to work and formalities were complete. As we left, the man told us to take our car to the inspection area, and pointed at a covered part of the complex staffed by two men. We got in the car and drove there.

Two men were working at the inspection area. One was an Arab man dressed in uniform, the other an Indian underling. When we parked and climbed out, the Arab man asked us to open the boot, which we did. The underling grabbed Angela's bag and placed it on the ground. When he unzipped it, both men regarded the contents without touching anything. They were looking for contraband: drugs, alcohol, pornographic material and, oddly enough, potted plants. Without bothering to rummage around, the Arab man turned to me. "What profession?"

"Teacher," I answered. "Both of us are teachers."

The man considered this, idly glancing at my bag, still in the back of our car. "Okay, finished. You can go."

What? But the men hadn't even opened my suitcase – the one packed with shrubs and terracotta urns filled with hashish and distilling equipment. We thanked both men and climbed back in the car. Finally, in possession of a whole bunch of Arabic-scrawled forms, including one that claimed to be temporary Saudi car insurance, Angela and I returned to the first man and handed everything over. With a stamp and a smile, he welcomed us into Saudi Arabia.

5

Judging by the amount of tyre carnage littering the side of the highway, blown tyres must be a daily occurrence in Saudi Arabia. But we weren't looking at the strands of rubber; we were looking at the expanse of aquamarine further on; the Saudi border was only a few metres from the Gulf: a quite gorgeous introduction to the Kingdom.

We stopped at the small Saudi town of Salwa, a service settlement just a bit further from the border. It consisted of a poky grocery shop, a small mosque, a couple of administrative buildings and a single petrol station. I was delighted to discover that fuel was even cheaper in Saudi Arabia than it was in Qatar. With a full tank costing about six pounds, Angela and I headed into the desert.

"Petrol is cheaper than water," commented Angela as she took a swig from the bottle we'd just bought. "How much would that have cost to fill up in England?"

I did a quick mental calculation. "About fifty quid."

The scenery south of the border was the same as in Qatar – brown sand dotted with scrub, and an occasional truck stop. In the distance were a few low-lying sand dunes and then a line of skeletal pylons, stretching towards unseen towns and settlements. Twenty minutes into Saudi Arabia, we pulled off the highway to have a quick bite of our prepared sandwiches. Just then, a lorry shuddered past carrying a cargo of camels. The driver looked bemused that we had stopped and craned his neck to look. I waved but he didn't return the gesture. I stepped out of the car to have my photo taken for posterity and then crossed the road to see the blue sign opposite. The closest town was Hofuf, 256 kilometres away. Riyadh, the Saudi capital, was 588 kilometres away, but the winner, located 1482 kilometres away, was the holy city of Mecca, the same distance as London is from Rome. With sweat dripping down my back, I quickly returned to the car as water-like mirages shimmered on the parched highway.

In my absence, Angela had removed her scarf. "How about I drive for a bit?" she asked.

"You'd risk driving here?"

"Just for a minute or so. Besides, who would know? It could be my own personal protest."

"Protest?"

"Against the ban on women driving here."

"Oh, I see."

Saudi Arabia is the only country in the world to ban women from driving. Saudi law also forbids women from getting inside a car unless they are with their husband or a close male relative. It was an archaic rule based on the belief that if a woman were to drive safely, then she would have to uncover her face, an unacceptable state for any Saudi woman. Secondly, if women were driving around, then they would be out of the house, possibly leaving children unattended and not keeping their homes in order. Thirdly – and this was the biggie – if a woman were involved in a traffic accident (and surely there would be many!) then this would lead to conversations with strange men. Women and non-family males conversing on the streets of Riyadh! No, never!

Despite this, in 1990, a group of Saudi women got together to stage a protest. Twenty of them climbed into their husbands' cars and took to the streets of Riyadh in a long procession. Someone called the police. Officers stopped the women in their tracks, arrested them all and confiscated their vehicles. The Saudi authorities only released the women after their men folk signed an agreement promising to keep the women on a tighter rein from then on. But things were not finished for the women. In Riyadh, someone printed off thousands of leaflets calling the women whores. The message also asked anyone who knew the women to shun their presence, sack them from their jobs and make their lives as unpleasant as they could. And people did. Such was the ferociousness of these reprisals that no other woman dared to drive a car for the next twenty years. It took until June 2011 before one brave woman gave it a go. In Jeddah, a Saudi city on the Red Sea coast, a woman in her thirties brazenly decided to get behind the wheel of a car and proceeded to drive it in full view of everyone. The police soon arrested her, throwing her straight in a cell. Then, in an unprecedented move, the Saudi courts sentenced her to ten lashes. World condemnation followed this draconian punishment, but the courts refused to back down. It took the intervention of King Abduallah himself who, fearing an international revolt if he didn't do so, decreed the punishment as unjust and ordered the woman be set free.

As well as not being allowed to drive, Saudi women are not normally allowed to travel on public transport either. If they are permitted, perhaps in a medical emergency, they have to sit in a special rear compartment so as not to offend the male passengers. When I told Angela this, she had grown mad, and thus the chance to drive in Saudi Arabia had probably been on her mind for some time.

"What if a policeman sees you?" I said. "We'd both be arrested. You'd get it worse, though. Do you fancy getting flogged?"

"I don't want to drive all the way to the border, only for a minute or so in the desert. Then we could swap back. But if a police car did stop us, I'd say it was an emergency."

"What sort of emergency?"

"I don't know. You're having a heart attack or something. You'd have to pretend to be unconscious."

I burst out laughing. I could just imagine lying with my eyes closed and mouth flopped open while a Saudi policeman questioned my wife. But what the hell, I thought. We waited for a gap in the traffic, which wasn't difficult due to the light movement, and then swapped seats. Angela glanced at me, and then pressed the accelerator. We moved along the dusty verge for a few metres and then came to a standstill. Angela's protest was over after four seconds.

6

With me back in the driver's seat, we set off again towards the Saudi/U.A.E. border. Aside from a few isolated dwellings, there was nothing to see along the way, but at least the drab brown sand seemed to be making way for a slight hint of orange. Five minutes later, the orange turned a shade of red and the scrub turned into sand dunes. For the first time since entering The Kingdom, we felt we were in the real Arabia.

The Saudi border was another small service settlement, largely deserted except for masses of trucks, all waiting in line to be inspected. Angela donned her headscarf again as we drove up to the customs booth, and, once our papers and passports had passed muster, our brief foray into Saudi Arabia was over. Next stop was the city of Abu Dhabi, a three-hour drive along the same stretch of highway.

Top row: A truck speeds past on a lonely Saudi highway; A small fire station just past the border
Middle row: Me, standing in the Saudi desert; Saudi Arabian riyals; Road sign saying it's 1482 kilometres to Mecca
Bottom row: Small, but geometrically pleasing, mosque on the Saudi-Qatar border; the small settlement past the border; Approaching Saudi customs

Chapter 3. Abu Dhabi: Capital of the Emirates

FCO travel advice: Most visits are trouble free. You should respect local traditions, customs, laws and religions at all times. Female visitors should take extra care when walking or travelling alone. Driving standards are not as disciplined as in the UK.

The gloriously white Sheikh Zayed Grand Mosque, the eighth largest Islamic place of worship in the world, shimmered in the heat. It was easily the greatest mosque either of us had ever seen. Abu Dhabi's greatest architectural triumph looked like a delicious mixture of the Taj Mahal and a lunar space pod. Driving on a stretch of highway caught up in the full throes of rush hour, I almost crashed into the car in front because I was trying to stare at it.

"Watch where you're going," snapped Angela, gripping her seat again. "You can see the mosque tomorrow. And shouldn't we be in the left lane? We need to turn at the next roundabout."

"Yes, backseat driver. Maybe the Saudis have got it right about women driving."

Our hotel was grand and spacious, a good place to end our road journey. For the next two nights, our car would not be moving; instead, we would use taxis. But not wanting to venture out on our first evening, we chose to eat in the hotel restaurant: a steakhouse with a menu designed by a celebrity chef. It was an exceedingly expat way to finish our evening.

The restaurant was pleasantly busy, partly due to its subdued decor, ambient lighting and celebrity billing. As we took our seats, the courteous Filipino waiter brought us a heated towel to moisturise our hands, and then fetched a small wooden table for Angela's handbag. Finally, he brought the menus.

"Have you seen the prices?" I whispered when he was out of earshot.

My wife nodded. I looked down at my menu trying to spot something within our price range. A medium-sized steak with a side order of vegetables was close to seventy pounds. If we factored in a starter, dessert and drinks, we would be looking at well over two hundred and fifty pounds for a quick evening meal.

"We should leave," I said. "It's too extravagant. Two hundred and fifty quid for a meal – we can't justify that..."

Angela looked around at our fellow diners. All were Westerners, laughing and carefree as they sipped on wine and cut into succulent steaks. "But it's embarrassing; we've only just sat down. And the waiter gave us some towels." She began to study the menu again.

"Who cares? We can go to the Italian next door. It'll be cheaper. Let's just get up and walk out while he's gone."

"Too late," said Angela. "Here he comes. But I've got an idea."

The waiter approached our table with his little pad of paper. He asked whether we wanted to order some drinks.

Angela closed the menu. "I'm afraid we'll have to leave," she said. "I'm a vegetarian and there's nothing on the menu for me."

My eyes widened. It was a good ploy. Though why a vegetarian would go into a steakhouse in the first place was a little odd. The man looked apologetic. "Oh...Ah...I'm really sorry...perhaps you can try the restaurant next door? I would like to apologise on behalf of the management for not having a vegetarian option."

"No need," Angela said, as she stood up. "And thank you, anyway"

We left the restaurant and headed next door.

Angela ordered beef lasagne while I ordered a pizza laced with enough meat to feed a family of five. As we sat with our drinks, I noticed the steakhouse waiter from next door standing by the entrance, scoping out every table. "Oh my God!" I hissed. "Don't look now, but that waiter's over there. I think he's looking for us. Keep your head down."

But it was too late; he'd already spotted us. "Hello, sir! Hello, ma'am!" he said a few moments later. "I've spoken to our chef and he says he can make a vegetarian meal for you. I can see you've already ordered some drinks, but you can bring them with you and we'll sort out payment between restaurants later." He beamed at his helpfulness.

I looked at Angela. What could she say now? She floundered but then gathered her thoughts. "Thank you very much, but we've already ordered from this menu."

The man bowed slightly. "Of course, ma'am. Sorry for intruding. Perhaps next time?"

When he was gone, Angela giggled. "Oh my God! How awful are we? What if he'd seen me eating my lasagne?" Suddenly her face dropped. "What if he comes back and sees me eating it?"

"He won't."

And he didn't, though I kept a wary eye on the entrance for the whole time.

2

Seven Emirates make up the United Arab Emirates, and Abu Dhabi is the largest. Abu Dhabi city is the capital of the whole country, and, like many cities along the Gulf, it began life as a humble pearl fishing community. It scratched out a living from the jewels it extracted from the shallow but fertile waters around its coast. Like the ebb and flow of its tidal waters, trade came and went, until its fortunes changed for good in the 1950s with the discovery of oil. Abu Dhabi and the other Emirates became richer than they could have imagined; Abu Dhabi now boasts some of the biggest skyscrapers, plushest hotels and fanciest shopping malls in the Middle East.

Since the 1990s, the population of Abu Dhabi has exploded due to the massive influx of foreign workers. Today, Emiratis make up less than twenty percent of the population. This has affected cultural identity, which is now blurred and often lost altogether. True, there are still mosques, palm trees and splashes of Arabic writing on every store front, but most of the pre-oil Bedouin homes, the old cooling towers that once channelled air through chambers to create rudimentary air-conditioning, and the original souqs where merchants traded frankincense, nutmeg and pearls, have been lost.

Abu Dhabi is not lacking in all cultural identity, though. The city possesses one piece of cultural identity second to none: the magnificent Sheikh Zayed Grand Mosque. And that was our first port of call.

3

The morning was hot and sunny, the same as the previous day and the day before that. Both of us were wearing long trousers and long-sleeved tops. When the taxi deposited us in front of the white mosque, we presented ourselves to an Indian security official, who looked me up and down and then nodded at my choice of attire. He then turned his attention to Angela. "You have scarf?" he asked, pointing at her head.

"I've got a hat," she answered, pulling out a floppy one from her bag. She put it on and the guard smiled, revealing a quite astonishing set of white teeth. They were almost as white as the mosque behind him.

"Perfect," he stated.

I couldn't get over how beautiful the mosque was: it was mesmerising. It dripped in delicious domes of white, its minarets towered towards the sun and thousands of marble columns flanked its sides. At ground level, a series of reflective pools rippled with the reflections of a truly magnificent architectural masterpiece, a building worthy of every superlative thrown at it. We walked past the pools to reach a shaded roofed walkway.

"Excuse me, madam," said a security guard, his tone less friendly than the white-toothed man near the entrance. He was looking at Angela. "You must get abaya please."

Angela pulled a face. "An abaya?"

The man nodded. "You need abaya to see mosque." He pointed at a small building behind us. "You go there to get."

"But the other man said I only needed a hat."

"No. You need abaya."

Inside the building, some escalators led down to an underground car park and then to a room dedicated to the lending of abayas. Five minutes later, Angela was wearing one, a full-length gown that came complete with black hood to cover her blond hair. I took a photo and then made her walk behind me as we made our way back towards the mosque.

4

We joined fifteen other people for a free tour that had just begun. In charge of the group was a thirty-something Emirati gentleman wearing a pristine white thawb and an equally white head covering. "This mosque," he said in near-perfect English, "is the largest in the United Arab Emirates. It is capable of holding more than 40,000 worshippers."

We followed him to one of the intricately patterned pillars that made up part of the outdoor corridor. Paintings of wispy flowers covered its length. Along the top of each column was a decoration of gold leaf. "Tell me," he asked us, "what do these columns remind you of?"

We all looked. No one said anything. To me, they looked like beautiful columns holding up a beautiful ceiling. I kept silent too.

"They are palm trees!" said the guide. "Look at the gold leaves on the top section, and see how they resemble the top of a palm tree."

"Is it real gold?" one young woman asked. Judging by her accent, she was Australian.

The man in the thawb smiled. "No, only gold paint. But the gold on top of the mosque's domes is real. Come, let me show you inside. Shoes off first, please."

Inside the great mosque, we all gazed up at the enormous crystal chandelier dangling like a jewel above our heads.

"That," explained our guide, "is the third largest chandelier in the world. It weighs twelve tonnes and contains forty million Swarovski crystals. And notice the carpet you are standing upon." Everyone's eyes swivelled downward. It was a mammoth expanse of green, pink and red, about the size of a football pitch. "It is the largest hand-woven carpet in the world. Iranian women, working day and night, seven days a week, for two years, made it."

We walked past a set of Korans, which the guide told us not to touch since none of us were Muslims, and then he asked us to sit on the carpet near a couple of carved columns. He stood before us like a schoolteacher. "Do any of you know who Sheikh Zayed, whom this mosque was named after, was?"

No one answered.

The man nodded, clearly used to such a response. "Sheikh Zayed was the first president of the United Arab Emirates. He ruled from 1971 until his death in 2004, and he is the man who turned the orange deserts of Arabia into the green and fertile land you see today. It was his idea for this mosque, although he never saw it finished. He is buried in an adjoining courtyard."

When the tour ended, Angela and I headed back outside. No matter how good the inside was, the outside was a hundred times better. We headed back towards a taxi.

5

Abu Dhabi city centre was a metropolis of skyscrapers, plush office blocks and top end hotels, all buzzed by a fleet of silver taxis. We could've been in Los Angeles or maybe Hong Kong. We drove amid the high rise buildings until we arrived at one end of the road that ran alongside the corniche. Our taxi pulled up in front of a huge shopping plaza – Marina Mall, one of the city's largest. While Angela went to look around the shops, I sought refuge in Starbucks.

With my latte in front of me, I began watching three Emirati boys. They were sitting by the window in their white thawbs tucking into large wedges of chocolate cake. I gauged their age to be around ten, and already they were heavily overweight. An upbringing of wealth and little exercise would be a recipe for later-life diabetes.

The boys finished the cakes and started on their cream-drenched drinks. One of them spotted something outside and pointed. All three burst out laughing. I strained to see but only saw a perfectly normal-looking African woman. The boys jabbered something in Arabic and burst out laughing again. With their drinks temporarily forgotten, they turned their attention to a trio of Western teenage girls, who, for some unfathomable reason, reduced the boys to even more guffaws. They were so raucous that the Filipino woman behind the coffee counter looked over. When she saw that it was Emirati boys causing the noise, she rolled her eyes and got on with cleaning the grinding machine.

The teenage girls stopped near the window, apparently deciding where to shop next. They were blissfully unaware of the scrutiny they were under. All three were stick-thin, wearing tiny shorts and sleeveless tops, a state of dress considered poor taste in most of Arabia. Qataris would frown at such open displays of flesh, I knew; Abu Dhabi, it seemed, was more tolerant. The boys grew tired of people watching and returned to their creamy milkshakes. Ten minutes later, they left, one of them carrying the latest iPhone in a new box: his latest toy. It reminded me of something a friend of mine told me in Al Khor. A little Qatari boy in her class had been absent for a few days seeing a dentist. Fair enough, nothing wrong with that, except that this boy had flown to Milan to see his family's Italian dentist by private jet.

It was a different world for Qatari and Emirati citizens, especially the younger generations who knew nothing except wealth and abundance. The world in which they lived was a place of no boundaries, where money was no object and no extravagance was too large.

As I sipped on the last of my drink, a young Nepalese woman in a grey uniform walked by the window. She stopped at one of the marble columns and started to polish it. Round and round her hand went as she circled the column with her cloth. She moved onto the next column, repeating the process with a glassy-eyed expression, a job she would be doing six days a week for two whole years. As she silently toiled, rich groups of Westerners and Arabs walked by with Gucci, Armani and Calvin Klein bags, filled with luxuries way out of her reach. I finished my coffee, left Starbucks and walked past her like everyone else.

6

"I found a gold cash machine!" I said to Angela. "Come on, I'll show you." She followed me around the corner until we came face to face with the *Gold to go: the gold ATM*, a vending machine that featured a gold exterior and a screen that displayed the price of gold based upon real-time prices. It was updated every ten minutes. Abu Dhabi was a relative latecomer to the world of gold ATMs. Dubai got its first gold ATM in 2010. It proved so popular that the owners had to replenish it twice a week. Clearly, Abu Dhabi was hoping for something similar.

"Shall we buy a bar?" asked Angela giddily.

I studied the screen. The ATM was offering gold bars ranging from 5 grams to 250 grams. "For a five gram bar, we're talking 1465 dirham, about 250 pounds."

"That doesn't sound too bad."

"Have you any idea how big a five gram bar of gold is? It's about the size and thickness of your thumbnail."

Angela looked at her thumb. "Forget it."

Abu Dhabi Marina was across the road from the mall, so instead of buying a gold bar fit for a gnome, we walked past the palm trees to look at the boats. Most were white and expensive-looking, the sort of vessels usually seen around the harbours of Monte Carlo.

"The super yachts are all moored over on Yas Island," I said. "These are just the baby ones."

Yas Island is Abu Dhabi's entertainment centre, a purpose-built, man-made island filled with designer shops, expensive restaurants, upmarket hotels, and, of course, the Abu Dhabi Grand Prix circuit.

"Do you want to go there?"

I shook my head. "Let's get a taxi to the corniche."

7

"You should make a will, you know," said Angela. We were standing at the edge of the water, gazing along Abu Dhabi's corniche, an eight-kilometre curve full of parks, bicycle routes and the occasional beach. Like Doha's corniche, it was perhaps the prettiest part of the city.

"Why? Are you thinking of bumping me off?"

"Maybe. But I was thinking about that poor woman we read about in the paper yesterday."

The woman in question was a twenty-eight year old British woman. She had been living in Abu Dhabi with her British husband and their two young children, happy and carefree. Two months previously, her husband left to go work in the morning, but never came back. He died in a road traffic accident.

For the woman, the next few weeks were hell on Earth. While she tried to come to terms with the loss of her husband, together with the fact that she would be bringing up two small children by herself, she had to deal with all the paperwork. Because her husband had not written a will, the authorities turned to Sharia Law – the moral and religious set of rules based on Islamic teachings – to deal with his finances. First, the couple's joint bank account was frozen. Even though there was money in the bank, the young widow had no access to it. Next, the state seized all his assets while they sought out a direct male relative who would be able to receive it all. It was this final aspect of Sharia Law that had caused the problems for the woman. The only direct male relative the courts could find was the deceased man's brother.

The brother had been estranged from the family for some time and when he received all his brother's money and assets, he refused to return any of it, as was his right. The article was urging all Western ex-pats to draw up wills in case the same thing happened to them.

"I'm going to leave all my money to the kebab shop around the corner from us," I said. "And decree that if you want any of it, you have to wear a veil for twelve months."

"Hilarious."

With evening fast approaching, the temperature along the corniche was reaching a pleasing level, and yet Angela and I found ourselves to be the only people there, apart from a lone fisherman and a young girl riding on a tricycle. The former was an Indian man dangling a thin line over the edge of the sea wall, the latter an Arabic-looking teenager in the process of landing on the ground. Angela and I watched her lock the front wheel of her bike, causing the rear to rise almost vertically. The result was that she ended up on the pavement under her chariot in a clatter of metallic clangs and thumps. The girl seemed uninjured, and looked more embarrassed than anything else. She quickly righted herself and then inspected the tricycle. It appeared to be fine because she got back on it and then looked at us.

"You okay?" I called out to her.

The girl nodded and glanced at the fisherman, but he was busy looking down into the water. She climbed onto her bike and pedalled away, leaving us in the heat of a developing Arabian sun.

In the distance was a dhow yard, with six or seven large, traditional wooden fishing boats moored for the day. Another was manoeuvring itself into position, blasts of black smoke puffing from its vertical exhaust.

A couple of jet skis zoomed past, generating a raucous noise and a huge arc of spray in their wake. We watched them race along the inlet before they turned back to pass the dhows. When the sun went down, we flagged down a taxi and asked the driver to take us to our hotel.

8

"Where are you from?" inquired the cheery young Pakistani taxi driver. His name was Omar, a 24-year-old man from the city of Peshawar. He told us he'd been working in Abu Dhabi for the past three years, and planned to do two more before returning home. "I've not had a day off in all this time!" he informed us proudly. "My wages go back home to my mother."

When we told him we were from the UK, near the city of Manchester, it brought about a quick discussion about Wayne Rooney, until Omar admitted he was more of a cricket fan. I noticed Omar had an American twang to his accent, a definite curl to some of the vowels. I asked him whether he'd been to school in the United States.

"Me? America? No, I went to school in Peshawar, but they didn't teach me English. I learn it myself by watching TV programs and listening to radio! I swear that's how I did it."

"Well you speak it really well," said Angela.

We stopped at a set of lights that were just as bad as the ones in Doha. In fact, with the skyscrapers and office blocks, we could've been in Doha.

"Do you enjoy working here?" Angela asked him. We were close to the hotel, waiting to do a U-turn towards it.

Omar pulled a slight face. "Mostly. Western passengers and Filipinos are very respectful. Not Arabs though. Very rude people." He didn't elaborate and we didn't press him. But it reminded me of a story an Indian taxi driver had told us in Qatar. He'd been driving along a road full of speed cameras and in the back were a couple of Qatari women. As he drove at the posted speed limit, the women ordered him to speed up. He refused, telling them about the cameras. They again ordered him to driver faster. When he refused, one of the women produced a mobile phone and rang the taxi company to complain. The upshot was he'd almost lost his job and had to pay a fine that amounted to his daily takings.

"Okay," said Omar. "Here is your hotel. Enjoy the rest of your stay."

We thanked him and climbed out. An hour later, after packing our bags in preparation for our return trip to Qatar the next day, we relocated to one of the hotel bars on the beach. As we sipped on our ten-dollar drinks, we looked back over the photos we had taken: the Saudi Desert, a dusty truck-stop border, a palm-fringed corniche, a gold-dispensing ATM and the best mosque in the world. Our first stop on our adventure across the Middle East had been a brief but enjoyable one. Abu Dhabi was an oasis of parks, shopping malls and hotels. True, it might not be a hotbed of Arabian culture, but it was a fun place to spend a little time, and it made us eager to see more.

Top row: The magnificent Sheikh Zayed Grand Mosque; An ATM that dispenses gold
Middle row: Looking along Abu Dhabi Corniche; The corridor of the Grand Mosque
Bottom row: Angela posing in her abaya; Panorama of Abu Dhabi

Chapter 4. Sightseeing in Qatar

The problem with sightseeing in Qatar is there is not much to see, unless you are a fan of posh hotels, shopping malls or building sites. Apart from a fort in the north, and a few sand dunes in the south, much of the tiny nation is stubbly beige desert or Doha.

Souq Waqif in Doha is worth a visit, though. It is directly opposite the Qatar Islamic Cultural Center: a gloriously spiralled building that looks like a minaret, a lighthouse and a fairground helter-skelter rolled into one. Used as a base for the teachings of Islam, it is one of the key landmarks of Doha; its image is found on everything from baseball caps and fridge magnets to mobile phone covers and drinking mugs.

As Angela and I drove along the corniche towards Souq Waqif, the Arabian Gulf, a gorgeous expanse of blue, filled our left-hand side A few dhows were bobbing up and down in the calm water and behind us, the skyscrapers of West Bay were gearing up for their evening light shows. On our right was the massive presidential palace, a gigantic beige building topped with a huge flag of Qatar. Fountains flowed from its walls and a blanket of green surrounded it, the grass kept healthy with the non-stop sprinkler system in operation. With the evening traffic surprisingly light, we passed the palace and then, when the yellow spiral of the Islamic Cultural Center came up on our right, we knew it was time to turn towards Souq Waqif.

The souq, like many others in the Gulf, had started its life as a small market place. Arabian fishermen and Bedouin came to hawk their goods there. Traders pulling their camel trains laden with spices, dried meat and cloth would gather to swap tales before trading their goods. With so many men standing around gossiping and shouting for custom, the bazaar became known as 'the standing market' or *Souq Waqif*.

Land Cruisers and tourists have replaced the camels and Bedouin. During daylight hours, only a few shops are open, but as soon as

4pm strikes, things open with a bang. The restaurants, a racy mixture of Lebanese, Iraqi, Turkish and Arabian eateries, fling open their doors so that waiters can lay tables and ready the lines of shisha pipes for later use. In the narrow alleyways behind the eateries, men will be setting out arrays of Arabic perfume bottles, specially angled to waft over passing customers, while their colleagues busily drape fancy cloth over wooden counters. Qatar fridge magnets and wooden camels, together with whole piles of cheap Chinese goods, lie waiting in front of storefronts, tempting the scores of tourists that will soon be passing through, and, further in, old men patrol the narrow aisles with wheelbarrows full of nuts, spices and bottles of water.

We had been to Souq Waqif plenty of times before, of course. Whenever any family or friends visited Qatar, we always made sure we took them to Souq Waqif, due to its *easiness*. Unlike the hectic bazaars of Marrakech or Tunis, Doha's souq offered hassle-free browsing, no hard selling and plenty to see. It also offered a nice introduction to the heritage of Qatar. Except it didn't do any such thing; the authorities pulled down the original souq decades previously. It took until 2004 before the Emir of Qatar decided to rebuild it. What the original Bedouin traders would make of the modern lighting system, the smoke detectors, the ATMs and the Haagen-Dazs ice-cream shop was anyone's guess.

In one section of the labyrinth was a pet section, the one part of the souq that Angela detested. Cages full of tiny chirping birds, all of them in bright pinks, blues and greens, waited for any passersby. They weren't the birds' natural colours, of course, but they did make them look pretty to children. The pet-stall owners had done the same thing with the baby rabbits and mice, and, whenever we brought visitors to see the special dyed animals, it always had the same effect: an initial look of surprise and amusement followed by a look of unease. We walked past the kittens and puppies, the latter with their tongues flopped across their mouths due to the heat, and the former sitting on elevated platforms to tempt passing hands. A perched macaw, a bucketful of terrapins, a large iguana in a glass cage and a colourful array of tropic fish – the bounty of the pet shop was as extensive as it was sad. We left the souq in search of the corniche.

2

At night, Doha's corniche is at its best: the lights of the skyline are simply amazing. Enjoying them are Lycra-clad cyclists, families walking with children, young Western women jogging in twos or threes and men walking hand in hand (a common display of close friendship across Southern Asia). Out in the water, the twinkling lights of dhows occasionally dot the blackness.

As well as operating as fishing boats, these wooden vessels are sometimes used for sightseeing trips. For a relatively small fee, a family can hire a dhow and set sail around the harbour to enjoy the sights of West Bay. These were the dhows we could see now. Friday afternoons are an even busier time for dhow trips. Friday is the first day of the weekend across much of the Middle East, and so groups of Westerners will collectively hire a large dhow for their own personal use. Between 2pm until 6pm, they will hunker down while the Indian crew sets sail. Despite sounding like a rich cultural experience, Friday afternoon dhow trips are a booze and food fest with a bit of drunken swimming thrown in for good measure. When the crew reaches a sufficient distance offshore, they drop the anchor, power up the barbeque and then watch as a hundred Westerners open cool boxes full of alcohol and get drunk.

"Maybe we should do a dhow trip," I suggested. A particularly gaudily lit one was powering back to its perch by the jetty. Blue and red neon lights covered its edges and yellow lights dangled from its rigging. It looked like a Christmas tree.

"You must be joking. Why would we want to do that?"

"Because everyone does one at some point."

"Well, I'm not. I can't think of anything worse. If I were in my twenties, then maybe I'd consider it, but not now. Sitting on a boat and getting drunk in the afternoon…I don't think so."

We wandered along the crescent-shaped promenade, once more marvelling at the skyline. One tower in particular looked like it belonged in Las Vegas or maybe *The Jetsons*. It flashed various neon in a rotation of splendid colour and lights. It was the Doha World Trade Center, one of the newest skyscrapers on the block, and maybe the best so far. Near the top, a circular section looked like a flying saucer had crashed into it.

"I was thinking," said Angela, "that we should visit that turtle place tomorrow: the one in the north. It's the hatching season. If we're going to see the sights of Qatar, then we should go there, don't you think?"

"Yeah, I'd like that." I was staring at the moon, a large disc of almost pure white. It looked distinctly Arabian. No wonder many of the flags of Muslim countries featured a moon.

We walked on for another kilometre or so, and then made our way to the Sheraton for a drink and some food. The Irish Harp's Guinness was second to none.

3

The next afternoon, with an hour to go until sunset, Angela and I drove north, passing the Ras Laffan gas complex, until we reached Fuwairat Beach, a small hawksbill turtle hatching site. Well away from any tourists or locals, the secluded beach was dotted with small flags that rangers had placed on the nesting sites. "Out of the thousands of baby turtles that hatch here," said the warden in charge of the beach, an Arabic man in his fifties, "maybe one or two will survive into adulthood. And if it is a female, it will return here in a quarter of a century to lay its own eggs. That is, if no one builds a hotel in the meantime."

We were with a dozen or so other eager ex-pats, all walking behind the warden. He led us along a thin strip of sand, windswept and bare, until we arrived at a cordoned off section of sand: the hatching area. Already, the sun had gone down and, if it hadn't been for the warden's torch, we would've been looking by moonlight.

We entered the cordoned off enclosure. "Yesterday, lots of eggs hatched, and the day before that was good too. So this evening, we are expecting even more." He told us that each nest contained about one hundred turtle eggs. "They only hatch when it's dark because that's when the sand is cool enough for them to waddle across." All of us peered down at the sand, hoping to catch sight of a flipper or a tiny squinting head. There was nothing. Maybe the torch light was scaring them.

"They should be hatching soon," the man said, sensing our impatience, switching off his torch. Moonlight shone overhead, offering just enough light for us to see. "When they do, the turtles will scurry along the beach to the ocean. Please do not touch them. Also, we must turn off all lights, especially torches and flashes because the hatchlings are programmed to follow bright light – which for these little ones is the moon reflecting off the waves. Sometimes we've found dead baby turtles up at the top of the beach. We think they've tried to follow car headlights. So let's make sure all our camera flashes are turned off."

Ten minutes later, with no sign of any baby turtles, the scientist whispered for us to be silent. Then, he did something surprising. He knelt down and began gently digging though the sand. After a few careful swipes, a few white eggs appeared, all of them perfectly spherical and resembling ping-pong balls. The sudden arrival of moonlight jolted the hatchlings into immediate action. At first, it was just a crack in one of the eggs, then a bigger crack, until an impossibly cute baby turtle emerged from a gap. It sensed the air around for a moment and then was off, flippers going like mad as it paddled down a specially constructed channel towards the ocean. Other eggs were hatching, and after only a few minutes, there were about thirty of the creatures, all clambering over one another in a bid for freedom.

The spectacle of the baby turtles propelling themselves along the sand was as amazing as we'd hoped it would be. One second they were on the sand, and then next, as an incoming wave washed over them, they were gone. Most would never be seen again.

Seeing the turtles turned out to be one of the highlights of living in Qatar.

4

Angela and I pulled into a petrol station. It was a fortnight after our turtle experience and we were on the way to Doha to meet the King of the Desert. We stopped by one of the pumps and handed the Pakistani man our car keys. Nobody in Qatar ever got out to fill their own cars, not with an army of paid attendants waiting to do so. Thirty-five riyals later (£6), we had a full tank, and handed the man five riyals extra for his effort. He smiled graciously, pocketing it in his overalls.

The highway from Al Khor to Doha took us past a series of major construction projects. One was a stadium for the 2022 World Cup; another was a train station for the future rail system. In the far distance was Lusail, a new city in the making, capable of housing a quarter of a million people according to reports. When it was finished, it would have yacht marinas, shopping malls, luxury housing and hotels, gold courses and a zoo dedicated to just giraffes.

"I can't believe we're going to see someone called the King of the Desert," I said. I was moving out of the way of a Land Cruiser: a black one this time. He'd been flashing his lights for some time and I'd made him wait long enough. When I was safe in the slow lane again, I recalled the phone call I'd had the previous evening.

"Hello," the man on the other end of the line had said in an Arabic accent. "This is the King of the Desert."

"Hi," I said. "Is this the company who organises 4x4 trips in the desert?"

"Yes. Would you like to book one?"

"Yes. Two people for tomorrow."

"Hold on, please." I could hear the man turning some pages, most probably a ledger or a diary. "Tomorrow at 2pm is available. Is this okay?"

I told him it was. Then I asked where we should meet.

"In the Sheraton lobby. That's where I will wait."

"And what's your name, please?"

"King of the Desert."

"King of the Desert?"

"Yes." There was no trace of humour.

"Okay," I replied. "But I'd prefer to use your real name."

"The King of the Desert is my name."

The man was clearly a fruitcake, and so, instead of arguing about what I should call him, I simply arranged the trip.

5

Like all five-star hotels in Doha, the lobby of the Sheraton abounded with opulence and grandeur. From the gigantic chandelier dangling above our heads to the marble floor underfoot, it was meant to impress, and it did: President Bush, Princes Diana and Muhammad Ali have all stayed in the hotel.

The Sheraton was the first international hotel in Qatar ever built, unveiled to the world in 1982 when Doha was little more than a dusty one-camel town. Photos from that time show a huge expanse of yellow sand spreading inland, edged by the Arabian Gulf. A single road ran past a few isolated dwellings – but apart from that, there was nothing. Except for one thing – on the corner of a headland sat a huge pyramid: the Sheraton. The innovative shape of the hotel would set the scene for all future developments in Doha.

We parked the car and entered the lobby. I lowered my eyes from the chandelier so I could look for the King of the Desert. A few Arab men were sitting around chatting and drinking coffee, and a few more were sitting inside the mock-Bedouin tents along one edge of the lobby, but none seemed likely candidates. In the end, though, we didn't have to worry because the King found us.

"Mister Jason?" a tall, gangly Qatari man said. He was about thirty years of age. The King's attire was the standard white thawb, designer stubble and red and white chequered headscarf. His thawb was so pristine that I wondered whether he carried a little iron and cloth to get rid of any creases while on the move.

We nodded and the King seemed satisfied. "Come."

His conversation skills were lacking, but his vehicle wasn't – it was a huge White Toyota Land Cruiser. We sat in the back and eyed the King of the Desert, who, without a word, set us off on our adventure. Pleasingly, he flashed everyone who got in his way and soon had us on the highway heading south. Outside, the outskirts of Doha were making way for open desert. Twenty minutes later, after not speaking to us once, I decided to engage the King of the Desert in conversation. I asked him whether he'd been a tour guide for a long time.

"Yes."

Okay, a little curt, but at least it was somewhere in the right direction. "And do you enjoy it?"

"Yes."

"And is this your car?"

His phone rang. "Excuse me," he said, cutting short our riveting conversation. When his phone call ended, I didn't bother trying again.

As the journey continued past Mesaieed, the most southerly town in Qatar, the scenery changed. For the first time we saw some real sand dunes. They were close to the road, pleasingly orange and rounded, busy with motorbikes and dune buggies. Companies hiring out buggies dotted the highway, as did ambulance stations. Small teams of paramedics waited in the stations, ready to deal with any sand dune related injury.

We came to a roundabout that the desert was trying to claim as its own. Orange sand covered the road edge and blew across it like liquid. We turned left, arriving at a large hotel and leisure complex called the Sealine Beach Resort. The King stopped the car and, without saying a word, climbed out. Five minutes later, he returned with two young Western women. They climbed into the back of the Land Cruiser with us, introducing themselves as Emma and Louise, sisters from Glasgow. They were visiting their brother, who worked in Mesaieed as a shipping coordinator. He had booked them a trip into the desert as a gift.

"He's a bit miserable, isn't he?" whispered Emma, a pretty, dark-haired woman, pointing at the King still outside. He was letting some air out of the tyres to enable better traction on the sand.

"And what's with his name?" sniggered Louise.

We all smirked.

6

One thing we did all agree on, though, was that the King was a skilled driver, well deserving of his moniker. For close to an hour he took us across the rolling dunes of the Arabian Desert, sometimes at improbable angles. Sometimes His Lordship would career up dunes at such death-defying angles that I felt sure gravity would win and send us toppling upside down. It never did. Other times we hung on for grim death and we raced vertically downwards, churning up clouds of orange in our wake. But the King judged each climb with precision and acute accuracy; at one point – for I caught it in the rear-view mirror – he even smiled at his own prowess.

To allow us to regain our composure, and to settle our cascading stomachs, the King drove us to the very south of Qatar, to an almost-closed inlet of the Arabian Gulf called the Inland Sea. He parked the Land Cruiser on top of a dune. "Take photos," he said, climbing out to perch himself on the side of the dune. He gazed out, surveying his kingdom.

The inlet looked like a huge lake surrounded by desert. In the distance, on the other side, was Saudi Arabia, an indistinct series of cliffs and highland. A slightly salty smell carried in the air as we climbed down the sand towards the water's edge. We were the only five people for miles. When we reached the water, I put my hand in, not surprised to find it as warm as bath water. If I'd brought my swimming clothes, I might have been tempted to go for a paddle. Less appealing was the litter strewn across certain sections of the beach. There were also small piles of charred wood and ash. People must sometimes camp out by the Inland Sea, I reckoned.

"What do we do now?" asked Emma, her Glaswegian brogue coming through loud and clear. All four of us were staring at the rippling water. It was almost hypnotic.

"Let's take a few photos then head back to the car," suggested Angela.

We all did, posing in faintly comical positions: jumping in the air, looking pensive, pointing at the lowering (and impossibly red) sun. When the King saw us returning, he got up from his perch and five minutes later we were following a set of tracks in the deserts made by other vehicles. The sand dune portion of the trip was over and now we seemed to be heading toward some sort of desert dwelling, perhaps a farm. An authentic-looking Bedouin tent stood close to an enclosure containing around fifteen camels. Three men were sitting outside the tent watching our arrival with interest.

"You want camel ride?" asked the King, in a rare moment of conversation. The girls said no straightaway. Angela and I didn't really fancy it either, but we did want to get out and see them. We told the King of the Desert this.

He nodded.

The beasts seemed a friendly bunch, and, while we wandered around their enclosure, the King and the camel herders sat talking and drinking tea. For the first time since we'd met him, he seemed amiable and animated. With the sun finally setting on a distant horizon, we all climbed back into the Land Cruiser for the return journey to Sealine Beach Resort and then Doha. Despite our driver's borderline rude behaviour, we all agreed it had been a great excursion. Angela and I arrived back at the Sheraton with the Doha nightlife in full swing. After a quick drink in the Irish Harp, we drove back to Al Khor.

7

"We should go to that fort," I said to Angela the following weekend. "That one up in the north."

"It's meant to be boring."

"I know. But it's one of the main sights of Qatar."

"I suppose so, then."

Even though the Zubarah Fort looked centuries old, a notion reinforced because it was a UNESCO World Heritage Site, it was actually an old coast guard station built just before the start of the Second World War. It looked like somewhere in which French Foreign Legion troops would reside – beige walls, round towers and tiny spy holes from which to shoot things. Composed of coral and limestone, and a roof manufactured from compressed mud, Zubarah Fort was now a historical museum.

The drive took us through the same stretch of highway where a Qatari man had once rammed us off the road. The road was busier now, mainly with fleets of trucks transporting water to and from Al Khor. Forty minutes later, we arrived at the top northwestern tip of Qatar and found the fort at the end of a rough sandy trail that almost led to the ocean. The Zubarah Fortress stood before us, looking well kept despite the ravages of the desert and sea air. We parked in the empty car park and climbed out.

"I can't believe it's closed!" I lamented as I tried to open the huge wooden door.

Angela sighed. "Typical."

Later we found out that the fort was only open on weekdays, and sometimes for short period on a Friday afternoon at the whim of the curator. We had stupidly arrived on a Saturday.

"I wonder if any new Qatari recruits will end up here."

"What do you mean?"

"Well, if I was in charge of the Qatari army, I'd get my recruits to work in this windswept place. It would be good for them. They could march up and down the battlements and keep a look out from the turrets."

"Good job you're not in charge, then."

The Qatari government had just introduced a new mandatory National Service scheme for all Qatari men aged between 18 and 35. It was an effort to instil some sort of discipline into an increasingly pampered and wayward section of society.

New recruits could expect to have their heads shaven and their diet of fast food curtailed, but could look forward to three or four months of driving around in armoured cars and learning to use assault weapons. Despite this promise of a Boy's Own adventure, the scheme went down like a lead balloon among many Qatari males. Some called it a 'collective punishment'; others said it would interfere with their employment prospects. To counter this, the government stated if a man already had a job, then it would remain open for him, and, anyway, they could always defer National Service any time up until the age of 35. Even so, men were reluctant to sign up, so, to deter any would-be draft dodgers, the government set out a few rules should any able-bodied man refuse or delay signing up until they were too old. First, they would go to jail for a month. Secondly, they would face a fine of 50,000 riyals (£9,000). Lastly, and worst of all, the men would never be allowed to get a job with the government – one of the best deals for any Qatari citizens. The government also told its citizens that army recruiters would be looking out for anyone turning up who did not appear legitimate, meaning that a Qatari man could not send his Nepalese driver in his place.

On a certain ex-pat website dedicated to Westerners, someone cleverly wrote a spoof article about Qatari National Service. It said that the scheme was being expanded to include Western men, because, after taking into account all Qataris who had been made exempt from the draft (for ill health, being too old or being too important), only nine Qatari men were left for duty. One imaginary ex-pat stated: "One minute I'm filing paper, the next I'm being drafted into the Qatari army. It really is true that in Qatar, anything can happen. At least I'll get an embroidered patch as a souvenir."

Angela took a photo of the cannon in front of the fort and then we drove to the abandoned town, only a five-minute journey away. Zubarah town, the namesake of the fort, used to be a major player in the pearl fishing industry. It once had a busy harbour full of dhows, a grid-like pattern of Arabian dwellings and a noisy bustling souq at its centre selling sugar from Bombay, dyes from Gujarat and cinnamon, turmeric and pepper from Arabia. But after a series of raids by Omani warships, culminating with a ferocious attack in 1811, which left the town almost destroyed, the people of Zubarah moved out, never to return. It didn't take the sand long to claim it. What remains are a series of archaeological digs.

Most of the village looked like piles of loose rubble in the sand. Without the roped-off trail, we would have trampled over most of it, thinking it was nothing special. Restoration work was going on in certain places, with bags of cement, trowels and a few pairs of discarded gloves, but there was nothing much to see apart from a few low walls that were once rooms. After twenty minutes, we had seen enough and decided to drive to The Pearl instead.

8

Dubai has *The Palm*: a series of artificial islands that, when viewed from the air, resemble a gigantic palm tree. Doha has *The Pearl,* which resembles a string of pearls.

The Pearl is full of luxury shops (including Rolls Royce, Maserati and Ferrari showrooms), expensive restaurants and a series of towering apartment blocks with names such as Florida, Monaco and La Riviera, all giving the impression that The Pearl is somewhere special. To reinforce this notion, the designers have incorporated sweeping canals, a huge marina for yachts, a series of bridges (including a replica of Venice's Rialto Bridge) and a set of open-air plazas, decorated in a faintly European style. The only problem is that for nine months of the year it is too hot in Qatar for anyone to appreciate them.

Another problem facing The Pearl is, since 2011, the Qatari authorities have banned all restaurants from selling alcohol. It was their way of saying: look, enough's enough, we tolerate booze in the hotels, and people drinking at home, but we want The Pearl to retain some semblance of Arabian restraint. This was fine, but the fact of the matter was that a high proportion of diners in The Pearl's restaurants were Westerners, who liked nothing better than to have an exorbitant glass of white with their meal. Not serving alcohol had a twofold effect: first, the restaurants lost money due to the lack of beverage sales and second, Westerners relocated to the restaurants in West Bay's hotels instead. Night after night, tables were left empty. Gordon Ramsay's *Maze* restaurant was one of the first to close. He moved his restaurant to the Doha St. Regis hotel, where customers could order wine by the bottle. Yet, despite the alcohol ban, The Pearl is still prime real estate, with an average apartment costing 16,000 riyals per month (£2800).

Angela and I drove along the road linking The Pearl to the mainland and parked in one of the subterranean car parks. We reversed between a red Ferrari and a purple Bentley. All around us were supercars and large 4x4s. Above ground, the high-end shops were largely empty (most people still preferred to shop in huge malls rather than the expensive boutique stores of The Pearl). The only people we could see browsing the jewellery, the designer bags and

Louboutin shoes were Qatari women with platinum credit cards. We bypassed the stores and walked towards the marina.

The water looked beautiful, a lagoon of clear turquoise filled with tiny shimmering fish. The yachts looked great, too: a fleet of white vessels anchored for the afternoon. When the weather cooled off later that afternoon, their Qatari owners would take them out for a spin, taking along their jet skis for a bit of aquatic fun.

We decided to get something to eat, and chose a Lebanese restaurant with an upstairs veranda. Our table overlooked the marina and the developments beyond. The Pearl was still a work in progress, with teams of men toiling all over the island, digging, planting, hammering and sometimes flashing their private parts at women.

In the local press, a story had recently emerged about a group of male flashers operating on The Pearl. According to one female witness, a 'scruffy-looking Indian labourer' had exposed himself and then proceeded to press his 'member' against her leg. Another woman described how a man of 'African origin', wearing a 'colourful robe', had grabbed his nether regions, grinned at her, and then referred to 'his manhood'. Keeping her wits about her, she swore at the miscreant, who walked away.

A few days later, a young British woman was walking towards her apartment when a man dressed in blue overalls started staring at her. This in itself wasn't anything unusual, but when the man walked in strange circles, the woman began to watch him closely. She saw him relocate to a bench just ahead of her. As she approached, the man removed his penis from his overalls and started to masturbate. Being level headed, she pulled out her phone to take a photo of the act, but before she could, the man ran away.

Three days later, the same woman saw another man with his penis out. He was leaning against a wall, grinning and masturbating. Again, the young woman tried to take a photo, but the man managed to block his face with his helmet – his construction helmet, that is – before fleeing. Because of the flashers in operation, the woman took to walking with her dog, which was a good job, because five days later, she saw a third man, again in blue overalls, up to no good. As he walked up to her, he was touching himself and grinning. Not wanting another penis performance, the woman picked up a stone and threw it, telling the man to stop whatever he was doing or she would set her dog on him. She told reporters that the man's grin disappeared. He fled soon after.

The construction workers on The Pearl worked hard, though, doing backbreaking shifts for six days out of every seven. No wonder some of them acted a bit strangely at times. And they were working for such small amounts of money. I'd read about a group of Nepalese, Bangladeshi and Sri Lankan workers who had actually gone on strike, an unheard of thing to do in Qatar. But they had a point. Before flying to Qatar, the men had signed contracts saying they would be paid 900 riyal per calendar month, plus 200 riyals for food, about £190 in total.

When they arrived in Doha, their employers ripped up the contracts. They forced them into signing new contracts stipulating that they would be paid 600 riyals plus the 200 riyals for food. But what could they do? They were already in the country and their wives and mothers were depending on their remittance. So they went to work, hoping that their employers would change the contract, which of course they didn't. The final straw was when their supervisor told them they had to work on their day off. They refused and a standoff commenced. The upshot was that the police came and arrested all the men. After a short period of incarceration, the courts deported all one hundred of them back to their point of origin.

Angela and I finished our late lunch in the Lebanese restaurant and headed back to our apartment in Al Khor. We had seen most of the sights of Qatar, and so we were keen to get out and see more of the Middle East. With the Easter Holidays almost upon us, the next phase of our travels was about to come into play. It would start with a flight to Dubai.

Top row: Dhows moored near the Museum of Islamic Art
Middle row: Angela posing outside the Museum of Islamic Art;
Souq Waqif; One of the glitzy skyscrapers of Doha – this one known locally as Tornado Tower .
Bottom row: A reproduction of an old Arabian cooling tower; Panorama of Doha

Part 2

Dubai – Muscat – Manama – Istanbul – Beirut – Istanbul – Amman – Damascus – Petra

Chapter 5. Dubai: Arabia made Easy

Virtually every Western expat who lives in Qatar will visit Dubai at some point. Some will board the first flight after work on a Thursday (the start of the weekend in all of the Gulf States) to jet off for a couple of days of pampering in Dubai's shopping malls and plush hotels. Some may even go for Friday brunch.

Brunch in the Middle East is a different thing from brunch in Europe. Brunch in Europe is a civilised affair: a little snack, mid-morning, and a nice cup of tea to wash it down with. Brunch in the Gulf States is an alcohol-fuelled extravaganza of gluttony. In Dubai, most of the top-end hotels offer something called Friday Brunch. For around 500 dirham (£80), a person can eat and drink as much as they can between noon and 4pm. Doha has its fair share of Friday Brunches too and Angela and I had been to a few. Each time, we had found the setting agreeable and plush, and our friends in high spirits, but we always ended up eating far too much delicious food and quaffing gallons of champagne. The rest of the day was ruined as a result.

A couple of our colleagues once flew to Dubai to sample one of its famous brunches. She told us that it was like a UK nightclub: flashing lights, blasting music, young women wearing the skimpiest clothes imaginable, and leering men hanging around by the meat counter. She told us she didn't want to repeat the experience. Angela and I commiserated; it sounded like hell.

For this latest trip to Dubai, we were going to steer well clear of the brunch brigade and try to seek out any culture the city had to offer.

2

When we boarded our late afternoon flight from Doha, the number of empty seats was surprising; usually flights to Dubai were full. Five minutes later, the reason became clear – a troop of Arab women boarding late. They entered the aircraft from the front, all black abayas, black veils and expensive handbags. One woman had impossibly beautiful eyes, large and hazel-coloured: as the only body part visible, they made her even more alluring. Even Angela noticed how striking she looked. A female member of the cabin crew was leading the women along the aisle, showing them to their seats. I looked down to read the in-flight magazine, but then looked up as a commotion developed. From what I could gather, one group of Arab women were refusing to sit in their assigned places.

"What's happening?" whispered Angela, straining to see.

"I don't know..." The young Korean stewardess was talking to the group but then turned her attention to some seated passengers. "I think the stewardess is asking some people to move so the women can sit together."

One Western man, in the row of three seats, one of which was empty, got up and moved elsewhere, allowing two of the women to sit together. They did not thank him or even acknowledge his presence; they were too busy barging their way into the row. That left three more women, all snaggle-toothed harridans by the looks of their eyes. They reached the row in front of ours and stopped. A trio of Indian men were sitting there. The stewardess leaned toward them. "Can you speak English?"

The man nearest the window said he did.

"These ladies would like to sit together and the seats they have been assigned are no good to them because they all are spread around the cabin and their seats are next to men. So I'm asking if you would all move for me. I'll show you where. It would help a great deal."

The man conferred with his pals. Then they all stood up, collected their things and spread out around the cabin. On their way, the Korean stewardess thanked them, which was more than they got from the Arab women. And so, after delaying our flight for twenty minutes, we finally went on our way to Dubai.

3

It was sizzling outside the passenger terminal of Dubai International, and our taxi driver was just as hot and bothered. More or less as soon as we'd left the airport road, a traffic snarl stretching as far as the eye could see had stopped us in gridlock. Beeping horns and wild hand gestures were the order of the day, with our driver being a particularly bad offender. As a truck tried to squeeze in front of us, he almost had a thrombosis, shaking his fists and ranting in a dialect of southern India. When he'd calmed slightly, he turned to faced us. "Traffic very bad. Few years ago, journey across city maybe take fifteen minutes. Now take one and half hour."

Angela and I nodded as we inched forward. Dubai had exactly the same problems as Doha, despite both cities' efforts at mass transit. Their highways simply couldn't keep up with demand. With nothing else to do, I studied the view outside. Dubai was known for its skyscrapers, hotels and palm trees, but the backstreets looked almost identical to the ones we saw every day in Qatar: tailors' shops, cheap kebab eateries, jewellery stores – most emblazoned with a mixture of Arabic and English – and convenience stores. Forty-five minutes after leaving the airport, we reached our hotel in the Deira district of the city. Without traffic, it would have taken only ten.

4

The next morning, I pulled back the curtains of our high-rise hotel room to reveal the sprawl of Dubai. The Radisson, across the street, was blocking a fair portion of the view, but we could still see enough to marvel at the sheer scale of desert engineering. Burg Khalifa, the tallest building in the world, was sticking up above the forest of steel like a sleek silver dart. It was a giant among giants. We were going to visit it later.

"What shall we do first?" I asked Angela, who had joined me at the window. She was gazing down at Dubai Creek, a slice of saltwater blue that separated Dubai into two sections.

"What are the options?"

"A boat trip on the Creek or visiting that souq you were reading about last night."

"The souq."

"I thought so."

After a leisurely breakfast, we jumped in a taxi towards Madinat Jumeirah, a modern and luxurious development of hotels, eateries and wind towers together with the aforementioned souq. The souq had been built in the style of a traditional Arabian town, and we'd read that the impression most visitors get when they visit it is that they are wandering through the Dubai of old, the *traditional* Dubai. I was interested in seeing if this was the impression we got too.

The journey took us past another icon of Dubai: the fabulous Burj Al Arab, the only seven-star hotel in the world. At £1000 per night, it was way out of our price range, even if it did offer a helicopter transfer from the airport for a one-way knock-down price of 10,000 dirham (£1650). But no one could argue about the sleek looks of the third-tallest hotel in the world, its curves of blue and silver representing the sail of a traditional Arabic sailing vessel.

"Why don't we go and have a look inside?" Angela suggested. "Maybe get a coffee or something."

"We can't. It's off limits unless you're actually staying there. They want to keep the riff raff out."

"Really?"

"I think the only way you can go in, if you're not a guest, is to go for high tea or something. But that costs about fifty quid per person."

"Fifty pounds for a pot of tea? Are they insane?"

I laughed. "You get sandwiches and cakes too."

"Oh, right. That's okay then."

We carried on through the traffic towards Madinat Jumeirah, telling the driver to take us directly to the souq.

5

A wooden, nautical-themed steering wheel that looked as if it had once belonged to an old dhow plying the spice route to India lay against an old teak pillar. Next to it was a small iron cannon. On the ground in front of the stalls sat copper teapots, golden candlestick holders, Arabian daggers, silver shisha pipes and large brass camels. The proprietors sat nearby, checking their phones or reading newspapers. Light came in through gaps in the wooden ceiling, or else shone from large metal lamps suspended from chains above our heads. The smell of incense, the sound of exotic chatter and the tinkling of metallic goods: Madinat Jumeirah was undeniably the nearest thing Dubai would get to a traditional souq, but, judging by the elevated prices, its main clientele were guests of the Burg Al Arab hotel. If Hollywood were to recreate a movie set for an Arabian market scene, Madinat Jumeirah would be it. It was squeaky clean, a sanitised version of the real thing, where comfort and cost were the main things on offer. Angela stopped by one stall, looking over some scarves, but the prices put her off. "We can get these same things in Doha for a tenth of the price."

We decided to go and see the tallest building in the world instead.

Sheikh Zayed Road, a mammoth twelve-lane artery, was the main route through the city. Many of Dubai's skyscrapers lined the road, but we could have been in New York, Tokyo or Hong Kong. That said, the massive Burj Khalifa looked like *pure* Dubai. If any building deserved to be an icon of the city, then surely this was it. It towered upwards at such an angle that it seemed as if we were staring vertically to see its upper reaches. It was so tall, in fact, that the top section was six degrees Celsius colder than the bottom.

"My God!" exclaimed Angela, trying to take a photo with her camera, but failing dismally because it wouldn't all fit inside the viewfinder. "That is *amazing*."

I nodded, my mouth hanging open. Dubai may have been a false Arabia, but it was certainly a spectacular Arabia. Burj Khalifa was an architectural masterpiece: a gleaming, glittering, shimmering silver rocket lined with blue. It towered almost three thousand feet, the same height as two Eiffel Towers balanced end on end, and then a little bit more for good measure. To stand underneath it was something else.

To go up to the observation deck, we had to buy a ticket from the adjoining Dubai Mall, the largest shopping mall in the world. At the counter, the Filipino woman told us it was twenty pounds each for a standard ticket, but that meant waiting an hour in the queue. "You can buy fast ticket," she told us, "for four hundred dirham." This was about £70 each.

"What do you think?" I whispered to Angela.

Angela screwed up her face.

We decided to leave it. Anyway, judging by the photographs behind the Filipino woman, the view from the 124th floor looked the same as we'd seen on approach to Dubai International.

6

For once, the thought of visiting another shopping mall didn't fill me with dread. In fact, going to the Ibn Battuta Mall was my idea. Named after a fourteenth century Arab explorer, the mighty mall was split into six themed courts, each reflecting a chapter of the great man's travels: China, Tunisia, India, Andalusia, Persia and the one I was really looking forward to: Egypt.

In the taxi, I asked the driver where he was from.

"India, sir, Kerala," he answered politely, staring at the traffic ahead. Like all taxi drivers, time was money for him, and the longer he sat in traffic, the less of the latter he would make.

"We've been to Kerala," I told him.

He looked at me in his mirror. "You been Kerala, sir?"

"Yeah. We loved it there," Angela said. "It's so green and...colourful."

"Yes! Very nice! My home!"

Angela asked if he had a family back in India.

"I have wife and two children, both boys. My youngest son is eighteen months. I not see him yet."

"Not seen him?" I said.

"I came Dubai just before he born. But I think I go back to India soon. He very ill. Heart problem, sir. Look, I show you." He reached into his glove compartment and produced an envelope. Inside, was a stapled jumble of A4 paper: a photocopy of a medical report written in Hindi and English. From the basic gist of it, I worked out the boy had some congenital heart problem, a difficulty so serious that surgery was the only way forward.

I passed it to Angela. She read it over. "You poor thing." said Angela. "What will you do?"

"I have money – but flight expensive. But what choice do I have? I need to go India for my son. All savings gone."

After twenty minutes of barely moving, we saw the cause of the jam. Half a kilometre in front, water covered the highway. Deep water. Nearby construction work was to blame for the sorry mess.

"Car will not get through, sir." said our driver. "Need four-wheel drive. Water too deep."

We sat and pondered our next step. The Ibn Battuta Mall was not far away; we could actually see it over on our right. But was it the correct etiquette to jump ship and leave the taxi driver marooned in a sea of traffic?

"Look, sir," said the driver. "Why don't you walk? Not far. Better than waiting in taxi."

"What about you?" I asked.

"For me, no problem. I get back to Jumeirah different way. Less traffic. Easy for me."

We paid him what was on the meter and then added some extra. "We hope your son gets better," said Angela.

"Thank you, madam."

We opened the door and headed towards the flood.

7

The flood was worse than we imagined. The highway was there, and then it was not, covered by a lake that seemed to be growing every second we stood watching it. Hundreds of construction workers, all wearing identical green overalls, and all excited by the impromptu disaster zone created within their work area, were standing by the side of the road, well away from the flood. Most were grinning as they watched traffic attempting to negotiate the deluge.

Cars beeped incessantly and, in the distance, we could hear sirens. Close to us, a truck driver leaned out of his window as he gushed through the flood, gesturing at the madness of it all. The water covered his wheels. To our right, perhaps at the centre of the flood, an abandoned car stood with water sloshing around its windows. It was a scene of turmoil: one that Angela and I somehow had to cross.

Angela grimaced as she stepped into the water. "It's hot!"

She was right. It was like wading through a cup of tea, and I could feel my legs tingling as I followed her across. For a moment, I wondered whether there were any chemicals in the deluge but realised it was too late to do anything about it. Another truck passed, its driver looking down at us with open astonishment, but two minutes later, after almost tripping on the hidden kerb, we made it to the other side where higher ground allowed us to escape the hot lake. I looked at Angela and she looked at me. We were both drenched and our legs were red from the heat of the water. But we had survived our first crossing of a bona fide Arabian flood.

Angela and I stepped inside the Chinese Court of the Ibn Battuta Mall. A large Chinese junk sat on a pedestal above a pool of water. Ibn Battuta had once sailed on the same type of vessel to China.

The next court, dedicated to Battuta's travels in India, featured mock white marble walls (representing the Taj Mahal, no doubt) and a massive *elephant clock* as its centrepiece. The clock was a working example of a medieval invention: a tall box strapped to the top of an Indian elephant. Every hour, a set of wooden figures moved in timely synchronisation, the same way they would have done in India a century earlier. A few people were looking at the contraption, but most were more interested in the stores, and I could tell Angela liked the look of them too. With forty minutes to go before the clock did its magic, I reluctantly followed Angela towards a clothes shop.

"Why don't you go on ahead," she suggested as I traipsed around the tenth aisle of clothes. I could barely hide my impatience. "I can tell you're bored. Go through the other courts and get a coffee. I'll meet you at the end in an hour."

It sounded like a plan, and so I left Angela to her clothes and shoe shops and rushed to the Persian Court, which was the best so far. A huge dome, painted in the style of a Persian mosque, made up the motif. It was intricately designed, painted with blue, gold and red geometrical patterns, and it reminded me of a mosque I'd seen in Uzbekistan. Yet, I was in the middle of a shopping mall. Whereas Madinat Jumeirah had disappointed me – largely due to its failed attempt at recreating a traditional souq – the Ibn Battuta Mall wowed me for the opposite reason. Here, the designers were not attempting to hoodwink anyone into believing they were actually in China or Iran: instead, they were offering a visual extravaganza with over-the-top grandeur. It was, quite simply, the most amazing mall I'd ever been in.

The Egyptian Court was a bit of a let-down. Apart from an authentic looking Egyptian stone gateway decorated with hieroglyphs and pictures of ancient pharaohs, it was all tacky plastic palm trees and fake arches. The next court, dedicated to Tunisia, was a disappointment too, home to fast food restaurants. The designers had tried to disguise the KFCs, Pizza Huts and Burger Kings by adding some upper levels that looked like old Tunisian town houses. It didn't work. The Andalusian Court, the final one, was home to silver arches, marble columns and a shop selling a 24-carat gold-plated Apple iPhone. It was sitting in a velvet-covered display box looking like a gold nugget. For three thousand pounds, it could've been mine.

An hour later, Angela found me in Starbucks. She had some shopping bags full of clothes and scarves. Soon after, we were in a taxi to the hotel. Instead of taking the usual fifteen minutes, it took two hours: the flood had caused chaos with the roads.

8

Friday morning was another hot and sunny one. It was our final day in Dubai before flying to Muscat and so we wandered down to Dubai Creek to hire a boat. Only a few water taxi drivers were in attendance, all of whom spotted us immediately. "You want thirty-minute tour of Creek?" one man asked, an Indian man wearing a white robe. "Only three hundred dirham!"

I laughed. "Three hundred? You must be joking!" Behind him, the other boatmen grinned.

"Okay, offer fair price," the man said, revealing a set of brown-stained, oversized teeth.

"Fifty dirham," I said.

It was the boatman's turn to laugh. "For that, I let you swim. Come on, offer fair price."

I decided to humour the man. "One hundred. Final offer."

"Two hundred."

"One hundred."

"One hundred and fifty."

"One hundred."

"Okay, one hundred and twenty."

We shook hands, and so Angela and I boarded a rickety open-sided vessel called an *abra*. The driver looked like he had cannibalised his seat from an old Ford Cortina. As soon as Angela and I took our places on the wooden seats in front of him, we headed into open water.

In the eighteenth century, Dubai's Creek would've been busy with dhows, stopping off on their way to India or East Africa, or else fishing the abundant waters. The Creek was the lifeblood of Dubai, the source of its economic boom. It needed it after the calamitous events of 1841, when a terrible smallpox epidemic struck the town, forcing many of its citizens to flee. Today, most of the ships have moved to the port of Jebel Ali, the world's largest man-made harbour, with only the old dhows remaining. If we ignored the skyscrapers, the set of white yachts and the sound of our abra's two-stroke engine, we might have been sailing an Arabian inlet from yesteryear.

"I love boat rides," said Angela, manoeuvring herself into a sunnier spot. "I love the feel of the wind on my face and the fresh air all around me. We should do more of them."

I nodded and leaned back in my seat, idly watching Dubai passing by on both banks of the water. Thirty minutes later, after a quick tour of The Creek, our seafarer dropped us off on the other side of the water near Bastakiya.

9

Once upon a time, Bastakiya had been a district of Dubai where wealthy pearl traders lived. They built traditional Persian-style dwellings as their homes, constructing them along twisting alleyways that led towards airy courtyards that were cooled by wind towers. It was the hippest place to live in Dubai. A hundred and fifty years later, things changed. With the discovery of oil, the rich people of Bastakiya became even richer. Abandoning their pearls for barrels of black oil, they left the traditional townhouses and moved into plush villas and palaces in the modern part of the city. They left Bastakiya more or less derelict.

With the oil came the sudden influx of low-paid foreign workers who moved into Bastakiya. The new residents did not maintain the already crumbling buildings and soon the area began to take on the air of a slum. By the late eighties, the government of Dubai decided enough was enough and earmarked the district for total demolition. One person stood in their way: a man called Rayner Otter.

Rayner Otter was a British architect living in Dubai. Bastakiya intrigued him, so much so that he acquired one of the old town houses for his own use. By using the original plans, Otter managed to renovate the home back to its former glory; when he heard about the plans to level it, he began a campaign to save it. His mission tied in with a timely state visit by Prince Charles. Somehow managing to persuade the Prince to take time out from his official work, Otter showed him around Bastakiya, pointing out that traditional houses were few and far between in Dubai, and that, if they were demolished, a great piece of Arabian history would be lost. The Prince agreed, and, with this royal approval, the municipality of Dubai reversed its decision to knock it all down. Better yet, they announced they would begin renovation work.

Angela and I wandered past art galleries, restored wind towers, cosy restaurants, souvenir shops and a mosque. A few men were hanging around outside a cream-coloured mosque, and when the call to prayer began, we stopped to listen. The muezzin was singing words familiar to us due to living in Qatar for so long: *Allah akbar, Allah akbar, Allah is the greatest, Allah is the greatest*, the man sang, his haunting melody echoing along the alleyway. The men went inside the mosque to pray.

"How about we have some lunch, relax in the hotel for a while, and then visit the old souq this afternoon?" Angela suggested.

"Why? Are you up for a bit of haggling?"

"No, but you will be, I hope."

10

Endless textile, trinket, perfume and spice stores made up the bulk of Dubai Old Souq, a semi-covered stone thoroughfare lined with stores. Traders loitered outside the shops, but, unlike Souq Waqif in Doha, making eye contact with any of the men was fatal. "Ah, hello! Come in my emporium! I give best price! *Best Price, I tell you!*"

We did go in one shop. As soon as we did, the man told us to feel the quality of the thawb material. I did so, and so did Angela. It felt like a piece of cloth to me and Angela seemed noncommittal. Even so, I wanted one. It might make a good fancy dress outfit sometime. "How much?" I asked.

"Two hundred fifty dirham."

I shook my head. "Too much."

"Quality merchandise! Make you good Arab!"

I shook my head and turned to leave, pulling Angela along with me.

"Okay, okay," the man said, flapping his arms. "One hundred fifty dirham. Best price! I have to feed family!"

"Fifty," I said, letting my steely gaze reach his. I wanted him to know I was not a man to be trifled with. I had cut my teeth in the haggling dens of Marrakech.

The man pretended to cry, which made us laugh. "Cloth worth more than fifty dirham! You put me out of business! I sell for one hundred dirham. But that is best, best price!"

One hundred sounded fair enough, almost seventeen pounds. And for that, I was getting the full works, white thawb robe, long headdress and black piping to keep it in place. Even so, I didn't want to appear a pushover. "I'll give you seventy-five."

The man grimaced, smiled and then nodded. "Eighty-five it is."

I nodded assent and the man began wrapping my outfit. Angela and I left the shop satisfied at a job well done. That was until we saw exactly the same thawb in another shop for thirty dirham.

11

Instead of getting a water taxi back across the creek, Angela and I decided to walk. It would involve a long trek around the northern tip of the city, but we didn't mind, since most of it would be under shade. What we didn't bank on was the sheer amount of men. Being a Friday meant that hundreds of South East Asian workers were hanging around in huge groups browsing the souq stalls, sitting on walls or generally just milling. Almost all of them were wearing their finest shirts and trousers, with their hair neatened and shoes polished. It was a similar deal to the men in Qatar, all of whom donned their Sunday best for their evening soiree. Angela and I reckoned they dressed up to prove to themselves that they were normal human beings and not just faceless drones. But men being men, whenever they caught sight of a woman, they would stare, especially if the woman had blonde hair.

"Jesus," I whispered as we squeezed our way through them. There had to be hundreds, perhaps thousands, of men. None of them seemed threatening in any way, and all were courteous as they moved aside for us, but every man, young and old, was staring and smiling at Angela. It was as if they had never seen a woman before.

"This is what it must be like to be famous," she said, clearly embarrassed. My wife was trying to keep her gaze fixed forward as scores of eyes followed her passage. "I suppose I should feel flattered...but this is really horrible."

As for me, I might as well have been invisible. I could have walked along with my tongue out and no one would've noticed.

We came to the pedestrian-only tunnel that crossed underneath Dubai Creek. In it, the crowd of men compressed into a furnace of heat, noise and sweat. But like the parting of the waves, the men allowed us passage. We emerged at the other side as fifty pairs of eyes swivelled in unison towards Angela. Finally, we caught a metro back to the hotel.

12

For some inexplicable reason, our hotel didn't have a bar. "You stay here," I said to Angela. "I'll nip over the road and see if I can get my hands on something." I left our hotel, crossed the busy highway – risking death by doing so – and wandered into the Radisson's lobby. I found the ground-level bar and went straight to the counter. I asked the barman, a Filipino gentleman, whether I could buy a bottle of white wine.

"Of course, sir" he replied. "250 dirham for the house white."

I took a sharp intake of breath. Over forty pounds for a bottle of plonk was ridiculously steep, but Angela was expecting me to come back with a bottle; besides, we were on holiday. I nodded begrudgingly at the man. He went to the fridge, picked out a bottle and placed it on the bar.

"One or two glasses, sir?"

The question stumped me. I didn't need any glasses. "None. I want to take the bottle to my room."

The barman looked at me quizzically. "I'm sorry, sir. If you want wine in your room, you must order room service. It is the same price. All the drinks we serve here have to be consumed in the bar itself."

My heart fell with a thud. I was so close to the wine I could actually taste it. The bottle stood on the bar with tiny bubbles of condensation forming on its exterior. I cursed my predicament and then looked imploringly at the barman. "Look, I'm not actually staying at this hotel. I'm in the one across the road. It doesn't have a bar and I want to take the bottle over there. My wife is waiting for me." And then I added something terrible. "She's disabled. That's why she can't come."

The man looked at me with pity. Perhaps he believed my outlandish story or maybe he didn't, but whatever, he still shook his head. "I'm sorry, sir. Security wouldn't allow you to take it into the street. It is against the law. And I'm sorry for your wife, too." He picked up the bottle and removed it from my sight, then went off to serve someone else. Crestfallen, I left the hotel and wandered back to our dry hotel. Angela was waiting in the room with the corkscrew poised. When I told her the whole sorry tale, she looked shocked, then erupted into laughter. "You told him I was disabled? Really? It's you who is disabled: mentally disabled."

So instead of wine, we had a glass of water each. "Here's to Dubai," I said, clinking my glass against Angela's. "We salute you."

We looked outside at the twinkling lights of Dubai. The Burj was there, lit up like a glittering firework, as were the other skyscrapers surrounding it. In the sky above, a ceaseless necklace of twinkling lights were making their way to the airport. We closed the curtains and said goodbye to the least *Arabian* of all the major Gulf cities, yet the one easiest to enjoy.

*Top row: Burg al Arab forming the backdrop of some man-made waterways in Madinat Jumeirah; A sunset palm shot of what looks like a mosque, but is actually the domes of Ibn Battuta Mall
Middle row: The magnificence of Burj Khalifa; Inside the Persian Court of Ibn Battuta Mall; A wind tower at Madinat Jumeirah
Bottom Row: McDonald's – Arabian style; Dubai Souq*

Chapter 6. Muscat, Oman – the quieter side of the Gulf

FCO travel advice: Most visits to Oman are trouble-free. Driving can be dangerous outside Muscat; there is a risk of hitting wandering camels.

A Fly Dubai Boeing 737 got us into Muscat's Seeb International Airport at around 4pm. As we taxied towards the terminal, I had high hopes for Muscat: it was supposedly the most traditional of the Gulf States. In contrast to its neighbours to the north, Oman had eschewed skyscrapers, favouring low-level and mostly white architecture. In photos we'd seen, the Omani capital looked beautiful and unspoilt in a rapidly expanding – petrochemical fuelled – Middle East.

The efficient airport authorities had us processed in no time, and we were in a taxi by twenty past. The pristine black highway was mostly free of vehicles and traffic jams. It was a world away from the roads in Dubai and Doha. Even the drivers seemed courteous.

"Welcome to Muscat," said the taxi driver in good English. He was an Arab gentleman in his early forties wearing a white thawb and rounded white hat embroidered with orange and brown patterns. I wondered whether he was Omani, but felt that he couldn't be. A local citizen would not be driving a taxi. I decided to ask him.

"Yes, of course," he answered jovially. Outside, the scenery was of desert sand and white settlements.

"And you were born here?"

"Yes. In Salalah. You been there?"

I shook my head. All I knew about Salalah was that it was Oman's second largest city and was in the south, close to the Yemeni border. It was reportedly a beautiful place to visit.

"You should go. It is beautiful. They have a rainy season there, you know – from the monsoon. The desert is transformed to green. It really is quite amazing to see. Between July and September, Salalah turns into India!"

I still wanted to know why an Omani citizen was driving a taxi for a living, so asked him.

"In Oman," the driver replied, "*only* Omanis are allowed to drive taxis. The government pays us very well. But watch out for some drivers. They won't use a meter and will try to rip you off. Where are you from?"

We told him we were from England but lived in Qatar.

The man nodded knowingly. "So that is why you ask if I am Omani! You cannot understand why I drive a taxi. Now I understand. Yes, it is different here from Qatar. We have people who work in everyday professions. Not like the Qataris, eh?" He laughed at his own accurate observation. "But there is one big problem with this. Much of the population in Oman is young, under twenty, I think, and there will soon not be enough jobs for them all. Also, many of the young people in this country do not want to work. They would rather sit at home and play computer games. The government is worried about this, but I'm not. I have job and it pays me well."

"So there are not many expat workers over here?" asked Angela, beating me to the question. On our right was the massive Sultan Qaboos Grand Mosque, named after the current king, the longest-ruling Arabic ruler. Its huge white minaret and golden dome were in direct contrast to the palm trees and beige mountains behind it.

"Yes, there are many, but the government restricts numbers. They want to – how do I put it – *Omanise* the country. This means training Omanis to do many of the jobs. The government needs to do something; oil is running out. The good times will not last forever."

I asked him about his hat, which, unlike the headdresses of Qatar and the U.A.E., looked like a white patterned fez. He told me it was a *kuma*, a prayer cap. "I think they first came from Zanzibar, which used to be under Omani rule. Mine was woven by a woman, but you can buy machine-made ones in the souq for a few rials."

We drove on through the outskirts of Qurum, a suburb of Muscat where most of the hotels were located. Five minutes later, we pulled up outside our place of stay for the next few days. We handed our friendly driver a wad of Omani rials and then, for the remainder of the day, lounged by the pool.

2

As expected, our first Omani morning was hot: the temperature needling 40°C. Our hotel was behind a beach road that ran alongside a deserted strip of sand dotted with a few palm trees and picnic tables. When the sun set later that evening, we would see scores of people on the beach – families cooking up kebabs on makeshift barbeques and Asian ex-pat workers playing football on the sand – but for now, there was nobody.

Further along was a rough-and-ready fish market where Indian men had laid out the catch of the day on the ground. At the edge of the water, a dozen or so small blue and white boats lay dormant, their work done for the day. A few people were looking at what remained of the fish, which wasn't much. The odour was pungent, a claustrophobic smell that made us wrinkle our noses. A small Indian woman didn't seem to mind, though, and bent closer to inspect one dried-up hammour fish. With a prod and a poke, she nodded to the man in charge, who grabbed it and flung the fish into a blue plastic bag.

We rounded a bend and came to a stretch of beach devoid of anything except sand. We wandered down to the ocean, where I took a tentative step into the surf. It was perfectly warm and I was soon wading up to my knees. I turned around to see Angela studying a few large rocks marooned in the low tide.

"Come and look at this," she shouted.

I sloshed over and found her pointing at a shiny black blob. It was about the size and shape of a large sausage and it was clinging to the base of a rock.

"What is it?" Angela asked.

"No idea." I leaned down to study it and then spotted another. Like its pal, the black sausage was clinging to the damp section of rock near the sand. "Maybe they're sea slugs?"

Further along from the slugs, or whatever they were, was an almost hidden stretch of sand full of empty sun loungers. It was the private beach of the Crown Plaza hotel. After a quick check that no one was around, we crept up to the most secluded loungers and claimed one each. For the next hour, we pretended we were on a real holiday, relaxing by a tranquil ocean populated by black sausage creatures.

That afternoon, we caught a taxi to the souq in Muttrah, the commercial heart of Muscat. As before, our taxi driver was a jovial and well-spoken Omani who seemed keen to engage us in conversation. After the usual chitchat about where we lived and why we were in Oman, I told him we were travelling to as many nations of the Middle East as we could. The man nodded approvingly. "How many have you been to so far?"

"Just four: Qatar, Saudi Arabia, U.A.E. and now Oman."

"Ah, so only the Gulf States?"

"No, we're going to Jordan and Lebanon later. Maybe even Iraq."

"Iraq? Are you being serious? Iraq has bombers and kidnappers. It is not safe for tourists. Tell me you are joking with me about Iraq."

"I'm not going," said Angela. "I've got more sense."

I changed the subject by asking the driver what Muttrah Souq was like.

"It is good for tourists. But take your time when looking at the wares on offer. And don't forget to haggle with the storeowners – they will expect you to do this. You will get many bargains if you remember this."

We turned onto the corniche road, with a long crescent of azure on one side and a sweeping line of white buildings on the other. Behind the corniche was a series of jagged brown mountains, the first high ground we'd seen on our travels so far. We came to a stop just past a large mosque. "Okay, here is souq. Remember to bargain with the men in there. Don't let them take you for fools."

3

Muttrah Souq turned out to be a compact area of tiny stalls dating back two hundred years. Originally, heavy wooden rafters had covered the maze of alleyways, primarily to block the heat from the sun, but also to keep the sand and flies out. Because it was so dark, traders and shoppers carried candles to see what was going on. Many Omanis still call the souq the Market of Darkness.

During this period, the Market of Darkness became a place of frantic wheeling, dealing and throaty conversation as wooden carts brimming with frankincense and silver paraded past. Spices and nuts, newly delivered from India, were bought and sold by the sack load. Nowadays, instead of the candles, electric lights illuminate Muttrah Souq, but the aromas remain the same: frankincense, perfume and incense. Compared to the souqs we had visited so far, this one seemed the real deal.

The first few stalls sold women's clothing, and the men in charge wanted us to look. "These are best garments in Oman," boasted one man. He flashed a wide smile but we bypassed him easily, not interested in his belly dancing outfits. The next man, an Indian, tried to cajole us into his scarf shop. "Air conditioned!" he said. "Very cool!"

The allure of some cold air pulled us in, and, after some good-natured haggling, heeding the taxi driver's advice not to appear too green, Angela bought three scarves, much to the delight of the proprietor. After passing some stores peddling frankincense, we came to a line of shops selling *Khanjars,* the curved daggers and national symbol of Oman. They looked like they could inflict serious damage, but I knew they were only used for ceremonial purposes. I was almost tempted to buy one, but, with the cheapest one costing fifty pounds, I reluctantly left them behind. Five minutes later,

Angela almost succumbed into buying a silver trinket box for a similar price, and so I suggested we leave the souq; otherwise, we might be tempted by the wares.

We emerged back onto the sun-drenched corniche road. We crossed it to stare at the ocean. Moored in the harbour were a few dhows and a single grey gunship belonging to the Omani navy. Dangling thin fishing lines over the edge of the corniche wall were half a dozen fishermen. All looked East Asian, maybe Pakistani or Bangladeshi. While we watched, one yanked up his line, deftly grabbing the small dangling crab and plopping it into a bucket.

Behind us was a mosque, a tall white building fashioned with a towering blue minaret and bulbous dome. Along from it sat a few old men eating kebabs and smoking cigarettes. Around their feet, a couple of cats scavenged for food, one of them getting lucky when a sliver of meat fell. It scarpered with its treat while its pal looked on in feline astonishment.

"I like Muscat," Angela said.

4

Vast pools of oil and gas do not lie underneath Oman as they do in some its neighbours, but it still has enough petrochemicals for its citizens to enjoy an enviably high standard of living. In terms of GDP per capita, Oman is richer than the United Kingdom, Canada and Denmark, and according to data collected by the World Bank in 2013, it is the twelfth most affluent country in the world. Before oil was discovered in 1956, Oman only had ten kilometres of tarmac.

We were in a taxi heading towards the heart of old Muscat. The highway was in the best condition of any road I'd seen, and that included roads in Europe and North America. What a difference oil made, I mused. Yemen, the country next door, had missed the gravy boat big time. Without any real store of oil, it was easily the poorest country in the Middle East, falling apart at the seams.

Our taxi pulled up in an area almost empty of people. The only person was a man walking up to the entrance of a small blue and white mosque. The taxi driver asked whether we wanted him to wait for us, but we told him no; we didn't know how long we would be. He shrugged and drove off.

We walked past the mosque, turned a corner and came face to face with the magnificent Al Alam Palace, official residence of Sultan Qaboos of Oman. It looked like it belonged in a science-fiction novel. Two white arches (the only nod at traditional Arabian architecture) and four gigantic blue and gold columns, which resembled oversized golf tees, made up the front section. It looked like the home of a futuristic king. Sitting on top was a giant slab of white marble, and on top of that, a tall flagpole. When we'd seen a photo in the guidebook, the Sultan's palace had looked small, but it was not; it was massive, deceptively so. We took a photo and decided what to do next.

"Where's the harbour?" asked Angela.

I sniffed the air, turned to my left and right, then announced that we should head back past the blue and white mosque. The road led us along a district of white residential villas hidden behind tall white walls. No one seemed to be around. There were no sounds of children playing, of dogs barking, or of any conversation. It was as if everyone had packed up and left. After another turn, with more of the same white villas, I admitted I didn't have a clue where we were and that we ought to flag down a taxi.

"Where from?"

Angela had a point. We had not seen a single moving vehicle, let alone a taxi, since the other taxi had dropped us off. The only cars in sight were a few parked Land Cruisers. With no other plan in mind, we walked to the end of the street and turned onto another residential street. We were getting deeper in what was probably a housing compound.

"I'm sick of this now," groaned Angela a few minutes later. "My feet hurt and I'm getting too hot. We have no idea where we are and there's nothing to see. Can't you use Google Maps on your phone or something?"

I'd already thought of that, but my phone battery had died in the taxi, rendering it useless. Angela didn't even have her phone. Just as I was pondering whether to knock on someone's door, a couple of ageing Westerners appeared from the gate further up the street. I looked at Angela and she nodded. We ran to intercept them.

5

"Hi," I said to the couple, a little more breathlessly than I'd intended. "I don't suppose you know the way to the harbour?"

"Harbour?" said the woman in her late sixties. She had a mop of white frizzy hair on her head and a long hippy-type green dress draped over a stout body. Her husband was tall and thin, wearing a neatly pressed suit. His most distinguishing feature was a large knobbly nose. Like his wife, he had an abundance of white hair upon his head. "Which harbour do you mean?" the woman asked in a matronly manner. Her husband silently appraised us.

I turned to Angela for help. She looked at me blankly. I turned back to the woman. "The one in the centre of town."

The man finally spoke. "I think they mean Muttrah Harbour." He sounded like an upper crust gentleman, the sort of man who spends time in country clubs sipping scotch.

I shook my head. "No, we've just come from there. We mean the main harbour."

"But Muttrah is the main harbour," the woman said.

Angela piped up. "We saw a photo of the harbour in our guidebook. Look, I'll show you." She handed it to the woman. Both old folks peered at the picture.

"Oh, I know where this is," said the woman. "And you're sort of right; it's not Muttrah Harbour, but it's certainly not the main harbour. By the way, I'm Margaret, and this is my husband, David."

After pleasantries, Margaret took charge again. "Look," she said, "if you give us ten minutes to visit the gallery, we'll take you there, won't we, David?"

David nodded uncertainly

She pointed at a dirty white 4x4 parked in the street. "Please get in the back. The gallery is only five minutes away."

I looked at Angela and she shrugged. We climbed inside.

David started the car and drove so slowly that we might as well have pushed it. But at least it was cool inside, and, besides, the couple seemed interesting. Margaret was giving us a commentary about their lives, saying they had lived in Oman for sixteen years, where she worked in finance, the same as her husband before his retirement. "But the country is changing so quickly that we hardly recognise the place. Isn't that right, David?" Before he had a chance to answer, she snapped at him to pick up the pace, informing him that we were on a tight schedule.

David muttered something under his breath, which his wife failed to catch; she was too busy telling us about how much rental prices had gone up in the last few years. "It's out of control," she said. "But I feel sorry for the low-paid expats. I don't know how they cope. At least we've got money and a housing allowance."

"They do all right," interjected David, saying nothing more.

I asked about the lack of people in downtown Muscat.

Margaret nodded. "It's the holiday season. Most expats have flown off to Sri Lanka or Dubai for a few days. Give it a week, and it will be back to normal."

A minute later, we stopped outside a house. It turned out to be the gallery. Margaret addressed us. "Fifteen minutes is all we can spare here. David and I are buying a piece by the in-house artist – a lady we know – so when you go in, please look around and be sure to see upstairs: there are some fabulous examples of wooden Omani doors. Any questions?"

I looked at Angela, who shook her head. I did too and so we followed Margaret and David outside.

6

As expected, the gallery was small. It was a converted villa full of sculptures, paintings and carvings. As Margaret had suggested we do, Angela and I went upstairs to see the doors. One in particular looked brilliant – a carved slice of wood full of spiralling patterns and leaves. The price tag was eye-catching enough to make us wince and so we wandered to a painting of an old Omani townhouse rendered in oil so thick it seemed almost 3D. It was equally expensive, well out of our price range.

Downstairs, we found David in deep conversation with a blonde-haired woman, presumably the artist. Aged about forty, she was waif-like, and talked with her arms a lot. Margaret was nowhere to be seen. Waiting for David and the woman to finish talking, we loitered by a painting of an Egyptian eye. Suddenly, Margaret appeared from a side room. "Come on," she summoned. "Time to go."

Back in the car, David was at the wheel, but it was abundantly clear that Margaret held the driving seat. "Left here, now! Slow down, David! Oh, for goodness' sake, you could've got in that space – such a shame!"

"Did you get your paintings?" Angela asked.

"Yes, we did," answered Margaret. "We'll pick them up when they've been framed. Did you look at the wooden doors?"

Angela nodded. "They were beautiful."

"We've got a couple in our villa."

David eventually found a parking space alongside a sea wall. High up on a craggy cliff was the Merani Fort, which we had seen in the guidebook. Margaret glanced at her watch and turned to face us. "We'll stop here for exactly two minutes so that you can take some photos. Don't dally, please!"

The Portuguese ruled Oman for a 143-year period during the sixteenth and seventeenth centuries and, to protect their interests along the lucrative Arabian Gulf, they built a series of forts along the coastline: the one we were staring at was one of them. Margaret told us the Muscat Garrison, a branch of the Omani army, used it as their headquarters. I managed to snap off a quick photo before we were shepherded back into the car.

It was almost dark when we reached the corniche road. The orange reflections in the water, the warm pink glow from the buildings, the palm trees, the minarets and the brooding ridges and valleys of the distant mountains made the scene almost irresistible. Doha and Dubai might have innovative skyscrapers, but Muscat looked like the real *Middle East*.

David turned off the main road and found a car park behind a set of shops. As we trundled along, trying to find a spot, a teenage boy, who looked Pakistani or Bangladeshi, approached David's window. David mumbled to himself.

"Calm down, dear," said Margaret. "We don't need another episode."

David brought the car to a standstill, pressed a button to lower his window, and, then, before the boy had chance to utter a single word, he let rip. "Listen here, Sonny Jim! I just want to park my car and not have any funny business from the likes of you!"

I looked at Angela who raised her eyebrows. David's bottled-up anger, no doubt caused by his wife's ceaseless nagging, was now fizzing dangerously.

David continued. "Are you listening, boy? Because I've lived in Muscat longer than you've been alive! I know all the scams; I've seen every one! And I've kicked plenty of arses too." David's gasket was about to explode.

The boy blinked. "Sir, I just wanted to say car park is free tonight. No charge like usual. No funny business, I promise."

David's window went up, his anger suddenly defused. "Buggers are always trying to extract cash from us. But I'll not have it! Not on your Nelly!" Margaret was shaking her head but was remaining uncharacteristically mute.

After thanking the couple for the lift, Angela and I walked around the souq for a while and then found a taxi to take us back to the hotel.

7

The next morning, we arrived at a marina south of Muscat to board a small boat. It was 8am and our vessel was packed with twenty other people, all of us eager to see some dolphins. With the hatches battened down, and bilge pumps cleared, we slowly powered across the still water of the harbour and then came to a juddering stop. At first I thought the engine had conked out, but when the captain pointed into the water on our left, I realised I was wrong. Easily visible in the clear water was a large turtle. Our presence did not perturb it because it carried on with its leisurely swim. Cameras flashed, voices oohed, and the turtle obliged by turning upside down to expose its belly. After a few lazy turns, it sunk into lower waters out of sight. The boat moved on, nudging its way beyond the harbour. Once free of the rocky headland, the captain hit full throttle, sending the boat into overdrive. The two powerful outboard motors provided enough thrust to send us skimming over the waves at breakneck speed.

Ten minutes of constant wave bashing sent everyone, apart from the captain and his wiry assistant, dizzy in the head. Then we slowed and there they were: dolphins by the dozen, swimming in pairs, in threes, some leaping out of the water in graceful arcs. Then another pod appeared: a more inquisitive group this time. Instead of keeping their distance, they swooped around the boat, some even poking their cute noses out of the water to do the rapid clicking sound for which dolphins are famous. And then, in the middle of the dolphin frenzy, another creature arrived, this one skimming across the surface. It was a sea snake, a poisonous one, according to the captain's assistant. Its black and white striped body rippled the water as it slid past the side of the boat. The dolphins didn't seem to mind the intruder, and carried on with their frolicking and playing, allowing us all to marvel at the sight of their enjoyment. All of us were happy when we returned to the harbour.

That evening, Angela and I wandered along Qurum beach to watch the sunset. The black slugs had gone, but now the beach was busy with people. Arabic men and women were sitting on blankets near impromptu barbecues while their children jumped over small sand dunes. A group of Asian ex-pat workers were trying to play cricket just beyond the waves, throwing a few overs before the sun went down. Angela and I found a wooden seat and brushed the sand off so we could sit down. The temperature was perfect, the sort of heat Brits craved on their summer holidays, yet seldom got. Instead of pot-bellied lobsters paddling in the Mediterranean, a trio of black-clad women with a small boy were sloshing about in the Gulf. Angela and I waited until the sun had set behind the distant mountains, and then retired to our hotel. It was time to pack for the next country of our journey, and the tiniest one in Arabia: the Kingdom of Bahrain.

Top row: Muttrah Corniche; A pretty mosque in Qurum
Middle row: Sunset falls over a Qurum beach; Al Alam Palace, official residence of the Sultan Qaboos of Oman
Bottom row: Wares for sale inside Muttrah Souq; The Grand Mosque of Muttrah; Two Omani men chewing the fat outside Muttrah Souq – the one on the left wearing a kuma cap, his pal wearing a wrap around massar

Chapter 7. The smallest state in Arabia: Bahrain

FCO travel advice: Demonstrations and protests are a regular occurrence in Bahrain. Some can be violent, however, most visits are trouble free. You should remain vigilant and if you encounter a large public gathering, you should leave the area immediately.

Bahrain isn't much bigger than the Isle of Man, but with its abundance of oil, it is one of the richest countries in the world. Its capital, Manama, has skyscrapers, a profusion of five-star hotels and a selection of white palm-fringed beaches; despite this, it doesn't receive anywhere near the visitors that Dubai, Muscat or even Doha gets. In fact, the only time Bahrain is busy with tourists is during the annual Formula 1 race. That was when the hotels are full of fans enjoying their motor racing with a Middle Eastern slant. Our visit to Bahrain was not on the race weekend, which meant our flight was largely empty. On the short ninety-minute hop from Oman, I counted nineteen people on board an aircraft with a capacity of 178.

Bahrain is not endowed with tourist sites; we knew this already. And so did the country itself. So instead of trying to tempt tourists away from the established Gulf hotspots, Bahrain has established itself as a financial and trade centre. Who needs tourists when you can have cash-laden businessmen!

Thus, apart from the Formula 1 crowd, few tourists ever bother with Manama, and the few people we knew who *had* been told us not to bother. One colleague described it as 'Bore-rain'. Well, we were hopefully going to prove the naysayers wrong.

2

Angela and I had almost been to Bahrain before. When we'd first arrived in Qatar, instead of securing working visas on our arrival at immigration, the airport official had issued us with thirty-day tourist visas. We didn't know this, of course, and only realised the error when our human resources manager called us into her office.

"You've both overstayed your visas. The fine is 200 riyals per day," the woman told us, checking her computer screen. "And so seventeen days over means you owe...3400 riyals each."

I mentally calculated this to be over a thousand pounds between us! The Indian woman saw the worry on our faces and told us not to worry. "School will pay the fine, but you'll have to pay for the flights."

"Flights?" I said. "What flights?"

"Flights to Bahrain. They're usually the cheapest. You'll have to do a visa run tonight." When she saw the uncomprehending looks on our faces, she explained what she meant.

Visa runs were common practice in the Middle East, she told us, whereby ex-pats unable to secure work visas will leave the country just prior to their thirty-day tourist visa expiring. They will exit Qatari immigration, fly to a neighbouring country and get stamped in by the foreign immigration. Then they will catch a flight back to Doha to obtain a new tourist visa from Qatari immigration. Every month, they will repeat the process. For us, it was slightly different. We would pay the fine, then leave Qatar. "When you arrive back in Doha," said the human resources manager, "you must explain that you are working in Qatar, and that you need work visas. Hand them this." She passed over an A4 piece of paper written in English and Arabic. It explained that we were employees of RasGas, one of the biggest petroleum companies in Qatar.

But in the end, we didn't have to do a visa run to Bahrain. Somehow, the human resources woman and Qatari immigration sorted everything out before we even got to the airport. We didn't even have to pay the fine. But deep down, I was disappointed. Doing a visa run had sounded exciting and a little bit edgy.

3

Manama is cut from the same piece of cloth as Doha and Dubai. It has a long, curving corniche full of super-modern glass skyscrapers, a network of palm-fringed highways and areas of construction going on everywhere. Some parts of the city look like a huge building site.

In the taxi, we passed a large billboard of King Hamad ibn Al Khalifa, the 64-year-old ruler of Bahrain. He was a heavy-set man with a thick black moustache. King Hamad had paved the way for radical changes in Bahrain. His rulings allowed women to vote and he sanctioned parliamentary elections. Hamad's changes made his country one of the most liberal in the Middle East; despite this, his subjects were not happy.

When Arab Spring protests began spreading across North Africa, Shia Muslims in Bahrain (the majority of the population) decided to get in on the act, demanding the same political power as their minority Sunni Muslim counterparts. In February 2011, when small protests broke out around Manama, Bahraini security forces were quick to act, using tear gas and rubber bullets. One campaigner died. When a Facebook page belonging to a group of Shia Muslims called for the 'Day of Rage in Bahrain,' protesters came out in their thousands. In response, government troops stamped down hard, shooting people, placing the city in lockdown and positioning tanks at key intersections.

But the protests would not stop. Day after day, more protests were held; at one point, forty percent of Bahrainis citizens were part of them. With government forces in danger of being overrun, King Hamad asked for Saudi assistance, who obliged by sending in a thousand soldiers. The extra troops managed to keep a lid on things, as did the newly declared three-month state of emergency. To this day, the peace in Bahrain is uneasy, and, according to the UK foreign travel advice, *'Following a fatal bomb explosion on 3 March 2014, you should be especially vigilant'*.

We looked outside. The streets of Manama looked peaceful and unthreatening. Workers were working, men in white thawbs were sitting inside their Land Cruisers, and, over on our right, a gorgeous blue ocean shimmered next to a region of palms and skyscrapers.

"Right," I said, grabbing my hat and camera, "let's see the sights of Manama." After dropping our things off in the hotel, and then studying the map, I was eager to go. We only had one full day in Bahrain before heading off to Lebanon.

Angela nodded. "Taxi or walking?"

I peered outside. It looked hot, but we were not far from the city centre. "Walk."

The second we left the air-conditioned lobby, our sunglasses steamed up with condensation. The humidity was incredible, like walking through an invisible mist. Within a few minutes, my skin was glistening and my clothes were damp. Compared to the dry air of Muscat, Manama was a sauna.

Hundreds of red and white Bahraini flags lined the highway we were traipsing along. Every few moments, a truck would thunder past, generating a breeze in its wake, rippling the flags further. A few car drivers stared at us as if we were mad for walking in the sun, and a group of Asian workers toiling at a roundabout gawped for a moment before resuming their digging, rolling and concrete pouring. Further along, we came to an amusement arcade that offered ten-pin bowling and bumper cars. It was a pity it was closed or we'd have gone in to buy a drink. But at least now I knew that we were close to the Bahrain National Museum – the map said it was the next building along.

It was, and just inside the entrance was a set of mannequins dressed in traditional Bahraini costumes. We bypassed them at top speed, heading to the cafe. When the waitress came over, I ordered three bottles of Diet Coke, all for me. Angela ordered a large bottle of water. Afterwards, we felt recovered enough to look around the museum.

Scale models of Bahrain's fortress filled the first room. The fortress was somewhere we hoped to visit later. Around the models was a collection of old pots and ceramic jugs. We'd seen hundreds of similar pots in other museums, so we quickly moved to a section full of figures doing traditional Bahraini jobs: pot making, sewing, beard trimming and tinkering with metal dishes. The next room was dedicated to the pearling industry in Bahrain.

In the 1920s and 30s, when Arabian pearls were in demand around the world, Bahraini boats would sail to the pearling grounds around the shores of the island to set anchor above the rich pearl fields. Bahraini pearls were the most coveted of all the Gulf pearls; because of this, thirty thousand men earned their living as pearl divers (many of them slaves from Africa). With a peg-type clip holding their nostrils closed, and leather bandages around their hands and feet (as protection against rocks), the men would descend to the seabed using sturdy ropes weighted down with heavy rocks. When they reached the bottom, they would disconnect the rocks, which men in the boats above hauled back to the surface. For the next minute and a half (the maximum time they could hold their breath), each diver would frantically search for oyster shells, depositing any found into the bag slung around their necks.

While the divers were doing this, they would be on the lookout for sharks, jellyfish and manta rays. Other dangers included popped eardrums, blurred vision and stray waves that could send them out to sea. But the greatest danger was something called a *shallow water blackout*.

Taking too many breaths before entering the sea caused shallow water blackouts. But no one knew this at the time. Taking these breaths did not affect a diver at the bottom of the sea; only as they returned to the surface. As the diver's handlers pulled them upwards, some men simply blacked out and their lungs filled with water. By the time the divers were out, they were already dead or suffering from severe brain damage. And the thing about a shallow water blackout was that no one could predict it; anyone could suffer from it, even the healthiest of divers.

For most divers, however, the trip to the seabed usually went without major mishap. When they had finished at the bottom, they would give a sharp tug on their rope, and the puller would hoist them up. They would empty their booty onto the deck for the ship's captain to inspect. The vast majority of shells would be useless but, every now and again, one would contain the prize of a pearl, which would be a cause of jubilation. But not for the pearl fishermen – they were at the low end of the ladder concerning remuneration. No, their job was to dive up to forty times a day so that the ships' owner might make a pile of cash.

By the end of the 1920s, pearling was the mainstay of many economies around the Gulf. This way of life might have continued had it not been for the Japanese. In the 1930s, they developed a way of creating pearls under controlled conditions, which meant cheaper pearls, more choice of colours and fewer imperfections. Almost overnight, the Arabian pearling industry was rendered obsolete, sending economies into meltdown. Luckily for them, they had something far more precious under their desert sands.

5

The best part of the Bahrain National Museum was the section dedicated to ancient burial mounds. At first, when we entered the large room, Angela and I thought the mounds were piles of loose rubble, perhaps part of an unfinished exhibit. One of them even had a large plastic lizard sitting on it, left there as a joke, we presumed. We almost left, but were glad we didn't.

They were not piles of desert rubble; they were examples of ancient burial mounds belonging to the Dilmun people, an ancient civilisation who, between 4000 BC and 800 BC, lived in an area stretching from Bahrain to Kuwait and into the eastern part of Saudi Arabia. Collectively, their mounds formed the largest prehistoric cemetery in the world, with over 350,000 of them covering the landscape like gigantic stone molehills. Today, less than one percent remain, the rest levelled to make way for new housing developments, highways and office blocks. Later, we found out that

Bahrain's surviving burial mounds were located at the edge of a highway cordoned off with old barbed wire. Across the road from them was an urban development. According to people who had seen them, plastic bags and piles of litter were all over the mounds.

Angela and I stopped at the two reconstructed mounds in the middle of the room. The information told us that archaeologists had found a man's skeleton inside the mound. He'd been laid on his side with two smaller skeletons next to him. The man's age was estimated to be around forty (the typical life expectancy of the Dilmun people), but the other skeletons were both infants, most probably his children. How they died was a mystery.

6

Inexplicably, there were no taxis outside the museum. Resuming our trek, we turned along the King Faisal Highway, home of the glitziest skyscrapers in town, including the spectacular Bahrain World Trade Center, surely one of the best skyscrapers in the world. It consisted of two huge blue and silver triangular towers (representing sails), joined together by three sky bridges. If Dubai had the Burj Khalifa, and Kuala Lumpur had the Petronas Towers, then Bahrain could hold its architectural head up high with its World Trade Center. And as well as looking fabulous, it was the first skyscraper in the world to integrate wind turbines as part of its design. Fifteen percent of the energy needed to power the building came by way of the wind generated from the Persian Gulf.

"I'm dying," I croaked as we passed underneath the massive skyscraper. My mouth was bone dry even through my body and clothes were soaked. A road sign told us that if we carried on walking the full length of the highway, we could eventually arrive at the Saudi Arabian border. The twenty-five kilometre long King Fahd Causeway connected the two countries, a bridge that 25,000 vehicles used every day. The bridge was especially busy at weekends when

Western ex-pats working in Saudi headed over to Bahrain for some rest and recuperation in Manama's alcohol-friendly hotels.

We turned into a small square where a small sand-coloured mosque sat wedged between a McDonald's and a branch of the Al Salam Bank of Bahrain. We rushed towards the burger joint, but then detoured to Hardee's instead when we saw the queue. Hardees's was empty, and as we staggered inside, weary and red, the Filipino woman behind the counter immediately told us to sit down. "I bring water," she said.

We gulped the water down, laughing with giddy relief from getting out of the sun. God knows how people coped when their car broke down in the desert, and they had to walk. No wonder they died after only a short time; we had both felt delirious after just thirty minutes, and that was in a city centre.

I rubbed my forehead; it was completely dry. The air conditioning had dried my face totally. I could see tiny beads of white on Angela's face: salt crystals. The sun had evaporated a gallon of water from our bodies, leaving only the salt behind. To replace it, we ordered hamburgers, fries and double Cokes.

7

The next morning, over breakfast, I flicked through the *Bahrain Daily Tribune,* which led with a story about the heat wave over the Gulf. Unseasonal winds had caused it, and they warned residents that things would be uncomfortable for the next few days. Another story was about a 29-year-old Bahraini woman who had been jailed because of a car accident. She had been driving a minibus full of children, and during the final stop of the day, outside one of the children's homes, she somehow ran over a four-year-old Bahraini girl, killing her instantly. Instead of stopping, the woman fled the scene. Police quickly caught up with her. She had been driving without a licence and so a Bahraini court had found the woman guilty, sentencing her to one month in jail.

Another headline was to do with prostitution – a subject I'd never once encountered in any Qatari newspaper. The story talked of two Arabic women (though it didn't say which country they were from) who had been working together as a prostitution double act. Police had arrested the pair during an undisclosed sting operation. Both women were sentenced to four months in prison for engaging in 'immoral activities', three months longer than the woman who had killed a child.

Another story involved a Bahraini woman jailed for assault. When I'd finished reading it, I explained the gist to Angela. The woman had tied her Asian housemaid to a chair and then shaved off her hair.

"No!" said Angela.

"She claimed the maid had fleas. After she'd shaved her, she dragged the poor woman back to the recruitment agency and told them she wasn't fit for work. The agency saw the state of the maid and rang the police. The mad woman got ten days in prison."

"Ten days? Is that all? That poor maid."

We finished our breakfast and decided to hit the mean streets of Manama again.

8

"What is wrong with all the ATMs in Bahrain?" I snapped. We had just arrived in City Center Mall, a large, standard-issue Middle Eastern shopping parade full of western brands and infernal cash machines that refused to dispense money. When the third machine spat out our card, I grew agitated.

"We'll have to pay for things by credit card from now on," said Angela. "At least we know they work."

I looked at the notes in my wallet, counting out thirteen dinar, worth about £22. Our plan had been to have some breakfast and then get a taxi to Bahrain Fort, an old Portuguese fortress sitting on the outskirts of Manama. We could pay for out coffees with our card, but then would have to hope thirteen dinar would be enough for the taxi. With this plan sorted in our minds, we found a Starbucks.

Half an hour later, we were standing on a street corner near the mall waiting for a taxi to pass. None did. Just as we were about to give up and go back inside, a white pick-up truck stopped. The Arab gentlemen in the driver's seat looked at us. He was about sixty with a weathered face full of wrinkled skin poking from under his white headdress. His lengthy thawb couldn't conceal a large stomach bulging towards the steering wheel. He reached over and opened the passenger door. "Taxi?" he bellowed in a thick accent.

Angela and I regarded his vehicle. It looked in okay condition, but the rear section was full of junk: an old tyre, various tools and random pieces of cloth. And nowhere on his vehicle was any indication it was a taxi.

"Are you are taxi?"

"Of course, taxi," he said. Traffic was swerving around him, most of it beeping at his sudden standstill.

I looked at Angela. There were no other taxis in sight, and besides, if he were an unlicensed driver, then his price would be lower than a regular taxi. I gestured to the lack of seating. "Where do we sit?"

"Of course!" he boomed again, ignoring the question. "Get in!"

"Where do we sit?" I repeated.

"Here!" he patted the seat beside him. He wanted us to squeeze into the single passenger seat. It actually looked about doable and so with Angela looking more amused than anything else, we agreed on a price of three dinar for him to take us to Bahrain Fort.

Angela was pressed against the door while I was pressed up against the Arab man. When we set off, the man's arm brushed against my leg when he changed gear.

"My name Hameed," he said in broken English. "Who you?"

We told him, adding that we lived in Qatar.

"Qatar not like Bahrain. There peaceful. Here, not peaceful. There, Qatari are rich people, here only few Bahraini are rich. Most poor, like me."

As we negotiated our way along the highway, a troop of ex-pat workers were toiling at the flowerbeds, their heads and faces covered in towels as they tried to block out the worst of the sun and fumes. Even though our driver had referred to himself as poor, he was a damned sight better off than the men outside.

We pulled into another shopping centre, this one called Bahrain Mall. Hameed stopped at the entrance, garnering another set of beeps for blocking one lane of traffic. He ignored them. "Three dinar, please!"

I looked at him as if he were mad. "This is not the fort."

"Bahrain Mall! Of course! Three dinar!"

I shook my head. "No! We want Bahrain Fort! Not Bahrain Mall. Look!" I showed him a picture in the guidebook. Hameed grabbed it and peered at it up close, his nose almost touching the page. Then without another word, he engaged the gear and off we set again. Next to me, Angela looked more confused than amused now, but I was getting annoyed. We had probably been driving in the wrong direction, and God only knew how much the journey was going to cost now. Soon we were back on the highway, then driving past a petrol station and a few industrial-type buildings, before veering sharply into scrub and desert. The road abruptly turned into a dirt track but the car did not stop.

My eyeballs rattled as we crunched and dipped across the scrubland. Hameed didn't seem concerned that his car was taking a battering, and, if anything, seemed to be revelling in the bumpy ride. Up ahead was a metal fence, which we stopped at. Beyond it was the fort. A guard appeared and, after a brief discussion with Hameed, opened the fence by a car-width to allow us entry. We trundled up to the fort where Hameed stopped. I told him that, if he waited for us to look around the fort, and then took us back to our hotel afterwards, then we would pay him double.

Hameed considered this. "How long you stay at fort?"

I shrugged and looked at Angela. After a brief conference, we told him that half an hour would be sufficient.

Hameed nodded. "Twenty five dinar for all."

I laughed and shook my head. Twenty-five dinar was over forty pounds, double what we had anyway. Hameed lowered his price to seventeen dinar until I showed him the contents of my wallet. He then did something surprising. He grabbed all the money and counted out the thirteen dinar with his big sausage fingers. Then he stuffed it all in his robe. "Thirteen will do."

I was taken aback. "Hang on," I snapped. "We'll pay at the end."

"No! Money is for Hameed," he announced. He then pointed to where the guard station was. "I wait there for you."

Short of fighting him inside the confines of his pick-up, we had no choice but to trust him, and so Angela and I climbed out, watching his pickup drive off, possibly to Saudi Arabia. As he left, a cloud of dust billowed in its wake.

9

In ancient times, the Dilmun civilisation used the site of Bahrain Fort as their capital. When the Portuguese took over Bahrain in the sixteenth century, they found the site of the old capital agreeable to their needs too. On top of a sandy hill, they built a fortress, which actually reminded us of the Zubarah Fort in Qatar. It looked well-kept and surprisingly large, and, now that we were walking closer to the entrance, we could see that we were not alone: scores of huge black beetles walking on spindly elongated legs were crisscrossing the pathway.

"What if he drives off?" asked Angela, voicing the concern of the moment. "He's got all our money."

"We'll go to the guard, get him to ring a taxi, and then sort it out from there."

"I'll blame you if he's not there."

We walked through the arched entranceway to find a set of open-air ruins. They were mainly broken sections of wall, a few crumbling arches and a series of stone corridors. We wandered through most of them, keeping an eye out for the black beetles until we found a good vantage point at the far end. In the distance were the skyscrapers of downtown Manama. The Arabian Gulf beyond them provided a gorgeous line to the steel and glass forest. At sunset, Bahrain Fort became busy because of the view we were staring at.

With our thirty minutes up, we made our way back to the wire fence. There was no sign of Hamad or the white pick-up. Just before Angela could unleash her ire, Hameed came bounding out of the guard house. He'd parked his vehicle further along the sandy track behind a couple of buildings. As promised, he drove us to our hotel at the other end of the city. It was a pity we couldn't give him a tip.

10

Our day in Bahrain had come to an end, and we had not even had time to see the Tree of Life, a four hundred year old tree that had miraculously sprouted in the middle of the Bahraini desert one day despite having no known water source. Nor had we visited Manama Souq, home to cheap Chinese goods masquerading as traditional Arabic offerings. But we had seen most of the sights, and had enjoyed the company of an unlicensed Bahraini taxi driver to boot. The next country on our travels promised to be as different from Bahrain as France is to Greece, and would be our first trip outside the wealthy and relatively safe Gulf States.

Lebanon has a history of danger: a nation ruled by fear, terror and kidnap. Its image has changed somewhat in recent years, but even so, many tourists do not regard it as wholly safe, with areas of its capital defined as no-go areas. With thoughts of car bombs and Hezbollah running through our minds, we packed our suitcases in preparation.

Top row: A monument to pearl divers at the back of the Bahraini National Museum; Manama sprawling into the distance
Middle row: The closest we came to a camel; Bahrain Fort
Bottom row: Al-Fateh Grand Mosque, Bahrain's largest place of worship; The magnificent Bahrain World Trade Center

Chapter 8. Beirut and Byblos

FCO travel advice: The security situation in parts of Lebanon can deteriorate quickly. There is potential for further violence, which would restrict departure options. There is a high risk of attacks by Islamic extremist groups.

Perceptions of Beirut are so deeply ingrained that, even though the civil war ended a quarter of a century ago, many people still associate the city with bombings, kidnap, carjacking and bloody massacres. The word *Beirut* is also a generic term for a place less than perfect. 'It's like Beirut here' is a common phrase used by Brits when they arrive at their Spanish hotel and find it in the middle of building work.

The occasional war-mongering story still blights Lebanon. In 2005, a car bomb killed the Lebanese Prime Minister, Rafiq Hariri, igniting a series of protests across the country. A year later, there was a conflict with Israel when Hezbollah, the Islamic paramilitary and political organisation with strong support in Lebanon, sent rockets across the border, killing three Israeli soldiers. Israel responded with rocket attacks of its own, targeting bridges, roads, petrol stations and Beirut international airport. By the time the UN managed to broker a ceasefire, a thousand Lebanese people, and two hundred Israelis, were dead.

In 2012, a car bomb exploded in Beirut, killing almost thirty people and injuring hundreds more. The following week, insurgents blew up two mosques in the northern town of Tripoli, killing forty people. In January 2014, a pair of suicide bombers struck the capital, killing nine people, and a month later, not long before our visit, two more suicide bombers unleashed their explosives during the Beirut morning rush. It was all very worrying, and, in the weeks leading up to our trip, I had been keeping a close eye on any developments in Lebanon, reading the UK Foreign and Commonwealth Office travel advice on a daily basis. As we flew from Bahrain to Beirut, the advice was to be careful, something we intended to do religiously.

2

"Have you ever been to Israel?" barked the middle-aged security official at Beirut Rafiq Hariri International Airport – a man sporting a khaki uniform and some thick black eyebrows.

I shook my head. Angela was answering the same question at the next counter.

The man turned through every page of my passport, studying every stamp, visa and ink marking. I knew any evidence I'd ever visited Israel would bar my entry into Lebanon, but, since I had never been there, I knew I was safe. The security official eventually realised this and placed a red stamp on a blank page, and finally welcomed me into Lebanon.

After collecting our luggage, Angela and I headed towards one of the parked airport taxis. Outside the terminal, we could feel the dip in temperature now that we'd left the searing heat of the Gulf States. It felt amazing.

The driver was a forty-something man with a thick black moustache and pack of cigarettes on his dashboard. Like most Lebanese motorists, he preferred aggressive driver techniques: forcing his way into lanes that he had no right to be in and then grumbling and shaking his hand whenever someone did the same to him.

The airport road took us through a district of Beirut called Dahieh, the headquarters of Hezbollah. Instead of being a hotbed of terror activity, it seemed perfectly normal, with people going about their business. Phone shops selling top-up cards, a line of stores selling women's garments – some offering a 70% sale – as well as an assortment of grocery stores, made it just another part of the city.

"Is it safe around here?" I asked the driver, now onto his third cigarette.

"Safe?" he answered. "Of course it's safe. This is not Iraq or Syria."

At the moment, that may be true, I thought, but if Israel ever resumed airstrikes, then Dahieh would be their number one target.

We carried on driving northwards, leaving Dahieh behind as we hit the busy streets of downtown Beirut. It was a place of high-rise buildings, shopping malls and spindly minarets. It had the palm trees and urban sprawl of Dubai, but it lacked the overbearing glitz and glamour of the super skyscrapers.

With a sudden veer to the right, our taxi turned off the main highway. We passed a large billboard advertising Almaza, the local Lebanese beer: a strange sight after the almost blanket prohibition in the Gulf. Then we came to a sudden stop at a busy T-junction. After the fifth car passed without letting us out, the driver shook his head and lit another cigarette. Two cars later, he banged his fist on the dashboard, sending his cigarette packet flying to the floor.

"Women are the worst drivers," he sneered. "So aggressive." Finally, he had enough of waiting and barged into the thick of it.

Ten minutes later, we arrived outside the hotel.

3

"It looks grim," Angela said the next morning. We were making our way along a street close to the hotel. The overcast conditions were giving the buildings a dark and shadowy hue. I nodded at her observation but knew it had nothing to do with the weather. Many buildings were grubby and grey, some crumbling so badly that they ought to be condemned. Except they weren't, at least judging by the washing dangling from their balconies.

Bullet holes peppered a few buildings – a legacy from the civil war – and further along, two unshaven men sitting outside a dingy storefront eyed us as we manoeuvred past baskets of fruit and large bottles of cooking oil. We got past them and regarded the fleet of bangers beeping and lumbering their way along the road, one so bad that it looked like its driver had stolen it from a scrapheap. It had dents on every panel and a cracked rear window. Its taillights were smashed or missing and the driver's door looked like it had been repaired with gaffer tape. The car was brown with more rust than paint. How it was going was a miracle.

After walking downhill, we reached the corniche road, which was far prettier than the backstreets. High ground flanked the city around us, the hills in turn leading to a set of distant and snow-capped mountains. In the winter, they were popular with skiers. The coastal road was busy, and not just with old rust buckets, but with brand new 4x4s, shiny new saloons and modern buses. We followed it up a curving incline until we arrived at Beirut's most famous tourist site: Pigeon Rocks.

Geographically, Pigeon Rocks are a large chalk arch and a slightly smaller stack. I knew this because I had once studied A-level geography. They were both sitting in the sea with little tufts of vegetation growing on their tops.

"Why are they called Pigeon Rocks?" Angela asked. "Because I can't see any pigeons."

"I've got no idea." I turned to look at the buildings opposite. A few high-rise hotels, a set of restaurants, the Bay Rock Cafe and a collection of palm trees gave this part of Beirut a modern feel, with a definite Mediterranean vibe. It looked like Spain, Italy or Greece, and certainly not Arabia.

Angela took of photo of the rocks and turned around. "What now?"

"I reckon we walk back along the corniche. There's a marina at the other end with some nice cafes."

We headed back down the hill.

4

It was a working day in Beirut, so the main group of people on the corniche were pensioners stretching near outdoor exercise equipment. The next largest group were women wearing sweatpants, power walking their way along the palm-lined pathway. There were two smaller groups as well: older men playing backgammon and young women wearing heavy black eye makeup, long black boots and tight blue jeans. This latter group seemed to enjoy nothing more than sauntering along the corniche in their sunglasses and lip-gloss.

"They're not like Qatari women, are they?" I said to Angela, referring to the lack of hijabs and veils. "They are actually Western looking."

"They look like they're about to go night clubbing."

The corniche was full of elegant streetlights hanging over the well-kept pavement. Out in the sea, just past the coastal barrier, were layers of sedimentary rocks, some jutting up above the water line. A couple of children, who probably should have been at school, were enjoying themselves on one set of rocks, paddling in the rock pools and then jumping down in the water below. At the far end of the corniche was the large marina, home to expensive yachts and tall-masted boats.

We found an outdoor cafe near the boats and sat down. Opposite us was a set of modern glass skyscrapers that would not have looked out of place in Dubai. Beirut, it seemed, was a city of contrasts. First, there were the bullet-ridden buildings and crumbling backstreets, areas that looked war-torn and ragged, and then there was the sparkly affluence of the corniche. I could not recall a city where the contrast was so stark and proximate.

5

We passed a soldier brandishing a heavy automatic weapon. He looked bored, shuffling from one foot to another, occasionally glancing along the street to see what was going on. Not much, he surmised, and so he began staring out across the Mediterranean instead. The entire corniche had a military presence, with soldiers either standing at intersections or sitting on top of heavily armoured, camouflaged tanks. None of the men seemed particularly jumpy, which reassured us.

I pointed out a shell of a tall building to Angela. It was set back from the corniche. Long abandoned, its concrete exterior was covered in thousands of bullet holes and shell marks. It was the former Holiday Inn hotel.

When the Holiday Inn first opened its doors in the early seventies, its designers had built it to withstand earthquakes and hurricanes, but not civil war. When the bloodshed started, holidaymakers fled and snipers moved in, using the top floors as their base. No wonder that section had sustained the most damage. When the war ended, and restoration work began across Beirut, the Holiday Inn stood vacant and broken, unable to find financial backers to restore it to its former glory. Today, it is a grim reminder of Lebanese history.

The civil war lasted almost fifteen years, between 1975 and 1990. It turned the 'Paris of the Middle East' into a city of lawlessness and bloodshed where the root problem boiled down to religion – Christians against Muslims, of which there were roughly equal numbers. Both sides committed atrocities, but perhaps the worst were the Karantina and Damour massacres.

Karantina was a Muslim slum located inside mainly Christian East Beirut. It was a stronghold of the Palestinian Liberation Organisation, but also home to thousands of innocent people, mainly Palestinians, Kurds and Armenians. On the 18 January 1976, in the midst of Lebanon's dramatic breakdown of order, Christian militias stormed into Karantina to flush insurgents out. Instead, they simply killed any Muslim they came across. By the end of the day, 1500 people lay dead.

Two days later, the Muslims got their revenge.

The Christian suburb of Damour used to be home to around 25,000 people, with churches, chapels, hospitals and schools. The first thing that the militia did was cut off the water and electricity supply. This done, they stormed in, looting and torching building after building, raping and murdering Christians in their way. At one point, they dug up a Christian cemetery, smashing coffins open and scattering bones.

Largely because of these horrendous atrocities, Beirut separated itself into a Muslim and Christian half, their respective districts split by the infamous Green Line. It was named for the vegetation that grew in the no-man's land: one of the few places in Beirut where plants could grow without danger of being blown up. Today, the Green Line is gone, replaced by a busy road running alongside Martyrs' Square. In the middle of the square is a bullet-ridden monument: bullets holes from the civil war.

Angela and I walked up to the large dark grey statue. It was dedicated to a group of Lebanese soldiers executed in the First World War. The four figures were preserved in heroic poses, one of them holding a flaming torch aloft. Sunlight streamed through gaping holes in each figure and one had part of its arm missing. It was a fitting testament to what had happened.

Across the road was the blue-domed, Mohammed el Amine Mosque, based on Istanbul's more famous Blue Mosque, a building we would be seeing in a few days' time. The mosque was huge, with four rocket-like minarets pointing up into the now perfectly blue sky.

"What do you reckon that is?" Angela asked, pointing at a bizarre-looking structure a little further on from the mosque. It was a concrete monstrosity that had been left to rot. If the Holiday Inn had looked bad, then this was ten times worse. Cracked concrete beams, exposed reinforced steel and bullet holes and shell marks pockmarked virtually every inch of the strange bomb shelter shaped oddity. A few hardy weeds were sprouting from gaps in the blackened concrete, an indicator of just how long the building had been left derelict. I wondered whether the owner of the rust bucket we'd seen earlier lived in it. They would go together well. It was easily the ugliest building in Beirut, and by quite a long way.

Later we discovered that it was called 'The Egg' and had, for a short time, been a grand cinema. Architects had designed the novel shape to incorporate a rounded dome (hence the name), but they had timed its opening horrendously badly, as it coincided with the outbreak of the civil war. Like other tall buildings in Beirut, its lofty position made it a favoured haunt of snipers, and, instead of being an arena of entertainment, it became a place of death and fighting. Rockets, shells, mortar attacks and thousands of bullets attacked its exterior for years. And like the Holiday Inn, it remains an eyesore of Beirut, but a historically significant one. Indeed, many of the citizens have demanded that the cinema remain in its current state, to stand as a monument and a memorial to Lebanon's turbulent past.

Angela and I crossed back over the old Green Line, flagged down a cab and went to get something to eat.

6

The next day, we caught a taxi to a downtown area of Beirut called Saifi Village. Because of its proximity to the Green Line, bombs, bullets and shells had virtually destroyed the district, but after the war, the Lebanese government redeveloped Saifi into a colonial French-style village, possibly in an attempt to recreate the time when the French had been in charge between 1918 and 1943.

It did resemble a French town, albeit a manufactured and slightly sterile one. Instead of bullet holes, it had pretty town houses, flower laden verandas, cobblestone streets, stylish outdoor cafes and plenty of palm trees. Twenty thousand French citizens lived in Lebanon, and quite a few of them lived in Saifi Village, though at the time of our visit, the streets were quiet. We did walk past one expensive-looking boutique shop, though, just as a couple of middle-aged Frenchwomen emerged. They *looked* rich and elegant, and, as they swept themselves along the cobbles, in a cascade of rapid-fire French and clickety-clack heels; just for a moment, we could have been in Paris.

Nejmeh Square was another pretty part of the city, this time busier with people. A group of outdoor cafes and bars surrounded the square, which had a tall Rolex-powered clock tower in the middle. Unlike the sterile feel of Saifi, Nejmeh Square and its surrounds felt alive, mainly due to the laughter, the flocks of pigeons and families with small children. We walked past a few Roman ruins, a series of olive groves and a Greek Orthodox Cathedral. Anyone visiting this part of Beirut would be hard pressed to imagine that during the war it was almost destroyed

A soldier watched us approach. When we got closer, he stepped in front, beckoning to my backpack. I removed and opened it, allowing the young man to see inside. After a cursory inspection of my guidebook and camera, he waved us on.

"Look at that board," I said to Angela, pointing at a large hoarding featured a young woman posing in skimpy red underwear. It was advertising a nightclub called Aphrodisiac.

"What about it? Do you want to go or something?"

"I wouldn't mind."

Angela laughed. "As if they'd let you in."

"No, what I'm saying is how strange to see something like that in the Middle East. I mean, you wouldn't see it in Qatar. Even a website showing it would be banned."

Angela looked at the snarl in the road. Even though nobody was moving, engines were revving and horns were blasting. Every lane was two abreast, some drivers holding prayer beads out of their open windows, hoping that blessings to Allah would somehow help them complete their journey quicker. At one busy intersection, a policeman controlled the traffic, but everywhere else, drivers were fending for themselves. We walked past them all in what we hoped was the direction of the hotel.

7

"I'm too tired to walk any further," I lamented. We'd been hiking for close to thirty minutes and we were still miles away from the hotel. I stuck my arm into the street, hoping a taxi would stop, but none did. It was like Manama and Muscat all over again.

"I thought you knew where we were going," Angela said.

"I thought I did. I'm going to ask that soldier."

The soldier was standing outside a small grocery shop. He was in his mid-twenties and had a dark layer of stubble on his thin face. He seemed startled when I approached him. "Do you speak English?" I asked.

"A little."

I explained our plight, naming the hotel where we were staying, which brought a nod of recognition. "Walk is too far, I think. Taxi much better." He then surprised me by stepping into the busy three-lane road. When a taxi approached, he raised his hand and stopped it. His action caused an immediate and cascading blockage to everyone behind the taxi, followed by a rabid cacophony of beeping. The soldier ignored the beeps and walked to the taxi driver's window, conferring with him as streams of traffic tried to swerve around him. A moment later, he beckoned us over.

Angela and I crossed to the old Mercedes taxi, garnering looks of annoyance from every driver the soldier had delayed for us. "I have told him where you go," said the soldier. "Do not pay more than five thousand lira."

That was about two pounds. We thanked him and jumped into the back of the taxi. Before we'd even closed the door, the driver screeched off. When we arrived at the hotel a short while later, I handed the driver a ten-thousand note, wondering whether we'd receive any change. We did, and it amounted to 8000 lira, and so for his honesty, I gave him 3000 as a tip. The taxi drivers in Beirut often got bad press for ripping off tourists, but this one had done us proud.

8

"Jason, you've got to see this," said Angela. We were in our hotel room, about to retire for the night. Angela was watching TV. As the end credits rolled, a man in a bright shirt and braces, with a ridiculously frizzy wig on his head and weird glasses on his face, was prancing – for that was the only word to describe his antics. While he pranced, he was playing a hideous tune on a tiny electronic keyboard, the sort of tune only a madman would play after one minute of tuition. With him were two pals. Their role was not to play anything musical but to cavort. And cavort they did, with wanton abandon. One of the cavorters, the strangest of the trio, was wearing a golden wig that came complete with Timmy Mallett-style glasses. He provided the raucous vocals. It sounded like he was having an acid trip.

"What the hell is this?" I asked, laughing at the absurdity of the program. If it had been broadcast in the morning, I'd have assumed it was a children's program, but this was late night TV.

Angela switched it off. "So what shall we do tomorrow?"

I picked up the guidebook. A small town forty kilometres north of Beirut called Byblos sounded promising. The guidebook described it as a picturesque fishing harbour with a side order of Roman ruins. I showed the small photo to Angela. She nodded. That settled it. Byblos it was.

9

The Beirut bus station lay below a busy underpass. It rumbled and groaned with the sound of bus engines and the vibrations from heavy traffic passing overhead. A dense smell of diesel and burnt oil lingered in the air. It became thicker as we neared the lines of parked buses and minibuses.

"You want taxi?" said a moustachioed man. We waved him off, but he was persistent, following us towards the buses. "Where you want to go? Bus very slow and break down many times! My taxi very quick!"

We ignored him and found a small minibus that had a piece of card taped to the front. The name of the destination was scrawled on it: Tripoli, Lebanon's second largest city, and the ultimate stop on a bus route via Byblos. We climbed aboard to buy a ticket from the driver. He was an unshaven man in his early thirties who looked like he'd just woken up. His hair was ruffled, his shirt was crumpled and he had huge bags under his eyes. He understood English, though, and soon issued us with one-way tickets to Byblos for 3000 lira (£1.20) each.

Our fellow passengers, of whom there were eight, all looked like locals. There were a couple of elderly women sitting together a few seats behind us, clutching shopping bags, but everyone else was male and travelling alone. With a jolt and a rumble, the bus powered into life and set off northwards along the coastal highway, up a gradual gradient until we reached the outskirts of Beirut, where we began to descend again. Every now and again, the bus would stop to allow a few people off and a few more on, and then, after forty-five minutes, the bus stopped once more. No one got off. The driver turned around and looked at us. "Byblos," he mumbled. "Get off bus." We did so, finding ourselves on a lonely stretch of road lined with cedar trees. Wondering whether there were two Bybloses in Lebanon, because surely this was not right place, we watched the bus pull away with a belch of black smoke.

Our guidebook stated it should take new arrivals to Byblos only a few minutes to get their bearings. We set off walking, wondering why the Byblos bus stop was nowhere near the town. After walking four kilometres, and with no sign of Byblos or anything else of note, apart from a few car repair shops and a petrol station, we admitted defeat.

We walked over to a couple of men in overalls standing near the petrol pumps. After showing them the photo of Byblos in our guidebook, one man pointed one way and the second man pointed in the opposite direction. It was a moment of comedy coated in pure frustration. I looked at each of them in turn until one took my book, knocked on a window hatch and had a conversation with someone behind it.

"Byblos that way," said the new man, poking his head from the small window and pointing in the direction we had just come from. We thanked them all, walked back to the bus stop, and then carried on past it. And then we found Byblos, almost an hour after arriving.

Unlike Beirut, Byblos was free of bullet holes and mortar damage. Instead, it had a beautiful little harbour overlooked by a collection of bars and restaurants and it was in one of them that we read that the Bible had mentioned Byblos, where it called it Gebel. The town also laid claim (with a fair few other places) to being the world's oldest continuously inhabited settlement. Its history dated back three thousand years before the birth of Christ.

After lunch in one of the harbour cafes, we decided to find the Roman ruins. The Romans had built a grand theatre, a set of magnificent temples and a huge number of civic buildings to house their citizens and troops. Carved stone walkways crisscrossed the town and massive columns lined them all. Byblos was one of the grandest cities in the Eastern Mediterranean.

We found the ruins at the southern end of the small town: stone columns, some standing upright, others scattered over the ground like discarded pipes, were everywhere. There were so many sections that, in some places, the remains had been piled up like rubble. Further along were the remains of an old amphitheatre, its step-like seats ringing the auditorium. In its heyday, the amphitheatre would have looked magnificent: a place of battle, blood and high enjoyment. Today, weeds and small lizards were the main audience.

When the Romans departed, the Ottomans came. They in turn left when the Crusaders arrived. They used some of the old Roman stones to build a castle, most of which survives to this day. Angela and I climbed one of the castle towers to stare out across Byblos. The moat had long dried up, but the vista was still worthy of a king, spanning the Mediterranean coastline: a scene of ancient ruins, palm trees and terracotta roofs.

"Well, I don't know about you, but I like Lebanon," I said. "I like the history, I like the sea, I like the way pensioners do their exercises by the corniche and I like Byblos. In fact ... I could live here, I think."

Angela nodded.

"And another thing: we've not felt threatened at all, have we? Beirut feels safe. Even wandering down the backstreets was okay. I was expecting it to be a bit more ... I don't know ... edgy."

Below us came the sound of people, talking and haggling. They were in Byblos Souq. After one lingering look at Byblos from our perch on Crusader Castle, we climbed down the stone steps to join them.

10

The restored souq area of Byblos was a pretty thoroughfare of souvenir shops selling tourist postcards, gaudy mugs, 'I love Lebanon' T-shirts and a whole range of cheap Chinese offerings. The men working the stalls seemed to know it was all rubbish and so didn't bother trying too hard to attract customers. The renowned Memoire Du Temps (Memory of Time) fossil shop was different, though. It was a store and small museum rolled into one, full to bursting with hundreds of fossilized sea creatures. Most were small fish, but there were a few special ones hidden among the shoals, including a few turtles, a selection of plants and even an octopus.

"This octopus is unique," explained one of the museum guides, a young woman who also doubled up as shop assistant. "Octopi have no bones and therefore don't usually produce fossils. But we have one here, as you can see!" We peered at the thing, trying to work it all out. It didn't really look like an octopus, but it did have some tentacle-like impressions near an elongated body part. Some of the fish looked great, though. One had been fossilised with its mouth open; another looked like a long and skeletal eel. A few pieces of rock had multiple fish in them, forever caught in their final swim.

"Lebanon has some of the best-preserved fossils on Earth," the young woman told us. "Archaeologists from all over the world come here to study them, and some of the best places to find them are not far from here, a place called Haqel."

The guide showed us the adjoining shop where fossils were for sale. Some cost as little as $10 – tiny pieces of limestone measuring perhaps 5cm by 3cm, with tiny fish fossils embedded into them. Angela picked up a piece of rock with four dark brown fish embedded into it. When she saw the price, she quickly put in back on its display stand. She picked a smaller one with a single fish. It was double the size of the tiny ones but five times the price. After handing over fifty dollars, we left the fossil shop with our own piece of Lebanese history.

Half an hour later, we were on the bus back to Beirut. When we got there, we spent our evening in the bars and cafes around Nejmeh Square. Despite the presence of armed soldiers, it was a fitting way to end our time in Lebanon, sitting among people simply getting on with their lives. As the sun went down and the shadows grew longer, we caught another cheap taxi back to the hotel. The next day we had another flight to catch, this time to a city not really part of the Middle East – for half of it was in Europe – but one we were both looking forward to, nevertheless. The city evoked images of minarets, bazaars and endless Turkish delights, but it was also famous for its cosmopolitan attitude and its openness. Istanbul was the next stop on our tour.

Top row: Beirut's corniche; a tank in the street
Middle row: Pigeon Rocks; The bullet-hole ridden Martyrs' Monument; The shell of the Holiday Inn
Bottom row: Mohammed el Amine Mosque stands behind the half demolished 'Egg'; The fish fossil Angela bought from Memoire Du Temps

Chapter 9. Istanbul: Where East meets West

FCO travel advice: Since 2013, there have been sporadic demonstrations across Turkey. Crime levels are low but street robbery and pick-pocketing are common in the major tourist areas of Istanbul.

Our afternoon flight from Beirut to Istanbul was interesting because of the man next to me. His name was Raymond, and he was a sixty-one-year old Englishman on his way to Istanbul to catch a connecting flight to Addis Ababa. Neatly folded by his side was an expensive Panama hat. In front of him was a gin and tonic.

"I'm marrying an Ethiopian woman I met on the internet two years ago," he told me. "She's forty-six and works as an accountant in Addis. I've not met her in person, but have spoken to her on Skype hundreds of times. The wedding's in a month's time and I can't wait. She's clever, witty and good-looking, but not a stunner. I avoid stunners for the reason that they do not make good wives. That's where I went wrong in my first marriage. I was constantly chasing the hounds away." Next to me, Angela raised her eyebrows, but carried on reading her novel.

As we descended towards Istanbul, Raymond told me he'd been an army photographer in his younger days, working in places such as Cyprus and Germany. "Then I became a civilian photographer for Saudi Arabian Airlines, if you can believe that. My first wife and I lived in Jeddah for seventeen years and loved every minute; brought our kids up there. We used to brew our own beer in huge containers in the kitchen." He had been working in Beirut as a freelance photographer for the past six months.

I asked him whether he liked the Lebanese capital.

"It's a bit grimy in places, but you can get a decent glass of white – which was more than I got in Saudi."

When we landed, I wished him well in his endeavours. With a nod and handshake, he put on his Panama hat – carrying it off with aplomb – grabbed his hand luggage and headed down the aisle towards his new life in Africa.

2

Istanbul, one of only a tiny handful of cities to straddle two continents, is home to fourteen million people, making it the sixth most populous city in the world. For almost a century and a half, it was called Constantinople: the centre of the Ottoman Empire, a city of trade, famed for its mesmerising architecture and forward-thinking ways. Nowadays, it might have lost its place on the world's centre stage, but it remains the powerhouse of Turkey, driving the country's industrial and commercial output, and, due to its historical significance, it receives over ten million visitors annually – making it one of the top ten most frequently visited cities on the planet.

Our hotel was nestled in a backstreet of Sultanahmet, the historic heart of Istanbul, on the European side. It was next door to a large Turkish restaurant. The fez-wearing waiters who worked there always looked bored when we passed. Opposite the hotel was a small convenience store. The proprietor was an elderly Turkish gentleman who possessed large leathery lips and dark-stained teeth. "Need water?" he said jovially the first time we went in. "Or maybe Efes beer? What about some chocolate or sunscreen? I also sell ice-cold lollypop! Whatever you need, Ahmet can get."

That evening, Angela and I sat on the terraced restaurant of our hotel, gazing out across a landscape of exotic red-roofed buildings, groves of trees and a grey domed mosque that was emitting the call to prayer from surround sound speakers mounted on its thin grey minaret. Behind the mosque was the fading blue of the Bosphorus, home to a fleet of anchored container ships. One was on the move, though: a large, elongated freight ship. Half of its red hull was shining gold due to the setting sun. Beyond the Bosphorus was Asia: a dark set of headlands rising on a far shore.

3

The next morning, the weather was agreeably warm, like the nicest summer days in England. Angela and I headed past the restaurant. The waiters were setting out tables, polishing windows and sloshing water over the cobbles in front.

We carried on uphill until we came to a busy street with a tramline running through the centre. Jewellery shops, fabric stores, and one shop, which boasted it sold 'women's apparel', were busy with tourists and locals. Like their counterparts in Beirut, the local women of Istanbul favoured T-shirts, jeans and uncovered hair instead of hijabs and abayas.

Hundreds of years previously, while Britain was wallowing in the Dark Ages, the Romans had been transforming Constantinople into a gloriously modern city. They constructed temples, amphitheatres and underground chambers to store water. One of the best subterranean water stores was for the Great Palace of Constantinople. Though the palace is no more, the water chamber, dating from AD532, still survives.

From the outside, Yerebatan Sarnici, the old palace water store, looked unimpressive: a simple square brick building in faded red and white stripes. In fact, it looked so uninspiring that we almost didn't bother going in.

When we reached the bottom of its fifty-two steps, a group of tourists were blocking things up. A Japanese man was in the process of getting dressed up as a Sultan so that a professional photographer could snap him posing in the atmospheric location. His family were finding this hilarious. When he finished, we moved forwards, declined the photographer's offer and marvelled at what lay ahead.

Yerebatan Sarnici was vast, larger than a football pitch. It was full of water, which rippled with red and orange reflections from the spotlights. Not that the place was bathed in light; the spotlights merely offered enough illumination so that visitors would not fall off the wooden gangways, or bang into the marble columns supporting the roof thirty feet above us.

Hidden speakers piped classical music into the underground chamber, water dripped from above, and, all around, voices echoed between the columns and across the ethereal pools. Together, this created a rather special ambience. In 1963, the producers of *From Russia with Love* had discovered the hidden ambience of Yerebatan Sarnici too. In the film, Sean Connery can be seen creeping furtively around the cistern in order to spy on some Soviet agents.

"Look at the fish!" I said. I was peering into the murky depths. Small fish were darting back and forth.

"What do they eat?"

"Algae."

Angela shot me a look. "Algae?"

"Green algae, to be exact."

"You haven't got a clue, have you?"

"No. But I do know how they discovered this place. During the Middle Ages, people used to drop buckets through cracks in the ground, because they knew that if they dropped them deep enough, the buckets would come up with fresh water and sometimes fish. None of them ever thought of digging down to see what was there, and this went on for decades until someone finally grew curious enough to have a look. This is what they found."

In one corner of Yerebatan Sarnici was a large concentration of tourists. All of them were nudging and jostling one another to see the Medusa Heads, which formed the base of two columns: one of the heads upside down, the other sideways.

We joined the scrum and, after a minute or so of jostling, we saw them for ourselves. Both Medusas had big heads with curly hair and stern expressions. A few people were reaching over to touch them, but we didn't, in case we slipped into the water. After taking a couple of photos, we decided to leave the sunken palace, passing through a tacky souvenir shop on the way out. It was time to see the hippodrome.

4

The Hippodrome of Constantinople wasn't quite as spectacular as the underground chamber, but that was because it was no longer there. All that remained of the massive U-shaped racing track were a few columns and the Obelisk of Thutmose III, a 3500-year-old monument plundered from the Valley of the Kings in the fourth century. It looked down upon scores of tourists.

Not far from the hippodrome was Istanbul's most iconic sight: the four hundred-year-old Sultan Ahmed Camii, otherwise called the Blue Mosque. To get inside its vast courtyard, Angela and I had to negotiate the steps crawling with tourists, all of them trying to take photos at the same time. One man, armed with a video camera, accidentally nudged me in the chest as I walked past. I stopped to glare at him and he lowered his camera to apologise. As we entered the archway, Angela nudged me. I gave her the glare too.

"Ooh, scary," she said, laughing.

"I'll shove you, if you want."

The Blue Mosque's courtyard was impressive – a huge expanse of cut stone surrounded by stone arches tall enough to allow seven or eight men standing on top of one another through. The mosque was the focus of attention, though, and it did look blue, or maybe grey, even though the reason for its name had nothing to do with its exterior. The blue tiles on the inside were what gave it its name. We wandered in to have a look.

Blue tiles coated the columns, arches, walls and ceiling of the Blue Mosque. The blue contrasted with the huge red carpet strewn across the floor. Sunlight streamed in through gorgeous stained glass windows, reflecting a thousand points of light from the giant chandelier suspended in the centre. Unlike the interior of the mosque we had visited in Abu Dhabi, which was underwhelming compared to its white exterior, the inside of the Blue Mosque was far greater than the outside.

"You need a shave," said Angela.

"Do I?"

"Yeah. That's probably why that man outside was wary of you. You look a bit rough and ready. A bit unhinged."

"Unhinged?"

"And I think you should have a proper Turkish shave– you know, one with a sharp knife."

I felt my stubble and agreed it did need a trim. "I might have one later."

"A Turkish one?"

"No, a normal one with my own razor."

"Go on. Be a man. I dare you!"

"Look, I'm not having some strange man go at my face with a knife. It's not going to happen."

"Chicken."

5

The term Turkish Shave does not adequately describe the hellish experience of going through one. Turkish Torture might be more apt. We found the barbershop fairly close to our hotel, but, before entering, I insisted we do a reconnaissance mission first. We walked past the establishment to ascertain that it was a) clean, b) empty of patrons and c) staffed by a barber who did not look like a psychopath. It got a tick from all three, but just to be sure, we did a second pass, more slowly this time. As we passed the window, I caught sight of the barber staring at me. He was standing right by the window. We hurried past, stopping a few metres past his little shop of horrors.

"Just go in," Angela said. "It looks okay."

While I dithered, the barber opened his door and beckoned us in. Five minutes later, I was in the hot seat with Angela sitting behind me on a small bench. Both of us watched as the barber picked up a scalding hot towel and began to abuse my face. First, he pummelled me as if I was some sort of clay model, singeing my neck and burning my cheeks. Then he put the towel down and picked up a straight razor from his counter. It gleamed, and then – quick as a flash – he whipped it across my throat. Such was the speed and dexterity of his movement that, in the mirror, Angela's smile immediately turned to horror. Then the barber laughed and showed Angela that he'd 'cut' my throat with the blunt side. The man *was* a psychopath.

Despite his theatrics, the barber certainly knew how to perform a close shave. Far quicker than I could've completed the same process with a normal razor, the barber rid me of my stubble, deposited the razor in a dish of antiseptic, and then smacked my cheeks.

"Good, yeah?" he boomed heartily. "Like baby arse!"

The treatment was not over, though. Part of every Turkish shave package was a face massage. I hated massages at the best of times, and to have a hairy-fingered man batter my eyebrows and forehead as if he was kneading dough wasn't my cup of tea. I tried to protest, but it was to no avail, because the barber pressed me back down into the seat. A few seconds later, with the man pummelling my neck, I'd had enough – the pain was simply too much. I told him to stop.

"No stop" he said, now digging into my eye-sockets with his knuckled fingers. "Good for you. Make you strong!"

I screamed when he squeezed my forehead. It felt like he was using a pair of pliers on me. I screamed some more when he pulled my ears, stretching them almost sideways before he started boxing them. Behind me, Angela was laughing her head off.

With my spirit broken, I slumped in the chair and waited for the torment to end. After finishing with the back of my neck, the barber picked up a cheap cigarette lighter and set fire to my nose. Whoosh, the tiny hairs inside my nose went up in smoke. Before I had time to react, he stuck the lighter in my ear, setting the flame to maximum. It was like someone had jabbed a large needle into my inner ear. He then started flicking them with his other hand. The pain was horrendous. Just when I was about to burst into tears, he stopped.

"Okay," he said. "Finish."

I nodded and closed my eyes. When I opened them, the man was beaming at me.

"How much did he charge you?" asked Angela as we left.

"Twenty-five lira. About seven quid. I'd have paid double for him to stop."

"All that for seven pounds?" She rubbed her fingers down my face. "My God. He's done a good job, though; it is like a baby's bottom. Your nose is a bit red, though."

6

"The Grand Bazaar is closed!" said the smiling man across the road from us. He was standing in the doorway of a large carpet emporium. Colourful throws of fabric hung all over his entrance, and on the ground in front of him. "But I am open. Come see!" We ignored the carpet seller and followed a sign that pointed to the Grand Bazaar.

It was our second morning in Istanbul, and we were en route to visit Istanbul's most popular tourist sight – the sprawling market place that was quite possibly the most famous souq in the world. Further along the street, another storekeeper said the same thing, that the Grand Bazaar was closed. Ha! I could smell prime Istanbullshit when it wafted in front of me. We waved him off, and then a third man told us the Grand Bazaar was closed. Their dismal attempts to get us into the stores was really rather pathetic.

"Are you sure it's not closed?" Angela asked a block later.

We stopped so I could fish out the guidebook. I flicked to the part about the Grand Bazaar. Then I sighed in annoyance. We should have checked the book before setting off. The bazaar was not open on a Sunday. It was written there in black and white. Shamefaced, we turned around and retraced our path, passing the men who had been trying to help. Both of us kept our heads down and our eyes fixed firmly forward. We decided to take a boat trip on the Bosphorus instead.

7

The blue of the Bosphorus was in a tumultuous mood. The boats tethered beyond the sea wall were pitching and rolling in the swells, their flags rippling in the hearty sea breeze. The wind had really picked up today, we'd noticed.

Before taking a boat trip, we took a detour. Near a busy trolley bus station, a set of shoe shiners were shouting for customers. One of Angela's sandals had been bothering her for some time; its bottom section was splitting, which would not have been a major issue except the sandals were here favourites. She walked up to one seated man. After inspecting the broken sandal with a practised eye, he nodded. "I fix." He then glanced at her other shoe, and, when Angela passed it to him, he said it needed a bit of work too.

He told us it would take about half an hour, and the price he quoted seemed fair. But there was a problem – Angela would be shoeless for thirty minutes – which would mean hanging around the cobbler or sitting in a nearby café. But then a third option became available. The cobbler produced a pair of sandal – spares for situations just like this. They looked like clogs, one dark blue, the other black, the kind of footwear prescribed to treat medical complaints. Each sole was about an inch thick. Angela accepted the temporary replacements, telling the man that we might be a little late getting back to him because we were going on a boat trip. Off we set, with Angela's gait a little hesitant.

"You look like an invalid," I joked when we were out of the cobbler's earshot. "People will stare."

"No they won't."

"They're not even the same colour. And they're miles too big."

We arrived at the edge of the Bosphorus and chose the first ferry that was leaving. Tourists packed it, most heading upstairs onto the blustery open-air deck. Angela and I did the same and managed to bag a seat near the railing. For the next hour, we powered past grand palaces, hilltop residential quarters and horrendous traffic jams.

With gusts of wind battering our heads, the boat passed under one of the bridges that connected Europe to Asia, the two continents barely a kilometre apart. Then we passed Yedikule Castle. Inside its old stone walls, Ottoman guards had once imprisoned the deposed seventeen-year-old Sultan, Osman II, until his grisly execution in 1622. While one man strangled him to death, another crushed his testicles.

Back on dry land, Angela caught a whiff of something in the air. "Mackerel!" she announced. The delicious waft was coming from a nearby stall where a teenage boy in a white apron was cooking fillets on a large, open-air griddle. Angela bought some, which came wrapped in a large piece of bread. With her mackerel sandwich and her odd shoes, we traipsed back to the cobbler who, as promised, handed her sandals back. They looked almost as good as new.

8

The next day, our last in Istanbul, we finally managed to visit the Grand Bazaar. We expected it to be like the souqs in Oman or Dubai but it was simply a sprawling flea market, most of it open air. Ceramic lampshades, endless rugs and handbags, T-shirts and Chinese-made kitchen utensils lined every store. Servicing them all were a series of men pulling box-laden carts.

Locals easily outnumbered tourists. Older Turkish women wearing headscarves shuffled around with plastic bags while men rummaged around hardware stalls with cigarettes dangling from their mouths. A little girl clutched the back of her father's shirt as he pushed his way through the aisle ahead of us. They soon disappeared in the throng. We passed some ducks locked up inside a tiny cage, prisoners until the dinner plate, and then saw a gaggle of children crowding around a rabbit hutch, gleefully trying to prod and stroke the animal inside. We moved on to the covered spice market where vendors had laid out mounds of colour in pungent pyramidal displays. At one, a grumpy proprietor reprimanded me for taking a photo of his saffron. We relocated to another part of the bazaar, this one the most bizarre of all.

"Jesus wept," I said, mesmerised and disgusted at the same time. I was staring at two large jars of water, each one rippling and writhing with forty or so green and black leeches. Some of them were hideously long, maybe twenty centimetres in length, others were smaller, but each one was disgusting and I shuddered to think of one sucking on my ankle. Ten of the horrid things were on the side of the jar, somehow gripping on with their mouths. I'd always imagined leeches to be sluggish creatures, lurking in muddy water, clinging onto any warm limb passing by, but, judging by these black creatures, they were quicker than eels.

"Who buys leeches?" Angela asked. The proprietor, an old man with a long white beard and skullcap, was watching us from his perch.

"Maybe they use them for medicinal purposes? You know, sticking a leech on a wound to suck out the badness."

The old man got up out of his chair and came over. "You buy leech? One lira each."

Both of us shook our heads. Even thirty pence seemed steep for such a revolting creature. Angela asked him what people used them for.

"For heart. Leech fix the heart."

I seriously doubted that. But who were we to argue? We left the leeches and went to find something else to do.

9

We jumped on a tram that took us across a narrow inlet of the bay. It delivered us to a tram stop close to a medieval structure called the Galata Tower. It was tall and round with a conical roof and spiky point on the top – the perfect medieval tower. Angela and I climbed to the top so we could see the view, just as Ottoman fire spotters had done hundreds of years previously. Ironically, despite their best efforts, the tower almost burned down when a fire broke out in 1831.

Galata Tower is also famous for its birdman, a chap called Hezârfen Ahmed Çelebi, who, in 1630, climbed the tower, donned some homemade eagle wings, and then, when a sufficient gust of wind came along, leapt from the top. Instead of dropping like a brick, Çelebi reportedly 'flew' for three kilometres before landing in a square on the other side of the river. As he unclipped his wings and bowed before the crowd, a guard came to arrest him. The birdman's daredevil heroics did not amuse Murad IV, the Sultan at the time. And this particular Sultan was not a man to annoy. Soon after becoming leader of the Ottoman Empire, Murad had banned smoking, alcohol and coffee. To make sure his citizens followed his draconian decree, he would often dress up in civilian clothes and patrol the streets of Constantinople. Whenever he came across anyone flouting his law, he would personally execute them on the spot. So when he heard about a birdman, he wanted him placed into custody immediately. As it happened, though, the Sultan was in a lenient mood and, instead of executing Çelebi, he sent him into exile in Algeria.

Angela I stared across at the flight path Hezârfen Ahmed Çelebi would have taken. How anyone could believe a man with false wings could have flown to the other side of the water, almost three kilometres away, was beyond imagining. Without doubt, he'd have ended up smashed on the ground at the base of the tower, or, if the wind had been strong enough and he'd flapped his arms, he might have possibly reached the water, which was half a kilometre away. But even that was stretching the realms of possibility.

If he attempted the same madcap flight today, he'd probably crash into one of the gigantic cruise ships anchored in the Bosphorus. We'd seen them the previous day on our boat trip, noting the people sitting in their cabin balconies. Instead of seeing as much as the city as they could in the day or so they had in Istanbul, they preferred to sunbathe aboard their ship.

"Right," I announced, looking at my watch. "It's time to go. Say goodbye to Istanbul. Say goodbye to Turkey. Next stop: Jordan."

Angela lingered at the safety fence, taking in the view of palaces, domes and minarets. I joined her, savouring one of the most magnificent cities in the Middle East.

Top row: The view of Istanbul and the Bosphorus from our hotel; The Egyptian obelisk in the Hippodrome area
Middle row: Leeches for sale!; Angela posing in front of Sultan Ahmed Camii, otherwise known as the Blue Mosque
Bottom row: Spices for sale in the Grand Bazaar (a few seconds after this photo was taken I was told to go away by the man in the striped shirt); The fantastic underground cistern called Yerebatan Sarnici

Chapter 10. Onward to Jordan

FCO travel advice: Most visits are trouble free.

"Oh my God!" I said, as I frantically patted down my pockets again. We were sitting near the gate for our afternoon flight to Amman, capital of the Hashemite Kingdom of Jordan. I couldn't find my phone.

Angela looked up. "What?"

"My phone! It's gone." I got up and patted my trouser pockets again, and then checked underneath the chair hoping it had slid underneath. It hadn't. I checked my bag. Nothing.

"It's got to be somewhere," said Angela. She stood up and helped me go through everything once more. When we came up empty handed, she looked as confused as I did.

I went through the ramifications of losing my phone. Apart from the phone numbers and photos, there were the emails of people in Jordan I might need to contact: the hotel; the man who was driving us down to Petra; the airline for our onward connection. It was a disaster. I berated myself for not being more careful.

"What about the cafe?" asked Angela. I remembered having a coffee. We'd had something to eat too. I'd been surfing the internet on my phone and that was the last time I could recall using it. I'd probably left it on the table and someone had stolen it. "Someone might've handed it in," Angela offered.

We rushed back to the cafe. The table we'd been sitting at was empty of people, and so we searched frantically for any sign of my phone. It wasn't anywhere. Distraught, I went up to the young man working behind counter and asked him whether anyone had handed it in. I was most surprised when he nodded. He went to a shelf and produced my phone. "A waitress found it when she cleared your table. I was hoping you would come back before your flight. It would have been tricky getting it back to you, otherwise."

I shook the man's hand, taking possession of a phone I'd thought long gone. I fished a fifty-lira note (about £14) from my wallet. "Give this to the waitress," I said. "And tell her thanks."

Angela and I walked back to the gate with our faith in humanity well and truly restored.

2

"This is the worst hotel I've ever seen!" said Angela, surveying the cracked wallpaper, the tatty fabric curtains, the mildew-infected bathroom, and, worst of all, the lack of air conditioning. "And what's that awful smell? I think it's ... urine. I'm not staying here." She glared at me.

"It's not that bad..."

"Not too bad?" My wife threw me an incredulous look. "Really? Not too bad? It's a flea pit. Look!" She pointed to the small plastic bin in the corner. It was full of somebody else's rubbish. She walked into the bathroom and pointed inside the toilet. It was a dirty brown colour and looked dry. "How much did we pay, again?"

"I'm not sure," I answered truthfully.

"Ten quid would be too much."

Before arriving in Jordan, a local Jordanian company had emailed me an astonishingly low quote. It included all our hotels in Jordan, the airport transfers, a private car journey to Wadi Musa, the entrance fees to the Petra ruins (with a guide), and a side trip to the Dead Sea. The price seemed too good to be true, and so I'd booked it immediately. But now I understood why it was so cheap.

Angela stood by her unopened suitcase. "And the manager was asleep, for God's sake. Asleep on a bloody hammock! You don't get that in proper hotels."

She was right. When we'd first arrived at the hotel, we had found the tiny lobby dark and empty. Around one side, which served as the bar area, a man wearing a string vest had been fast asleep in a hammock. When I coughed, he jumped up in surprise, rubbing his eyes.

Angela regarded a brown stain in the corner of the room. It looked like someone had crushed a bug. At least that's what I hoped. She said, "You can stay here if you want, but I'm going to that hotel we saw around the corner."

The hotel was the Le Meridian Amman. Twenty minutes later, we were safely ensconced inside it, relishing the cooling breeze of its modern air conditioning. It was expensive, but what the hell, we were on holiday, and it had a nice pool. I emailed Adib, the Jordanian driver who was going to take us to Petra in a day's time, and who thought we were staying at the hovel around the corner, telling him about the change of hotel. After that, we sat in the hotel bar sipping on a pint of beer and a glass of wine that cost ten pounds each.

3

"These pavements are stupidly high!" I said, stepping off a concrete ledge. "God help anyone in a wheelchair getting up and down these monsters."

It was the next morning, and Angela and I had just passed the large, blue domed King Abdullah Mosque. An armed soldier nodded as we traipsed by. Yellow taxis were everywhere, most of them beeping to attract our attention. When we waved them off, they rejoined the honking and fume-emitting traffic making its way to the city centre. We sidestepped a man with missing front teeth who was leaning backwards over the bonnet of an old Mercedes. His car blocked most of the pavement. He eyed us as we passed, but it wasn't a threatening stare. If anything, it was a gaze of boredom.

Further into the centre, the street got busier and the traffic did too. The beeping was almost on a par with India: a cacophonous orchestra of shrill white noise. Arabic lettering was scrawled across the shops, most selling clothes or else catering for men wanting to sip on tiny cups of coffee. We passed another bored-looking soldier and then, almost forty minutes after leaving the hotel, we came to the city centre.

The focal point was the Al-Husseiny Mosque, a large, beige place of worship dwarfed by its two tall minarets. Small, street-level shops, with only a few signs written in English, surrounded the mosque. One simply said: *Citizen*. What the shop sold we couldn't tell; it was closed. The other sign was for an upstairs eatery: *Sham Restaurant Originality* the establishment called itself. We looked back at the mosque; its front entrance was busy with ranks of old men sitting in the shade of its tall walls.

"It's not much to look at," I said, surveying the scene in downtown Amman. The mosque, the down-at-heel fruit and vegetable shops, the spice and hardware stores, the crowded alleyways, and the tired-looking apartment blocks behind them, all looked dull and past their best.

"At least there are no bullet holes like in Beirut."

We passed a shop specialising in black abayas. Outside the emporium, a set of mannequins were modelling the clothes, each one looking identical to the next. A man was lounging in the doorway smoking a cigarette and checking his phone. We turned left, heading west towards the first of three tourist sites we wanted to see in Amman, all of them Roman in origin.

4

The name the Romans gave to Amman was Philadelphia, a name now immortalised as a Jordanian beer. One of the key structures the Romans constructed was the strange-sounding Nymphauem. Instead of housing nubile nymphomaniacs, it served as a shrine to mythical water nymphs. Roman citizens would have found its intricately patterned mosaics, imaginative carvings and plush fountains much to their liking, and they certainly would have enjoyed the large swimming pool, a place to cool down after a hot and dusty day.

Angela and I found what remained of the Nymphauem on a street corner opposite a fruit and vegetable stall. A few local women were scrutinising the wares with experienced hands and eyes. Angela and I peered through the wire fence at the old Roman structure. All that remained of the two-storey complex were a series of tall columns and arches, and a few sections of carved wall. A backdrop of ugly apartment buildings overlooked the ruins. We decided to move on to the second Roman sight.

The Roman Theatre looked better. It was carved into the hillside of downtown Amman (to protect the Roman spectators from the hot Jordanian sun) and looked deliciously Roman-like. We paid the two dinar entrance fee, brushed off the men trying to flog Saddam Hussein-era banknotes by the entrance, and went in to see it up close.

There were surprisingly few people inside the open-air theatre – especially for the second most popular tourist attraction in Amman – and those that were in attendance were high up on the steps that formed the auditorium's seating. Almost two millennia previously, Roman citizens watched actors treading the boards where we now stood: rich people on the lower levels, poorer people further up, where the acoustics were worse. A tout walked over to us, initially masquerading as a helpful local, but soon switching to annoying shop vendor as he tried to coax us into his souvenir store across the road.

"Maybe later," I said – the standard response to such requests. He nodded and wandered away.

"Shall we climb up?" Angela asked.

I looked up. A young Middle Eastern couple were sitting close together in deep conversation. They were the only people I could see. They seemed a long way off. I told Angela I wasn't that bothered, especially since we still had to climb the most prime of Amman's attractions: the Citadel. She agreed and so we went to find it.

Most people visit the Citadel by taxi or coach because the hill it sits atop, Jebel al-Qala'a, is the highest piece of land in the city. Angela and I did not know about the twisting road on the other side of the hill – the route that taxis took – and so we found a set of steps between two shops and began to climb.

At the top of the first set of steps, we came to a thin alleyway flanked by cream-coloured buildings. We were in some sort of backstreet made up of wooden doors, cracked plasterwork and satellite dishes. We walked past them until we arrived at another set of steps. Adjacent to them, a woman emerged from an impossibly tiny doorway, so small that I had first assumed it was a window. She looked startled when she saw us, but carried on past, heading down the steps we had just climbed.

"Are you sure this is the right way?" Angela asked at the third set of steps: the steepest ones so far. I nodded, though it was impossible to tell. Around a narrow alleyway, lined with the same cracked plasterwork, we saw three small children throwing a tennis ball to each other. They were playing near a green metal door that was hanging from its hinges. The children stopped their game and smiled. "American?" a little girl aged about five said.

"No, England," said Angela.

The children smiled some more and then carried on with their game. Up more steps we went. The morning call to prayer sounded. It cascaded around the tight alleyways around us, reverberating into different timbres and pitches. We couldn't see the mosque, or, indeed, mosques, for there were at least three muezzins reciting their prayers, but the sound stopped us.

"I like the call to prayer," Angela said. "It sounds so...I don't know...exotic."

"Exotic?"

"Mysterious too. It's the haunting voice of the men singing. It sounds so mournful."

"But we hear it in Qatar all the time."

"I know. I like it there too."

We carried on walking up another steep set of steps until we finally reached the summit of the hill. There, we found ourselves in a large car park full of cars, taxis and a large white coach. The groups of tourists who had come up in the coach were milling about, nattering away in Spanish. We walked past them to get in before the rush.

The main things on offer in the Citadel were an old and long-abandoned domed palace full of cooing pigeons, a set of pillars that once belonged to the Roman Temple of Hercules, and a small museum. With a crowd of tourists hot on our tail, we beat them to the museum while they loitered by the tall pillars. Inside was a six thousand-year-old skull, a trio of ancient statues and a few Egyptian carvings, plus the usual pots and tools common to museums across the globe. We read the information signs and stopped to look at a few things, more to cool off than anything else, and then made our way back outside to enjoy the view.

At a quiet section of Citadel wall, we stared down at Amman. It looked beautiful, an endless array of white and cream buildings perched on the hillsides below us, a view that had probably remained unchanged for centuries.

Behind the residential dwellings of old Amman stood a few gleaming skyscrapers, most of them still under construction. In a few years, the skyline of Amman would look very different. For now, though, it was great.

I took a photo of the view, and the resulting image soon became one of my favourites of the whole trip. If anything summed up a city in Arabia, then surely that was it: the sprawl of Amman covering every available space on the hills.

We had some lunch is a small cafe around the corner from the mosque. The owner seemed pleased that we had chosen his establishment above all the others on the street. "What do you think of Jordan?" he asked us.

"It's great," I said. "The Citadel is amazing."

"Yes it is. It's just a shame more tourists are not coming to see it. By the way, we have tortoises on the top level. After you have eaten, go up in elevator and see them." He wandered off towards the kitchen.

My chicken shawarma was delicious, perhaps the best one I'd ever had. And the Philadelphia beer washing it down was a treat too. I ended up eating far too quickly and, before I could stop myself, I burped. A second later, Angela grimaced. "You pig. I can smell that. You're a disgusting animal."

I nodded. "Well, prepare yourself for another, because it's brewing as we speak."

Angela produced a look of pure disdain.

"When did I start to disgust you? I think it was about six months ago."

Angela laughed. "It was before that. You've been disgusting me for years."

I smiled.

Angela shook her head. "You're proud of that, aren't you?"

"I think I am."

After our meal, we jumped in the elevator to see the tortoises. Inside the compartment, there was a note stuck onto the wall: 'You can feed our pet tortoises on the roof. Please feed them lettuce and cucumber. No parsley please'.

The top level of the cafe overlooked the street, and we could see the Roman amphitheatre we had visited earlier. There were some empty tables and lots of flower pots. Angela spotted the tortoises first. Two of them were plodding around on the ground, searching out titbits of food, and then one of them started running. I'd never seen a tortoise running before and I couldn't help but chuckle. It scarpered under a table and stopped, catching its reptilian breath. It seemed they had a good life on top of the cafe. We left them to their rooftop adventures and returned to street level.

6

The next day, we wanted to visit Jerash, another ancient Roman complex, this time to the north of Amman. To get there, we acquired the service of a taxi-driver called Bassam. He appeared delighted when I outlined my proposal to him. He would drive us to Jerash, wait for a couple of hours, and then drive us back to the hotel. A good day out for us and a nice little earner for him.

Bassam was about forty, with a thick shock of black hair and a bushy moustache. We quickly found out his favourite word in English was 'crazy.' The first time he used it was when we swerved around an old woman crossing the road at a snail's place. "Crazy!" he yelled. "Crazy lady!"

Downtown Amman passed in a blur until we arrived at the back of another horrendous traffic jam. We were near the central mosque, and the black abayas were still standing sentry opposite it. While we waited, Angela asked Bassam whether he'd been to any other Middle Eastern countries.

"Only Syria," he said, fiddling with his air-conditioning, which was currently blowing slightly hot air. "It used to be a beautiful country: Damascus especially. I went three times before I was married. I had good times with the girls there. Crazy times! But since then, I have not been. The fighting in Syria has caused problems here too. People in Europe and America think Jordan is the same place and so do not come."

The traffic moved. We passed a few kebab and shawarma shops, and then a whole line of gaudy fabric shops. Then the traffic stopped again: three lanes completely gridlocked. From behind came the sound of an ambulance. No one moved over and I could see the emergency vehicle stuck in the traffic behind despite its flashing lights and tinny siren. "In England," I told Bassam, "people move over to let ambulances past."

Bassam glanced at the stationary ambulance in his mirror. "In UK, yes; in Jordan, no. Sick person might be dead by now. It's crazy, I know."

When the traffic got moving, the ambulance managed to break through, escaping the snarl by mounting pavements and edging past other vehicles with only millimetres to spare. As its siren receded into the distance, Bassam caught me staring up at the buildings on the hills. He told me that they were cheap houses. "Rent is maybe 100 dinar for one month (£85). Over in West Amman, it is very expensive. Rent is maybe 700 dinar. Crazy prices, mister!" With that, he lit a cigarette and simultaneously changed gear, leaving the steering wheel devoid of hands for three seconds.

7

The countryside of northern Jordan was a mixture of rocky hills, electricity pylons and the odd herd of goats. Occasionally, we passed police cars armed with speed cameras, but Bassam always spotted them in time. Carts selling huge watermelons stood by the side of the road, as did piles of ceramic pots. At one point, we passed a cart laid out with spices. How the array of powder was not blowing away was a mystery.

We passed a teenage boy holding a gleaming silver tray. Further on, we passed another. He flashed his tray in the sun to catch our attention.

"What are they doing?" Angela asked from the back seat.

"I show you." A minute later, there was another flashing tray. Bassam stopped. When the boy came around to his window, Bassam asked whether we wanted anything – drinks, nuts, fruit and the like. We shook our heads and he spoke to the boy in thick Arabic. The boy nodded and ran into a nearby shop, reappearing a minute later with a packet of cigarettes on his silver tray.

As we set off, Bassam lit a cigarette from his new packet, and, when he inhaled, he erupted into a coughing fit suggesting his pastime had been a lifelong hobby. "Maybe that ambulance come for me one day," he joked. "And it will be stuck in a traffic jam."

Forty five minutes after setting off from central Amman, we arrived in the small town of Jerash. It had dense clusters of beige buildings sitting on the hill slopes and a central core of dreary shops. It also had the first set of traffic lights we had come across for a long time.

Bassam stopped at the lights, watching a man move to the centre of the road. The man stood in front of the windscreen and produced a bunch of flowers from a sack. He proffered them at us like some crazed magician. When the lights turned green, Bassam waved him away in annoyance. "What a crazy man – standing in the road like that. He will need those flowers for his own funeral if he does not move!" The man scarpered and we turned left, pulling into a large car park. A party of green-uniformed schoolgirls wearing white hijabs were hanging around a large bus. The teenage girls were laughing uproariously at everything, the same way kids across the world did.

Bassam told us to enjoy ourselves. "Take as long as you like; I wait here in taxi."

8

Angela and I made our way through the tourist trap that formed the entrance to the Jerash complex. Bags, paintings, sunglasses, T-shirts, nuts, rugs and every kind of trinket imaginable were for sale. A trio of Arabic schoolgirls were walking in the opposite direction. "Hi," one of them said, her accent suggesting a childhood of watching American TV. She didn't wait for a response, because they were all giggling as they walked by.

More children were at the other side of the entrance building, younger ones this time. A single, harried-looking male teacher was trying to organise them into some sort of order; it was like getting snakes to fit into a bag. Whenever one set of children stood in line, the rest would fall out in loose straggles. In the end, he gave up and did what most teachers did when faced with a similar situation: he shouted at the top of his lungs until they were silent.

"Wow," said Angela, staring at the imposing spectacle of Hadrian's Arch. In the first century, Jerash established itself as a great trading centre and when Emperor Hadrian visited Jerash in AD 129 (just a few years after completing his ambitious wall project in northern England), the citizens of Jerash built a huge arch to commemorate his appearance. This was it.

It was a massive beige block, with a huge archway in the middle and two smaller archways to the side. Grand columns supported a triangular roof section; in its time, it had served as the gateway to the city beyond. We later found out that it was one of the largest arches built during the Roman period and had been lucky to survive. In AD 749, a terrible earthquake struck northern Jordan, demolishing countless Roman buildings to rubble and dust. Not so Hadrian's arch; it stood proud as a testament to the skill of its creators.

Angela and I followed everyone else heading underneath the arch. School parties were everywhere, some of the children inexplicably banging drums as they wandered around with their teachers. A few more girls noticed us and said hello. One brave girl actually came right up to us. "You American?" she asked.

"English," I answered.

"That is good," she said cryptically, before wandering off to find her friends.

Beyond the arch, the ruins of Jerash followed a more or less straight path, with men sitting under large parasols trying to sell overpriced bottles of water to anyone who passed. We arrived at the old Roman forum, a cobbled, open plan area surrounded by columns. A group of teenage girls were sitting between some of the columns singing and banging their drums. A few more were dancing to the impromptu rhythm, their teacher sitting off to one side with a mobile phone pressed to his ear.

"Do you think he's ringing his wife?" asked Angela with a smile on her face. "To tell her how much he hates school trips."

"Or maybe to organise a hit man for the person who sold them the drums."

We left the girls and wandered along the column-flanked pathway, trying to avoid tripping into the weed-ridden cracks. When we saw some steps, we decided to climb them. They led to a plateau. Single columns stood among piles of Roman rubble: earthquake damage. The tremors had reduced the grand palaces and the beautiful temples to Roman rubble, with only a few isolated columns remaining intact. We followed a well-worn pathway that brought us out at the top of an ancient amphitheatre. The stone steps that ringed the theatre did not have barriers or safety fences, and for a few moments, I suffered a disturbing bout of vertigo that forced me to sit down on one of the steps. Even then, the spinning did not stop, and it was only after I rested both hands on the stone and pressed my back into the stone seat behind that I felt normality returning.

9

"Ruins good, yeah?" said Bassam, smoking another cigarette. The smell of stale smoke hung in his car like a cloak. "I would have joined you but I have walked up and down them about one hundred times. Nothing new for me."

We set off towards the traffic lights again. I couldn't see the man with the sack anywhere. "If we go left," Bassam said, "we will reach the Syrian border in maybe twenty minutes."

"It's that close?" I asked.

"Yes. Maybe thirty five kilometres. But no one goes there now. Too much danger and crazy people."

I looked at Angela and saw the same look in her eyes. We had once been to Damascus. One weekend we'd decided to fly there and see what it was like. It was only a short flight from Qatar. It had been safe to visit then, with none of the civil war or Islamic State shenanigans going on. In fact, Damascus had been a great place to see, a little pearl set amid the mountains. Less than a year after our visit, the country would erupt into a sustained and bloody civil war.

The lights changed to green. Bassam engaged first gear and we turned right. As we traversed the rolling hills towards Amman, again I thought back to our trip to Damascus.

Top row: One of my favourite views of the Middle East, this one of downtown Amman taken from the Citadel; The Temple of Hercules in Amman Citadel
Middle row: Hadrian's Arch in Jerash; A busy street of downtown Amman
Bottom row: Me standing in the Roman Theatre; Central Mosque; Jordanian dinar

Chapter 11. The Road to Damascus

Current FCO travel advice: We advise against all travel to Syria. British nationals should leave now by any practical means. There is a very high threat of kidnapping in Syria.

Travel advice at the time of our travel: Developments in the region may trigger public unrest. Personal crime levels are low.

"Hello," said the nine-year-old girl sporting a huge brace. It covered her entire set of front teeth. She had long black hair and was wearing western-style clothing. Despite her brace, she smiled sweetly. "Please may I sit down?" she asked.

I was sitting in the departure lounge of Damascus International Airport while Angela was looking around the shops. We'd just spent a couple of days in Damascus where we had come across some of the friendliest people in all of our travels. I smiled at the girl and nodded, despite it being a most unusual request for a little girl to make to a stranger.

The girl sat one seat away from me. "My name is Tira," she said. "I want to be a dentist when I grow up."

"A dentist?"

Tira nodded earnestly. "But I am worried I will make a mistake in someone's mouth and go to jail."

"Jail? I don't think so. You seem too clever for that."

The girl pondered this. "How can you tell I am clever?"

"Because of the way you speak English and your confidence at coming over to speak to me."

The girl smiled, revealing her braces again. The dentist who had fitted them had clearly done a great job in enthusing the girl about the world of dentistry.

"Are you American?" she asked.

I told her I was from England.

"I thought you were from America. That is why I came over."

"Sorry about that," I said, smiling.

The girl realised what she'd said. "No, I did not mean to be unkind. I meant that I only came over because I thought you would speak English to me. And you are doing this. My teacher says I need to practise all the time." She changed the subject. "We are going to Aleppo to see my grandfather. He lives there."

Aleppo is Syria's largest city, located north of Damascus, not far from the Turkish border. During the time of the Ottoman Empire, it was their third-biggest city, with only Cairo and Istanbul beating it in terms of size.

A woman in a hijab, sitting a few metres away, turned around to look at us. She was with a little boy of about four. She studied me for a moment and then turned back to her son.

"She is my mother," said Tira. "I better go. But thank you for speaking with me. I have enjoyed our talk." She got up and returned to her mother.

Of all the people we met on our travels around the Middle East, Tira is the one I think about most. What happened to her when the war broke out? What happened to her mother and brother? Aleppo became one of the main centres of Syrian bloodshed and violence. Whenever I watch a news report on Syria, one of the most harrowing thoughts I have is that the girl with the braces is no longer alive.

2

Angela and I arrived into Syria on a warm and sunny September evening. Our visit tied in with the holy month of Ramadan. Our visas passed scrutiny at passport control and we quickly boarded a bus bound for downtown Damascus.

The journey took us through a series of parched brown agricultural fields before we reached the outskirts of the city, where white, grey and beige apartment blocks vied for space by the side of the pockmarked highway. They spread into the hillsides that surrounded Damascus, until the gradient became too steep to support any foundations. Further into town, the traffic thickened, mainly with old yellow taxis that zipped around with wanton abandon.

The bus dropped us off in the centre of town, a place that had become an outdoor market due to the influx of arriving and departing passengers. Arrays of ceramic pots, aluminium pans and fruit and vegetables were all on sale, piled up on the ground beside men playing backgammon. As we climbed off the bus, the heat hit us and the taxi drivers moved into position.

"Where you go?" one man asked in a thick accent.

"No," another driver snapped, pushing him out of the way. "Don't listen to him. He is a crook. I will take you." A couple of other drivers joined the scrum.

Being European meant we were the top choice for the taxi drivers. We didn't know the going rate and were therefore ripe for a fleecing. I pointed at the first man who had spoken, and the rest waved their hands in disgust, walking back to their seats in the shade. We followed the driver to his decrepit yellow taxi, an Iranian manufactured Saba.

"Afamia Hotel," I said. "How much?"

The man was manhandling our luggage into the car's tiny boot. There was no way it was going to fit. It would have to go on the front passenger seat.

"How much?" I asked again. I rubbed my thumb and forefingers together. "You have a meter?"

"No meter. Price: two hundred."

Two hundred Syrian pounds was less than three British pounds, which sounded a fair price to us. Later, we found out it was a grossly inflated price; over five times the usual price. As the man started the tinny engine, I regarded his dashboard. It had a layer of carpet along its length and a strange mirror dangling from the plastic radio. In the middle of the mirror, someone had painted a pair of eyes. They stared at us as the engine shook itself to life.

Even though the car looked on its last legs, it still propelled us through downtown Damascus at a surprisingly brisk pace, its small size enabling it to nip along side streets with ease. The buildings looked similar to the ones in Amman, except in worse shape and covered in dust and grit. Damascus seemed unloved and neglected but its people looked happy. We passed a man swinging his young son beneath his feet, an old woman playfully nudging her husband on the arm and then a pair of teenage boys laughing uproariously at something on their phones. Even our taxi driver seemed jovial now that he had secured his fare. He turned a dial on his radio and began humming along to the Arabian-style pop song blaring out from the speakers.

3

The Afamia Hotel was only a ten minute walk from Damascus's old town. Wasting no time in hitting the streets, Angela and I took our lives into our hands as we crossed a three-lane highway devoid of traffic markings. The only way to cross was to wait for a large enough gap in the traffic and then run like the clappers.

Ahead of us was the magnificent, Ottoman-built Hejaz Railway Station, a large brown palace of a building, dripping with grand columns, carved stone arches and full of red and blue stained glass windows. Originally built to transport pilgrims to Medina in Saudi Arabia, it was closed, possibly never to open again, especially since, about fourteen months later, a mortar shell exploded near it, killing a dozen people and injuring fifty more.

In front of the station was an old black steam engine. Once upon a time, hundreds of excited people had waited for trains like it to take them on the five-day journey to Medina. No one was waiting for the train now.

With darkness almost upon us, the mouth-watering aroma of open-air cooking was wafting over the streets. Soon, the people of Damascus would be breaking the fast of Ramadan, sitting down to eat in large and boisterous gatherings. Kebab stalls were ready, as were men selling large hunks of bread from mobile carts. Feeling pangs of hunger, we walked to the entrance of the Al-Hamidiyah Souq.

Even though the souq was wide and spacious, it was awash with heat and noise. Turban-wearing men were shouting for customers at their clothing stalls and, further in, so were the pomegranate juice sellers, who were also clinking glasses to attract passersby. A parade of wind-up dogs yapped at our feet, almost tripping us up. Angela pointed at a stall selling stuffed birds of prey. Falcons, buzzards and eagles, some with snakes clasped in their beaks, were sitting on a tablecloth-covered stand. A couple of women in abayas were studying one of the birds while the owner of the stall hovered nearby. In the end, they didn't buy one, and the proprietor sat down again to read his newspaper.

We strolled through what was possibly the most authentic souq in the Middle East. If we ignored the cheap Chinese and Turkish products, the market probably looked the same as it did when it opened for business in the early nineteenth century. We followed it around a corner where Angela noticed a small stall selling bottles of fragrant oils. As soon as we entered the tiny shop, the bearded man set to work, opening bottles from his extensive range, allowing Angela to smell the liquids. Whenever she nodded consent at one, the man's expert fingers would take another bottle from the shelf and place it before her. Angela liked the smell of one honey-coloured oil in particular. She asked the man what it was.

"Oud. Very high-quality and very pure oil, madam."

"Oud? What's it made from?"

"Agarwood, madam. Very rare."

It was also very expensive, with a tiny bottle costing well over one thousand Syrian pounds (£10), ten times the price of every other oil in his shop. Even so, Angela was so smitten by the aroma that she bought a bottle. The man sealed it up and handed it over.

We followed the main alley through the souq until we came to a large open air square. Tabletop stalls selling cooked food and fresh juices were busy now that the fast was over. At the far end of the square towered the Umayyad Mosque, the third most important place of worship in the Islamic world, reputedly containing the head of John the Baptist, a prophet in both Islam and Christianity. It also housed the Tomb of Saladin, one of the great Muslim leaders from the twelfth century. He had successfully fought off the Crusaders.

The mosque's courtyard was open to members of the public, and so we followed the crush of locals going through the narrow stone entrance. Strategically placed spotlights had bathed the square in a delicious golden-orange glow. The marble floor shimmered with lunar reflections. Above our heads, a tall, square-shaped minaret shone with green light, the colour of Islam. When the waft of cooking from outside became too much, we decided to find somewhere to eat.

4

We relocated to a rooftop restaurant recommended by our thin guidebook. The tall stone minaret of the mosque was just along from us, as was an attentive waiter who showed us to our table. Every diner was in a celebratory mood now that the fast was over, shaking hands, laughing and telling tales, but most of all, eating.

"Syria is better than I thought it would be," Angela said. She was staring at the table next to ours. A family of eight, including four children, were enjoying plates of kebabs, shawarma, feta cheese and hummus salad. All of them were digging in, arms crisscrossing each other, full of chatter and smiles. "It's so friendly. The people are so nice."

I nodded, savouring the mouth-watering smell coming from all directions. When the waiter approached with his pad of paper, we ordered a plateful of shawarma and kebabs for ourselves. I also inquired whether the restaurant sold beer because, even though the guidebook claimed it did, I'd not seen it on the drinks menu.

The man's eyes flicked to the side, as if searching out hidden observers. He leaned in close to me. "We do have beer," he whispered. "But we do not advertise the fact. I can bring you a beer in a metal jug. Is this okay?"

I told him it was and then he asked Angela whether she wanted a beer too.

"No, water will be fine, thanks." When the man disappeared, Angela glared at me.

"What's up?"

"You. There was no beer on the menu. They obviously don't like serving it, yet you still ordered one. And during Ramadan, as well! I can't believe you sometimes. No respect."

I winced. She was right – ordering a beer during Ramadan was immensely disrespectful. I was surprised they had even sold it to me. But what could I do now? The waiter was nowhere in sight. The beer was probably already on its way. "I won't drink it," I said.

As promised, it came in a metal jug, the same type of drinking vessel on the other tables. After taking a single sip to see what Syrian lager tasted like (bitter with a strong aftertaste), I left it on the table untouched. Our food came and was delicious. Afterwards, we left a hearty tip on the table before we left. Back on ground level, as night cloaked the buildings of the old town, Angela and I strolled back through the souq, past the old railway and towards our hotel.

5

The next morning, we were back in the old town. It was Friday, which meant most Muslim shops and businesses were closed until later that afternoon. With things so quiet, we decided to visit the Christian Quarter.

It surprised us to discover that Damascus even *had* a Christian Quarter, but back in 2011, close to one in ten Syrians were Christian. "That café is open," Angela said. A young couple were sitting on the top veranda drinking coffee. We climbed the stairs to take a seat ourselves. The couple smiled, said hello and then continued with their love-smitten conversation. Below us, a rabbit warren of stone alleyways was busy with people. The buildings lining them dated to medieval times, and reminded me of certain cities in England, places such as York or Chester. Most of them had arched wooden doorways with thick pieces of dark timber supporting wooden balconies. Their wattle and daub design made them look highly appealing even with electrical cables dangling over them.

"If bananas wear pyjamas," I said. "What do peas wear?"

Angela rolled her eyes. "What?"

I repeated the question.

My wife sighed. "I don't know."

"Come on. If bananas wear pyjamas, what do peas wear?" I was looking at a fruit and vegetable store below us. Piled up outside were bunches of bright yellow bananas. Next to them were carrots, melons, oranges and a whole pile of peapods.

Angela thought for a moment. "I don't know...keys?

"Peas can't wear keys. Peas wear dungarees."

Angela smiled despite herself.

We finished our drinks and headed back to the street. We saw three small boys, dressed in what looked like new clothes, maybe early Eid gifts. Each boy was holding a gun and waving about freely. These weren't real guns, of course, but toy ones that could shoot tiny little plastic orange pellets. Every small boy in Damascus seemed to have one.

"This is how children should play in England," remarked Angela, as they bolted around a corner. "Just like my brothers used to do when they were little. Not like nowadays when they all sit in front of a computer. I bet you played army games when you were a kid."

I nodded, remembering how my friends and I used to love playing with toy pistols in a time when it was politically okay to do so. Our mini-warfare games had all been innocent fun, and none of us had grown up to be terrorists or mad men. Nowadays, if a nine-year old was seen with a toy gun in the UK, he'd be facing an armed response unit within seconds, possibly with rubber bullets headed his way.

But it wasn't all fun and games for the boys in the Christian Quarter. Further on, we saw a group arguing, resulting in one boy running away in tears. I noticed he didn't have a plastic gun and I could only surmise that his pals had either taken it from him, or else pelted him, knowing he had no means of returning fire. He crossed the street and ran down a side alley where another group of boys was playing. Ten seconds later, he reappeared, tears gone, with a smile on his face. He was holding a large plastic gun, armed and primed with a fresh batch of pellets. As quick as a flash, he was off in hot pursuit.

6

After lunch, we decided to visit the House of Saint Ananias. It was the place where Saint Paul had supposedly been cured of his blindness. For anyone not familiar with the Bible, the story goes like this: a man called Saul was spending most of his time 'zealously' persecuting Christians in Jerusalem. One day, he decided to travel to Damascus so he could persecute some Syrian Christians instead. He never made it, at least not at first. Along the way, a terrible sound came from the sky: it was God punishing Saul for his crimes against Christians. By the time God was finished with his smiting, Saul was left blind and stumbling, and might have died had it not been for a man called Ananias. Ananias took pity on the blind man and led him along the road to Damascus.

When the pair reached the city limits of Damascus, Ananias guided Saul through a great Roman arch (part of which remains to this day) and walked along the Street Called Straight to his home. When they entered the abode, Ananias touched the scales on Saul's eyes and somehow cured him of his blindness. So overcome was Saul that he converted to Christianity, changed his name to Paul and became a saint.

Angela and I found Ananias' home on the corner of the Street Called Straight (now called Damascus Straight Street). It was nondescript and small, with a few potted plants beside its arched entranceway. After paying the small entrance fee, we made our way down some stone steps into a small oval-shaped chapel. A row of small benches was on either side of a tiny aisle that led to a little altar. A local woman was sitting on one of the seats, facing the altar, so we kept our whispering to a minimum while we looked at the icons depicting the conversion of Saul. It was the most Biblical place I'd been to in my life. If Syria were more relaxed about tourists visiting, it would have been packed.

We left the chapel and headed back to street level, where the labyrinth of alleyways and side streets, many without signs or any way of navigation, left us stumbling blind ourselves. Not that we minded; Damascus' old town was gorgeous.

7

Damascus was a hotbed of pirate DVDs. The old town's souq was full of stalls selling the latest Hollywood blockbuster for as little as fifty Syrian pounds (75p). Like the previous evening, the souq was packed to the extreme. One shop in particular, selling ice creams sprinkled with nuts, was doing a roaring trade, and so were the orange and pomegranate juice sellers, who were squeezing fruit like robots on a production line.

Further along, a jam of cars was causing gridlock. It was so chaotic that people were climbing out of their vehicles to shout at one another. We sidestepped one vehicle whose driver was beeping in frustration at the queue ahead of him. Dangling from his window was a set of prayer beads. They weren't doing him much good. A few metres further, we arrived at a junction and saw the cause of the jam. Cars were coming from all four directions at once and meeting headlong in the middle. There was nowhere for them to go.

The next day was September 11th, and over in Florida, America, a mad pastor was threatening to burn copies of the Koran. In Damascus, things looked calm and so Angela and I decided to visit the modern part of the city. When the taxi dropped us off, we saw a district characterised by quiet roads, lush green palms and large residential villas. We could've been in Greece or Spain. The only indications we were in an Islamic nation were a few minarets poking above the palms, and a huge Syrian flag standing next to the large five-star Dedeman Hotel. Behind the hotel and villas were the brown hills that surrounded Damascus, the same hills where rebel fighters would soon launch guerrilla attacks.

Angela and I walked past the villas until we came to a large roundabout full of terraced fountains. The sound of water trickling and of birds singing filled the air. "It's got to be around here somewhere," Angela said. Opposite us was the Turkish Embassy, and the cafe she'd read about in the guidebook, the one that served the best coffee in Damascus, was supposed to be near it. We retraced our steps and walked up the other side of the road. There was still no sign of the cafe. Once again, we stopped at the roundabout, wondering what to do.

"I reckon that way," I said, pointing along a main road.

Angela nodded and so off we set. Two minutes later, a man with an assault rifle appeared. He was wearing combat fatigues and black sunglasses. He might have been a policeman, a soldier or a terrorist for all we knew. He babbled at us in Arabic, but switched to English after seeing our uncomprehending looks. "You must leave," he said sharply. "You are near American Embassy. Do not take photo. Go now!"

"Are you a policeman?" I asked.

"Yes."

"Why can't we walk down here?"

The man looked annoyed. "No questions. Go back down hill."

We complied and gave up on the cafe. September 11th was clearly making the Americans jumpy, and that had filtered down to the police officers guarding them. We walked to the Dedeman hotel, had a coffee in there instead and then caught a taxi back to the old town.

An hour later, we were on our way back to Damascus International Airport so we could catch our flight back to Doha.

A few months later, Angela and I watched TV reports about bombings, street warfare and endless atrocities going on in Syria. Whenever a new update was broadcast, I would find myself thinking about the little girl I'd met in the airport, the little Syrian girl called Tira who wore braces and who hoped to become a dentist one day.

Top row: Inside the sprawl of Damascus Souq; One of the more modern parts of the city
Middle row: One of the huge minarets of the Umayyad Mosque, as seen through an old archway; The Chapel of Ananias where Saint Paul converted to Christianity; A street just outside the old town
Bottom row: Statue of Saladin; An alleyway in the old town

Chapter 12. Petra and the Dead Sea

The road journey from Amman to Petra passed in a blur of sand and phosphate factories. Spindly scaffolding and tall chimneys blighted the orange hills and rocky plains beyond the highway. With Jordan being one of the world's largest exporters of phosphate, its factories were working at full pelt to extract it as quickly as they could.

In the driver's seat was Adib, a well-built man with receding hairline. His job was to drive us to Wadi Musa, the town that served as a base for the Petra ruins. There, he would drop us off at the hotel and then introduce us to our guide the next morning. A day later, he would drive us to the Dead Sea, and then back to Amman. Adib was fine with all of this except the hotel part. According to his company brief, he was supposed to be delivering us to a small hotel on the edge of Wadi Musa, and when we told him we had booked ourselves into the Movenpick, he was confused.

"Our hotel not good for you?"

"It has no air conditioning," I told him.

But this was only half of it. Following the fiasco with our initial hotel in Amman, Angela had checked out our proposed hotel in Wadi Musa. A quick search on the internet revealed that the rooms were tiny and its carpets stained. It didn't have air conditioning but it did have thin, dirty windows. But what did we expect? It was only twelve dollars a night. We booked ourselves into the Movenpick instead.

"So you don't need this hotel we booked for you?"

"No. We're staying at the Movenpick. Is this okay?"

Adib nodded but still looked confused. Five minutes later, he was on his phone speaking to someone, presumably his boss. When he'd finished, he addressed us again. "My company say they will not pay for Movenpick."

"Don't worry. We've already paid for it ourselves."

This seemed to settle Adib down. He concentrated on his driving. Outside, the phosphate factories were giving up their claim on the desolate Jordanian landscape. Our journey south continued.

2

Three hours after leaving Amman, we arrived in the town of Wadi Musa. It was a small brown town nestled in a valley of equally brown terraced hills. The town's existence was entirely down to tourism. Cheap hotels, cheaper cafes and gangs of touts, all of them trying to milk another dollar from the cash cow that was Petra, were all over the town. One shop proudly boasted it sold the *Best Tours of the Ruins in Jordan*; its faded blue sign told a different story.

"You know what Wadi Musa means?" asked Adib.

We shook our heads.

"Wadi means valley, and Musa is the Arabic name for Moses. So it means Valley of Moses – you know, the man from the Bible."

"Moses?" I asked. "He passed through here?"

Adib nodded.

We followed the road downhill. Like everywhere in Wadi Musa, small convenience stores and backpacker hostels lined the road. Then we came to a stop outside some large gates. We had arrived at the Movenpick. It was next door to Petra.

"I come back tomorrow at eight," said Adib. We thanked him and spent the rest of the afternoon and evening wallowing in luxury.

3

The next morning, good to his word, Adib led us from the hotel lobby into the heat of the desert. I asked him whether he'd driven all the way from Amman or stayed in town for the night.

"I stay in Wadi Musa with my cousin," he told us. "He live with his wife here. He is taxi driver. I always stay with him when I work in Petra. Sometime he stays with me in Amman."

I wondered why he hadn't stayed in the cheap hotel we'd been booked into. Maybe it was too low for his standards, or, more likely, his company had cancelled the booking and reclaimed the money.

Outside the hotel gate was a well-oiled set of hawkers gearing up for the morning. Men with donkeys were milling about by the entrance of the Petra complex while groups of women wandered around trying to flog nuts and fruit. A tacky stall called the *Indiana Jones Gift Shop* was next door to the *Indiana Jones Snack Shop*; their owners were busy sweeping dust from their entrances. A group of small children stood outside the gift shop begging for money.

"Come," instructed Adib, leading us through the melee. "Ignore everyone." A small child tried to grab my arm. He was about six years old, already a professional beggar, abandoning school and study for the more lucrative work of gaining money from tourists. I peeled his hand away. He pulled a face and scanned the crowd for a more willing victim.

Angela and I followed Adib into a large white building adorned with Jordanian flags. Inside were some ticket counters. After getting our passes, Adib told us to wait. A minute later, he returned with another man, a thirty-something Jordanian wearing sunglasses and a sports cap. He introduced himself as Khaled, an official guide of the ruins.

"I will pick you up tomorrow at 8am," said Adib. He turned tail and left.

We followed Khaled until we emerged from the other side of the white building. There, another group of men with donkeys and horses waited. Khaled exchanged words with one man. He was the oldest of the group, wearing a white thawb and traditional chequered red and white head covering. After a few seconds, the old man came towards us.

"Hello," he beamed, shaking my hand. The man had a cracked and wrinkled expression; the face of a man used to toiling under the sun for long periods. "It is time for horse ride. Giddy up!" He cracked up laughing at the expression he'd used. Behind him, two teenage boys were holding onto a couple of horses. Neither looked very amused.

Neither was I. The last time we'd ridden on horses was in Peru, and that had almost ended in disaster. My horse had nearly killed me and Angela's had thrown her to the ground. I looked at the old man in front of me. "I think we'd rather walk. But thanks, anyway."

The man looked astonished. His eyes widened and the lines around them momentarily smoothed. "But you already pay! And look, all tourists enjoy the horse ride."

Almost every Westerner was on horseback, making their way along the flat, rocky terrain ahead of us. It seemed the way things were done in Petra. I looked at my horse and it looked back. I narrowed my eyes and it swished its tail. I stroked its brown head and, when it didn't bite my hand, I looked at Angela. She was already climbing onto her steed. What the hell, I thought, and jumped into the saddle.

4

One of the teenagers took up station beside me. He was a toothy individual with an unruly mop of black hair. He clucked and swatted my horse to get it on its way. The other boy was doing the same thing for Angela.

"You ride?" the teenager asked, passing me the reins.

I shook my head. "Never been on a horse before," Behind me, Angela was setting off, looking more comfortable in the saddle than I felt. She glanced over and smiled.

"You want to go fast?" the young man asked, despite what I'd just said.

"No!" I shook my head to emphasise this. The teenager nodded and ambled alongside saying nothing. To pass the time, I took a few one-handed photos of some camels sitting along the edge of the dusty trail, and then pointed the camera at the scenery behind them.

It was mainly jagged, orange-red tinged rocks. It looked like the surface of some distant planet.

"Where you from?" asked the teenager.

I told him.

"Ah, England! I know Scotland and Isle of Wight!" He then proceeded to give me what he thought was an authentic Scottish accent but sounded more like Japanese. I smiled anyway. A quarter of an hour later, we arrived at the end of the trail. Angela and I climbed down and looked around for Khaled. He was sitting down on a rock some distance away, though how he'd managed this was a mystery since I'd not seen him pass. With the young guides waiting for their tip, I opened my wallet and fished out ten dinar ($14), five each, which I handed over. Mr Toothy grabbed the cash then gave me a look of such distain that I wondered what I'd done. The answer was simple: I hadn't given him enough.

"We want ten dinar each!" he snarled, waving the note in my face. I couldn't believe the audacity of the man.

"You're lucky to get that," I snapped back. "That's ten dinar!" I grabbed Angela's hand and walked away. When I turned around, one of the teenagers shouted something at me in Arabic, then spat on the ground. Angela told me I ought to grab the banknote back. I was tempted, but by now, Khaled was walking towards us. He'd noticed the altercation. When I explained what had happened, he rolled his eyes. "Very common problem. They think tourists will give them a big tip if they shout and stamp their feet. Every year, they demand more and more. Anyway, enough of those boys, it is time to see Petra. But first, we must walk through the Siq. Come, I show you."

5

The Siq is a narrow, meandering pathway that cuts through the middle of sheer sandstone cliffs. Walking through such a high-walled chasm meant we were in relative comfort, shaded from the sun. "Look at this," said Khaled. It was a furrow carved into the rock at about knee height. "This is an old channel that brought water from the wadi into the city of Petra. It dates from the first century and is one of the reasons that Petra became an oasis in the desert."

We walked on, then pressed ourselves tight against the rocky wall to allow a horse to pass. In a carriage behind it were two young Western tourists, speeding to reach the prize at the end of the Siq

"You want postcard, mister?" said a young boy proffering a range of different scenes of Petra. He'd been lying in wait around a bend ahead. "Only one dinar!" I waved the boy away, but now he'd made his move, others were rushing up to join him, most offering donkey rides. We shook our heads at all of them, and they soon gave up.

Finally, though, the Siq opened to reveal the most majestic structure of Petra: the Treasury. If anyone has ever seen a photo of Petra then this is what it will be: the two thousand year old carved structure built with one purpose in mind – to impress.

And impress it did. When Bedouin traders and visiting merchants arrived at the mighty carving, they must have gaped in awe at the sheer size and complexity of the thing. And the way it seemed to reveal itself through a gap at the end of the Siq, all at the very last minute, made it all the more special. The passage of two millennia could not diminish the effect of seeing it for the first time.

"Wow," said Angela.

I said nothing, staring upwards. Wow indeed. It was the same feeling of awe I'd experienced when I'd seen the Taj Mahal for the first time. No wonder Petra had been included in the new list of Wonders of the World. It deserved its place. Khaled allowed us to gaze freely for a few moments, waiting until we'd had our fill of the huge rock carving. I couldn't believe it had survived the passage of time so well. Every column, every pediment, every decorative element – including a trio of carved human figures – all looked pristine and free of erosion.

As if reading my thoughts, Khaled explained. "Although Petra as a whole is under threat from rain and wind erosion, the Treasury is almost perfectly protected from the weather because of its position. But if you look closely, you may see a few bullet holes."

"Bullet holes?" said Angela.

"Yes, up by that carved statue. They were made by Bedouin rifles. They were trying to find hidden treasure behind the statues."

Before we could question him further, a camel snort brought our gaze to ground level. Two beasts of burden, their humps draped in red and blue cloth, were lazing in the sand near their handler. When the large tour groups arrived later that morning, the camels would be busy, but for now, they looked content to wallow in front of the pink carving. We walked past them towards the Treasury. Beyond its grand columns was a dark stone chamber, into which we followed Khaled: it was devoid of objects, with only a few striations on the walls offering decoration. Angela asked Khaled what the chamber's purpose was.

"Most historians believe that the Nabataeans built the Treasury as a crypt for their people, and this was where they laid them to rest. The name, the *Treasury*, is misleading though. It has nothing to do with the Nabataeans, but from two later legends: one is that this chamber used to house Egyptian treasure; the other is that bandits may have hidden their treasure here."

"Which one do you believe?" Angela asked.

"Neither. The thought of a Pharaoh from Egypt transporting his treasure across the sands of the Sinai Peninsula in order to store it here sounds absurd! Why would he do that? The legend about the robbers sounds more probable, but is almost certainly false, too. No one has ever found evidence of this so called pirate loot. But that is why the Bedouin shot at parts of it and left their bullet holes. They were trying to find this so-called treasure."

The legends and intrigue have appealed to Hollywood film producers. In *Indiana Jones and the Last Crusade*, the Treasury formed the entrance to the Holy Grail's final resting place. In one scene, Harrison Ford and Sean Connery ride through the Siq on horseback until they arrive outside the Treasury. The look on their faces was much the same as ours had been: open astonishment.

"Come," said Khaled. "It's time to see the rest of Petra."

6

Before arriving in the town of Wadi Musa, I thought that the Treasury *was* Petra: just that carving on the rock face and nothing else. But there was so much more, and over the next hour or so, Khaled led us around an ancient theatre, some Royal Tombs and a large crumbling structure that might once have been a temple. Everywhere were ruins and more ruins.

"My dream," said Khaled, "is to go back in time and see Petra as a living and breathing city. I would buy spices from the markets, eat food from the stalls and see water gushing along the rivers into gardens. All of this," he said, sweeping an arm from left to right, "would have been green and lush. Not like the brown it is today. What a dream, eh? To see how the Nabataeans actually lived!"

"What happened to them?" asked Angela.

"Two things. One: the Romans came and took Petra as part of their empire, and two: a terrible earthquake destroyed much of the water channels and cisterns. Without water, the city began to die."

After delivering us to a restaurant in the midst of a jungle of donkey touts, camel handlers and trinket sellers, Khaled told us that he would be leaving us. "The way back to the Siq is that way, but further along this trail is the Monastery. It is a hard climb but well worth it. You could always take a donkey if you are feeling tired."

We said goodbye to him, grabbed something to eat and then pondered our options. A scrawny adolescent dragging a pair of miserable-looking donkeys approached. "You want ride to top?" he asked. "It take one hour if you walk; my donkeys take twenty minutes! Air-conditioned taxi!"

I didn't fancy sitting on a donkey with my feet dragging along the floor, and, besides, the donkeys looked old and knackered. We declined his offer and set off walking, stopping to read a sign written in Arabic and English. *Venturing beyond this point without a guide is dangerous*, it said. Away from the sign was a rough trail snaking up into the highlands. We passed the sign and began our trek towards the Monastery.

7

The eight-hundred step trail wasn't really dangerous, but it did have some sheer drops that would have killed us had we slipped. Some people faced a greater danger though: those on donkeys. One Western man passed us with terror in his eyes. As his donkey carted him along the edge of some precarious rocky steps that overlooked a cliff, he looked like he was about to scream. Conversely, the teenage boy running alongside him was in high spirits. When the donkey stopped at a particularly steep section of the trail, he relished giving it a whack on the rump to make it bolt. This time the man did scream as he flew upwards, disappearing from sight.

Forty gruelling minutes later, we reached the top, where a splendid view of the valley awaited us. It reminded me of old Western films I'd watched as a child, scenes in which cowboys had hidden in high cliffs waiting to attack the stagecoaches below. Everything was beige – the rocks, the ground, even the sky, with the only colour being clumps of dull green from the hardy bushes that had somehow taken root in this most inhospitable of places. A few rock lizards and a herd of goats, their bells tinkling as they roamed the plateau, made up the local wildlife.

Like the Treasury below, the Monastery had been carved into the rock face. It seemed mirage-like, the sort of vision an unhinged mind might see after wandering the desert without water for three days. Unlike the Treasury, though, it had suffered the effects of weathering far more, especially on its columns. They were worn and raw. At its base was another darkened chamber, empty apart from a few discarded Coca Cola cans and our echoing voices. "Do you know what I'd love to do?" I said. "I'd hide in here and when someone came in I'd bellow: WELCOME UNDERLING! I AM YOUR MASTER

AND YOU MUST BOW DOWN TO ME NOW! WHA-HA-HA-HAAAA!"

Behind the Monastery stood a drinks stand selling bottles of water for the scandalous price of three dinars each, five times the cost of at the bottom. But then again, someone had lugged them all the way up. Angela and I found a shaded spot and gazed out over the valley. It looked untouched by man. If I scrunched my eyes, I could almost imagine ancient caravans, transporting spices, textiles and incense, coming through the mountains to trade with Nabataean merchants. Nowadays, the only trade coming through were the tourists.

"I can't believe we'll be back in Qatar in a couple of days," Angela said, taking a sip of the meagre water we had remaining.

"I know. But what a trip. How many countries have we done?"

Angela counted them off on her hand. Qatar, Saudi Arabia (sort of), U.A.E. and Oman. Then Bahrain, Lebanon, Turkey and now Jordan. Eight countries in all: each with its own unique flavour and colour. We stood up, looked at the Monastery for the final time and then made our way back down the slope.

8

It is not often that childhood dreams come true, but in Jordan, one of mine did.

As a child in the 1970s, I remembered watching a program about the Dead Sea. I could vividly recall footage of a man lying on his back, floating around without any effort, even reading a book as he bobbed up and down in the mystical water. It seemed like magic and I could not comprehend it. My dad explained that, due to the high quantities of salt in the Dead Sea, it was impossible to sink. This thought intrigued me and I immediately wanted to go there, to try it out for myself. But, of course, we couldn't go to the Dead Sea. Flying to Israel (the country the travel program had focussed upon) was too expensive and exotic for the average family in the 1970s. And so that was that: floating in the Dead Sea was to remain a childhood dream for the next three decades. But now, my dream was finally going to come true, except not in Israel; in Jordan.

The next morning, Adib picked us up from the Movenpick for our trip to the Dead Sea. Ten minutes later, we were passing the same tourists shops we'd passed on the way in. Then we left the town behind.

Apart from the sliver of meandering black tarmac, the landscape beyond Wadi Musa was beige rocks. Sometimes they hung over the highway, as if threatening to unleash their bounty of stone upon us, or else they rose majestically in the distance. As we negotiated a hairpin bend, we descended through a wide gorge where the landscape took on a lunar appearance. Rocky outcrops, bare ground and a desolate landscape, devoid of human contact, made it seem other worldly. Except there were a few humans around. Occasionally we passed tiny nomadic settlements, sometimes with herds of goats wandering under the supervision of a single-robed man.

After two hours, we descended into the lowest point in the world, over 1200 feet below sea level. It was also an area of Jordan quite close to the Israeli border. It flanked our left hand side. I asked Adib whether he's ever been.

He shook his head staunchly. "No." I didn't pursue the reason why.

Our first sighting of the Dead Sea gave us a glimpse of just how salty the huge lake was. White sediment caked the shoreline, and, in some places, where the shallow water had almost completely evaporated, the surface looked white, as if a layer of snow had somehow fallen in the desert. We stopped to have a look, and Adib agreed to pose for a photo. After I'd taken it, I reached down to touch the salt in order to taste some. It was bitter and horrible, nothing like regular salt. I tried to spit it out, suddenly wondering whether it was poisonous, but when I saw Adib laughing, I knew it wasn't. Back in the car, we continued northwards, towards the up-market hotels that had sprung up around the Dead Sea. The Crowne Plaza, Marriot and the Kempinski all had establishments along the

Dead Sea's eastern shore, which we bypassed in favour of a public resort on the north-eastern edge of the lake. It was time to realise my childhood dream.

9

"Bloody hell, it's hot!" I babbled as the water went up to my knees. "It's like being in a bath!" The Dead Sea was also stinging like mad. I had a tiny cut on my leg, which the saline solution was attacking with vigour. And yet, I was grinning like a fool! I was actually in the Dead Sea!

Angela followed me as I trudged deeper, dunking my hand into the warm water, finding its oily texture unlike any other water I'd felt before. It seemed almost slimy. When I reached a suitably deep point, I bent my knees and then leaned backwards. And then I floated like a cork in a pond. It felt such an alien way to be in water and one I was so utterly unused to. Angela was also floating on her back, smiling as she propelled herself with only minimal arm movements. I stretched my arms and feet upwards so that they were sticking out of the water. I did not go under. A man floated past reading a book. His wife was laughing as she tried to take a photo.

I noticed a family of four a little further in. Mum and Dad were watching their two sons, both of whom were wearing bright orange armbands. I couldn't believe it! Why did they need armbands in a sea where it was impossible to sink? I couldn't fathom it. It was only later that we learned that it *was* possible to drown in the Dead Sea, and people did so every year, usually as a result of swimming too far from the shore and trying to swim on their fronts. This resulted in their legs being forced upwards and their heads downwards.

I kicked my legs in the soupy sea and propelled myself into deeper waters. There was no risk of a denizen of the deep biting me though, because nothing, apart from some algae and bacteria, could survive in the lake. "I reckon I could swim to Israel," I quipped to

Angela, pointing towards the mountains on the other side. "Because this in no effort at all."

We splashed about for another half hour, with Angela taking a photo of me reading a book that we borrowed from the other couple, and then we dragged ourselves out. Slimy, oily grey sand covered us, some of which I decided to slap onto the top of my head. "It's supposed to reduce hair loss," I explained,

"You'll need a bucket then, not that measly amount."

After we'd cleaned ourselves up and got dressed, we met up with Adib, who had been waiting in a cafe further along the public beach. Ten minutes later, we were on the road to Amman. Our trip in the Middle East was coming to the end for the time being. One more night in the Jordanian capital, and then we would be flying back to our home in Qatar. After a few days of rest and recuperation, I would set off by myself on the final segment of the journey, a trip that would see me visiting some of the lesser travelled parts of Arabia, places such as Kuwait, Palestine and Iraq.

Top row: The Monastery, almost like a mirage; A close up of a camel
Middle row: The Treasury starting to appear; Our guide, Adib, showing us the Dead Sea
Bottom row: A horse and carriage makes its way through the sun and shade of the Siq; A woman selling trinkets in Petra; The best preserved building of Petra – the Treasury

Part 3

Kuwait – Israel – Palestine – Iraq Kurdistan – United Arab Emirates

Chapter 13. Kuwait City

FCO travel advice: Most visits are trouble-free. Protests take place sporadically in Kuwait. Landmines are still present in Kuwait. You should avoid off-road driving. Driving is hazardous. Many drivers pay little attention to other road users.

With the fasten seatbelt sign chiming, I looked out of my window and saw the endless expanse of sand finally giving way to a few desert dwellings and a series of slick, black oil fields – the powerhouse of this small Gulf State. Seconds later, the sand gave up entirely as the urban sprawl of Kuwait City, home to over two million people, came into view. A few minutes ahead of the posted arrival time, the wheels of the Qatar Airways Airbus touched down on the runway of Kuwait International Airport with barely a bump. It was time to start the next phase of my Middle Eastern Adventure.

Kuwait City seemed similar to other Gulf cities I'd visited. It had big shiny skyscrapers, big shiny 4x4s and a long stretch of corniche fringed with palm trees. It also had patrols of Asian men in brown overalls doing all the menial jobs that the locals couldn't be bothered to do. Troops of them toiled over the attractive flower beds and gardens that added colour to the otherwise lacklustre highway central reservations.

My taxi driver was speeding and swerving like a maniac, despite being over seventy years of age. As in Oman, he was a Kuwaiti, one of an ever-increasing number of nationals forced into working for a living due to the government's *Kuwaitization* program. His white headdress was flapping around as he swung his head from side to side, gesturing wildly to any driver in his way. He was particularly fond of his horn, which he blasted at anyone foolish enough not to set off the split-second the lights changed to green. With mad men like him on the road, no wonder Kuwait's traffic accident rate was soaring. In fact, the most dangerous job in Kuwait was to be a fast food motorcycle delivery man.

"You here on business?" he asked as we careened along the hard shoulder. His voice was calm despite his antics.

"No. Tourist."

He didn't comment, as he was too busy trying to barge his way into the line of waiting traffic he'd just bypassed. When nobody allowed him leverage, he simply pushed in, anyway, forcing the car behind to brake and blast its horn.

"From Europe?" he asked.

"Yeah, England. But I work in Qatar."

We came to a standstill in a traffic jam. All the Gulf States, I was noticing, were suffering from the same traffic problems – the existing infrastructure simply could not cope with the influx of new vehicles.

"Qatar, eh?" The man harrumphed and tutted. Whether it was because I worked in Qatar and he didn't like this fact, or whether it was just a reaction to Qatar as a whole, I didn't know. Whatever the reason, the mad Arab dropped me off outside the Oasis hotel and accepted his hefty fare without further comment.

2

A few days previously, in our apartment in Qatar, I had been checking through my plans for the final jaunt around the Middle East, confirming flights and hotels. Angela was not going to accompany me for one main reason: Iraq. In fact, she couldn't believe I wanted to go.

"It's safe," I told her again. "I keep checking the Foreign Office website and they have no restrictions for Kurdistan, beyond the usual keep your eyes open and avoid demonstrations."

Angela was unconvinced. "There's no way I would go to Iraq. Just be careful."

"I always am. Anyway, Israel bothers me more than Iraq."

Israel bothered me a lot.

After spending the night in Kuwait, I was returning to Amman in Jordan. Amman was only a short distance from Jerusalem, where I'd arranged my day trip to Israel. The land border crossing was the only place on Earth where both the Jordanian and Israeli customs officials did not stamp passports, either when entering or leaving. This was hugely important for me. If an Arabic immigration official found evidence of me ever visiting Israel, then they would ask questions. They might even deny my entry into their country. Kuwait would definitely bar my entry, as would Lebanon, and so that was why I'd arranged to visit those countries before even attempting to cross into Israel. But having an Israeli stamp in my passport could potentially cause problems for me in Qatar too. And that had been a major cause of anxiety for me in the weeks leading up to my trip, because even though the chance of it happening was highly unlikely, it was not impossible. A border official might be having a bad day, or might take a dislike to me, or when they saw that I had a resident's permit from Qatar stuck in my passport, then who was to say they wouldn't stamp my passport just for the hell of it.

If they did, I had a back-up plan of sorts. I'd have to 'lose' my passport in Jordan somewhere. Then I'd go to the British Embassy, who would issue me with some emergency travel documents. It would cost about a hundred pounds, but at least I'd be able to get back into Qatar. Then I'd have to apply for a new passport. But the worst thing about this scenario was that it would mean cutting short my trip. Iraq would have to go, and so would Ajman in the U.A.E. I tried not to think about this too much.

3

According to recent World Bank statistics, Kuwait is the third richest country in the world. The only nations above it are Luxembourg and Qatar. The United Kingdom languishes in 26th place, with a GDP less than half that of Kuwait. But it hasn't always been like that.

During the eighteenth and nineteenth centuries, Kuwait had been doing okay for itself. It had established itself as the best boat-making centre along the Arabian Gulf, and as a transit point for goods travelling between Arabia and India. Its thriving pearl fishing industry was adding money to the coffers too, and so, for a while, things were looking good for Kuwait. Things came off the boil with the outbreak of World War One. When the Kuwaitis sided with the Ottomans, British warships began a prolonged blockade, cutting off vital supplies to the burgeoning desert country. Then came the Great Depression of the 1920s, which kicked Kuwait when it was down. Trade was drying up and people didn't need as many boats. The Japanese delivered a further blow when they flooded the market with cheap, but better quality, pearls. Almost overnight, its one remaining source of decent income was gone. With Kuwait on its knees, Saudi Arabia decided to go in for a sly kick, grabbing a huge portion of Kuwait's territory, an area it still holds today.

By the 1930s, Kuwait was a shadow of its former self. Many of its citizens were living in poverty, eking out existences as fisherman or subsistence farmers. Then something miraculous happened – someone discovered vast quantities of oil. The rest is history.

After dropping my luggage off in the hotel room, I was in a taxi, heading to the most famous sight in the city – the iconic Kuwait Towers. My driver was an affable fellow from Kerala who had been working as a taxi driver in Kuwait City for the last fifteen years, which explained his good English. "There nothing to do here. But the money is good and the work is easy, at least compared to what it would be like in India."

I asked him how often he returned to his home country.

"Every two years. I have wife and two children, both boys. I want them to get good education so they do not have to drive a taxi like me."

We were driving through the backstreets of Kuwait City, home of rundown grocery shops and a mixture of Turkish and Lebanese eateries. One of them had an advertisement for a non-alcoholic brand of beer in its window, reminding me that Kuwait was a totally 'dry' country. Not even the upmarket hotels sold alcohol. I wondered whether the taxi driver knew of any backstreet booze retailers. If anyone ought to know, it should be him.

"No, sir, there is nothing like that. I think some residents make own drink at home, but they do it in secret. If caught, big trouble. But I have heard of people who smuggle bottles of whiskey into Kuwait, which they sell for two hundred dollars! For that kind of money, a person could fly to Bahrain and drink all day!"

Kuwait Towers stood on the tip of the corniche and did indeed look striking, composed of three towers, two of which had huge spheres attached to their lengths, both filled with water. The tallest tower contained an observation deck, a restaurant and a small photo gallery showing the damage caused by the Iraqi invasion in 1991 when the 'barbaric invaders' had used the towers as target practice.

We parked and the driver asked for three dinar. Three Kuwaiti dinars sounded like a bargain, but it wasn't. The Kuwaiti dinar was the highest valued currency in the world, meaning that one dinar was worth more than any other base unit on the planet. One measly Kuwaiti dinar was equivalent to about £2.20, which meant my short taxi journey had cost me almost seven pounds, possibly the most expensive taxi rate I'd faced in all my travels. The driver wished me well and drove away, leaving me as the only person in the vicinity.

4

I gazed up at the sleek white spikes of the towers and their bulbous blue domes. Upon closer inspection, they resembled giant disco balls popular in the 1970s, especially with their blue, white and green polka dot patterns. Maybe it was intentional, I mused, because the Kuwait Towers had opened in 1979, about the same time that the Village People were presenting the world with *YMCA,* and Earth, Wind & Fire were proclaiming that there was a *Boogie Wonderland* somewhere. Perhaps Kuwait City was it. Perhaps not.

When I approached the ticket booth, I discovered why there was no one around. Kuwait Towers had been closed for renovation since 2012. I looked up at the spheres, but couldn't see any work going on. Perhaps the renovations were all interior. I walked towards the sea front, instead, stopping at a high wall that overlooked a gorgeous line of azure blue. In the distance, a jet ski ripped over the water, sending an arc of spray behind it. Across the other side of the bay was a clump of partially constructed skyscrapers: new apartment blocks, probably. I turned in the other direction towards downtown.

Despite the heat, Kuwait City's corniche was fairly pleasing for an afternoon stroll. When a taxi stopped to see if I wanted a ride, I waved him away, wanting to see the deserted beaches at my own pace rather than speeding past at one dinar a second. That said, twenty minutes later, I was starting to overheat and so decided to stop for something to eat in a café.

"I'd like a spicy chicken sandwich please," I told the waiter. "But without mayonnaise." The Indian man nodded and repeated my order. As he wandered away, I began to read the *Arab Times*, one of the English language newspapers I'd picked up earlier at the hotel.

Whenever I'm in a foreign country I always try to peruse the local papers, and the *Arab Times* was turning out to be quite good. One headline read: *Street Violence on Rise*, which seemed at odds with the perception that street crime was low in the Gulf States. The report described numerous fist fights, beatings and brawls in Kuwait City, all involving local Kuwaiti men. Police had arrested one man, who the newspaper described as a transvestite, for the crime of 'beating a car'.

Another article described the hierarchy in Kuwaiti society, which, as in most places in the Gulf, was based upon wealth. It consisted of five tiers, with the Kuwaiti royal family at the top of the triangle, followed by Kuwaiti families whose ancestors had once been rich merchants. Former Bedouin nomads, who were lucky enough to settle in Kuwait just before the country struck the oil jackpot in the 1950s, made up the third tier. Next up were people from neighbouring Arab countries, places such as Jordan, Syria, Yemen and Lebanon. These citizens had lived in Kuwait long enough to establish families and businesses, making piles of money along the way. They were almost Kuwaiti citizens. At the bottom of the pile were foreign workers. But in this lowly pile, there was still a hierarchy in operation.

At the top of the expat pile were Western professional employees, people who worked in finance, education, construction and medicine. Below the Western expats were Arab workers from neighbouring countries who had not been in the country long. They ran businesses and held positions of power in industry. Below this level were the Indian and Pakistani businessmen. In Qatar, many Indians ran stores around Doha, or were in charge of backstreet restaurants. Some ran limousine taxi services, and others taught in the Indian schools. Some of them could afford to have their wives and children with them, something denied to the people at the bottom of the expat tier. Filipino expats came next: most of them well educated and well versed in English. The majority of this group worked in Kuwait's (and Qatar's) service industry: waitresses, supermarket checkout workers, airport check-in staff, McDonald's servers and the like. And then there was the bottom rung of the ladder: unskilled men from Sri Lanka, Bangladesh, India and Nepal, the majority of the Gulf's workforce, living together in work camps, toiling on construction sites, lugging suitcases around airports or packing people's shopping in supermarkets.

I looked up from the newspaper when the waiter arrived with my food. He looked apologetic even before he spoke. "I am sorry sir, but the chef has put some mayonnaise on your sandwich. But only a tiny bit!"

Damn, I thought. It reminded me of a trip to Kosovo when I'd been in a similar mayonnaise-induced situation. How the horrible white sauce had taken over the world was beyond me especially since even the smallest amount of the stuff in my mouth would induce a gag reflex. The waiter stood waiting, a hopeful expression on his face, but it was no good, I looked in the sandwich and saw large glistening globules of mayonnaise everywhere. There was no way I could eat it and I told the waiter so. He nodded in resignation and removed the plate, saying he'd get me another spicy chicken sandwich with no mayonnaise.

Incredibly, the next sandwich contained no chicken! Surely this couldn't be right. But it was even worse than that. Instead of chicken, it contained *only* mayonnaise! What was it with mayonnaise? And how could my simple order of a chicken sandwich with no mayonnaise turn out to be a sandwich containing just the cruel condiment itself?

It was a hideous joke and I was about to leave when the owner of the cafe noticed my discomfort. After explaining my plight, he nodded and apologised. "It is our chef," he explained in deferential tones. "He doesn't understand English! But I will make sure you get the sandwich you want, and then I'll beat the chef to death with a stick covered in mayonnaise."

I thanked him, only wishing the last part was true.

I set off once more along the corniche, this time armed with a spicy chicken sandwich with no mayonnaise.

5

I finished my sandwich and carried on along the curling corniche. To my right was Kuwait Bay, a body of turquoise water that fed into the Gulf of Arabia. To my right were the skyscrapers, mosques and busy highways. I arrived at a large building on the seafront that looked like a beige palace but turned out to be a sprawling fish market. Different kinds of fish were laid out for customers to haggle over, including sharks, rays, parrotfish and long silver things called belt fish. Indian men wearing aprons stood next to analogue weighing scales while their colleagues, armed with knives and meat choppers, stood waiting to scale, skin and fillet any purchases made. I wandered up to one man and asked whether he'd caught the fish himself.

"No, sir. I no catch fish. I only sell and clean." He pronounced the word 'fish' as 'fiss'.

By cleaning, he meant chopping off the head, discarding the innards and cutting out the fillets. I asked him where he was from.

"Kerala, sir," he answered, flashing some white teeth at me. "You want fish, sir?"

I shook my head and smiled. "Not now. Maybe later."

I recalled an article I'd read about men from Kerala in the Gulf. Because of the money they sent back to India, the Indian press had dubbed them 'Gulf Men', men of means, eligible bachelors and men to watch out for. With their wealth, they could build their own houses, buy their own shops, and could seek out the daughters of higher caste families, who welcomed them as potential grooms. When these Gulf Men returned home after their stint in the Middle East, they were self-made men, and enough of them accomplished this to perpetuate the myth that anyone who went to work in Kuwait, Saudi Arabia or Qatar would come back a Gulf Man. Many would be disappointed.

I went outside, passing a dhow yard, staffed mainly by fishermen from Kerala. With the fishing trips over for the day, the men were now checking nets and lobster pots or cleaning engines. After taking a photo of the Grand Mosque, Kuwait's largest, I had my first interaction with a Kuwaiti policeman. He was sitting in a Land Cruiser outside the gates of the Sief Palace, the official residence of the Emir of Kuwait. I asked the police officer whether I could take a quick photo, but he shook his head. "I'm sorry. The prime minister is about to leave the palace."

I lowered my camera and looked. Apart from a few more guards at the far end of the driveway, there was no activity.

"But when he has left, perhaps ten minutes from now," the policeman added, "a photo should be okay. As long as you stay on this side of the fence."

I thanked the officer, considering this, when suddenly a third man in a red beret rushed over. Where he'd come from, I wasn't sure, but I later learned that his uniform signified he was a military policeman. He was carrying a gun and a stern expression. "No photo! No photo! You go now!" He waved his arms dramatically. The regular police officer spoke to my red tormentor. The military policeman listened for a moment and then shook his head emphatically. The man in the car said something else, and the man shook his head some more. Soon, they were having an argument in thick, guttural Arabic. Suddenly, Red Cop marched up to me, stopping an inch from my face. "Go!" he said with undisguised rage.

Raising my hands in acquiescence, I turned around and walked off.

My final stop for the afternoon was one of the last remaining examples of pre-oil architecture in Kuwait. Bayt Al-Badr, a mid-nineteenth century town house that had once belonged to a rich merchant, was made of mud and stone and had a large, ornately decorated, wooden door as its entrance. Most of the buildings along the corniche would have looked similar before they turned to steel, glass and concrete.

The old building housed small exhibitions and sold local handicrafts, but when I tried to open the door, it refused to budge. I walked around the other side, where I found a window. The glass was dark and stained, an indicator that no one had cleaned it in a while. After walking back to the door, knocking hard but hearing nothing within, I finally gave up and walked to the hotel.

6

A few hours later, I decided I wanted to watch the sunset from the corniche. I couldn't be bothered walking, and so got the hotel to order a taxi for me, despite knowing how much it would end up costing me. My driver was an Indian man called Naveen. He was in his thirties, and, like my driver from earlier, he hailed from Kerala.

As we turned the corner, a thickset man speaking into a mobile phone suddenly stepped into the road in front of us. It was a wonder we didn't hit him. As we screeched to a halt, the white-robed pedestrian didn't even turn in our direction. This clearly displeased Naveen, because he turned from friendly Indian to angry Indian, shouting and gesturing through the window. The fat pedestrian didn't notice and crossed to the other side.

"Did you see what he did?" Naveen asked me, shaking his head.

I nodded.

"I almost killed him." Naveen tutted and put the car in gear. As we moved off, he glanced in his rear-view mirror. We went about a hundred metres before the brakes were slammed on again. Before I knew what was happening, Naveen threw open his driver's door and charged back towards the man in the white robe. I strained my neck to watch them pointing and yelling at one another. Then, as quickly as the fracas had begun, it ended. Naveen returned to the car and slammed his door closed.

"That man is a fool!" stated Naveen. "Crossing the road like that! And then laughing at me! A fool, I tell you! "

I nodded in agreement and called the jaywalker a crazy man.

"Yes! That is exactly what he is – a crazy man!"

What happened next took me by surprise. Naveen reversed his taxi back along the street like a lunatic. When he reached the fat man, he stopped the taxi, pressed a button and lowered my passenger window. Before I could gather my wits, he began yelling at the man through my open window. The pedestrian looked nonplussed for a moment, but then his expression turned to anger. With a swish of his robes, he rushed over: furious and large, glaring at me. He yelled something at me, and then turned to Naveen, beginning a fresh tirade of shouting. They were both crazy men, as far as I was concerned.

Twenty seconds later, the large man waved his hands in disgust and walked away. My window went back up and the taxi moved on once more. Naveen, bizarrely, began laughing, and I joined in too, more with relief than anything else. I asked Naveen what the man had said.

"He called you a motherfucker!" he answered. "Because you called him a crazy man!"

We both burst out into a fresh burst of guffaws. Mercifully, the rest of the journey went without incident.

7

Naveen dropped me off near the fish market, where I arranged for him to pick me up forty minutes later. With the lights of downtown Kuwait City starting to illuminate, I could get a sense of just how modern Kuwait City was. Night-time was always when the Gulf cities really began to shine. The bill for powering the sea of neon, the lines of street lights, the offices and hotels had to be phenomenal. But they looked fantastic.

With the drop in temperature, more people were out and about. A few Westerners jogged past, as did a couple of Arabic teenage girls, staring into mobile phones. I remembered my own phone and rang Angela.

"I'm looking at the skyscrapers of Kuwait," I told her. "They look amazing."

"Better than Doha's?"

I regarded them. There were curved skyscrapers, giant column skyscrapers and a gigantic TV tower that rose above them all. Kuwait City's skyline looked like something from an advanced alien land. "They're not far off."

I could hear Angela doing something on the other end of the line. I asked her what.

"Just taking a sip of wine."

"Cruel."

"Why...oh, yeah! No alcohol in Kuwait for you! But you can have some tomorrow. You're in Jordan, aren't you?"

"Yeah. And then Israel the day after."

"Good luck with that one."

"I know. If they stamp my passport..."

"They won't. You'll be fine."

Angela wished me luck. I told her I'd ring her from Amman the next day. I then walked back to the fish market to wait for Naveen. There was one thing that I wanted to see, and when he arrived, I asked him to take me to the Musical Fountains, the fourth largest set of fountains in the world. When he looked nonplussed, I told him they were near the ice rink.

"I have never heard of such a thing? Musical Fountains? Near the ice rink?"

"That's what it says in the guidebook."

8

The fountains were eluding us. It was as if they had been demolished or something. Naveen did a U-turn and travelled back up the same stretch of road past the ice rink, while we both looked for the mysterious fountains. Naveen told me that he'd driven along this particular stretch of road hundreds of times and had never seen any fountains, musical or otherwise. "Also," he added sagely, "no one has ever asked to see them before. You are the first person! Perhaps they were never here at all."

I tended to agree with him and so we called it a day, especially with the meter going hell bent for leather. Back at the hotel, I shook hands with Naveen, wished him well and paid him his fare. An hour later, I was eating some kebabs in a cheap restaurant in a street behind my hotel. The meat skewers were delicious, and the water refreshing, though I would have preferred a beer. Then it was back to the hotel to pack. I had a flight to catch to Amman the next morning.

*Top row: The skyline of downtown Kuwait City; The Kuwait Towers – iconic, but closed for restoration when I visited
Middle row: Close up of Kuwait Towers; Along Kuwait City's corniche; The ornately decorated door on the Bayt Al-Badr
Bottom row: Kuwait Grand Mosque; Kuwait City's Skyscrapers*

Chapter 14. A Day trip to Jerusalem

FCO travel advice: The situation in Jerusalem remains tense. Stay alert in the old city of Jerusalem. Rocket attacks and sporadic gunfire have occurred without warning.

I collected my Jordanian visa from Queen Alia International Airport and grabbed my bags from the carousel. Forty minutes later, I was sitting in my hotel room in West Amman. After telling Angela that I'd arrived safe and sound, I grabbed some lunch at a nearby café, and confirmed my plans for the next day. According to the email I'd received from the tour company, someone would pick me up at seven AM and drive me to the Jordanian border. From there, I would get on a bus to the Israeli side, and if all went well, I'd pass through security where another driver would be waiting. His job was to drop me off in Jerusalem. Six hours later, I would make the same journey in reverse. A straightforward trip that was giving me the jitters.

Since January 2013, it has been Israeli protocol not to stamp passports and to instead issue foreigners with border cards that acted the same as entry/exit stamps. It was the same with the Jordanian authorities: they would not stamp passports either, mainly because they did not see the crossing as an international border, anyway.

I reread the email. The tour company told that in over one thousand crossings, this year alone, not one passport had received an unwanted stamp. The only issue they could foresee was that I was a resident of Qatar, which might bring about some hard questions by the Israeli authorities. But this would not, in their opinion, cause any real problems for me. I returned to the hotel to brood.

2

Moya picked me up at seven in the morning. He was a barrel-chested man in his thirties who enjoyed chain smoking as a pastime. Because it was so early, the streets of Amman were quiet. Moya asked me where I was from.

"England," I answered, "but I work in Qatar."

Moya nodded "I have business associates in Qatar. Good people."

I asked him whether he'd ever been there.

"No. But I've lived in Kuwait. I've also been in Iraq and Syria."

"Iraq? Were you a solider?"

"No. I lived there with my brother. He sold cars in Baghdad. But this was long time ago. Not safe in Iraq now."

I decided not to mention that I was heading to Iraq in a few days' time.

We passed a shop called *The Treasures of Jordan*. Underneath the sign was written: Fine Gifts for Sale! Further along, Moya pulled over near a line of smaller shops. Men sitting at plastic tables having an early morning coffee made up most of the patrons. From out of one of the shops ran a teenage boy. He rushed over to Moya's open window and stood waiting expectedly. Moya turned to me. "You want coffee? Tea?"

I shook my head. "No, thanks."

Moya spoke to the boy in thick Arabic. The teenager ran off into the shop and emerged a few minutes later with a small cardboard cup of coffee and a new packet of cigarettes. After a swift slug of his brew, we were off again, joining the early morning traffic out of Amman.

3

On his fifth or sixth cigarette, Moya switched on his radio, where an Arabic radio station was broadcasting. It was two men talking in rapid-fire Arabic, and after a minute of listening, Moya turned it off. "They talk about new roads and new buildings in Amman. Nothing very interesting."

Our destination was the Allenby Bridge Crossing, one thousand feet below sea level. As the dual carriageway snaked its way downwards, a sudden traffic jam appeared. An overturned lorry had spilled its guts of rubble and soil into one lane. The driver and trio of policemen were furiously trying to shovel it away. We got past the accident and carried on our way.

Outside, the Jordanian countryside turned from rocky outcrops to flat lowland filled with tufts of hardy vegetation. Then a series of farms appeared, mostly small orchards of banana trees. And then we arrived at the Allenby Bridge Crossing, a hotbed of car rental companies and money changers.

"You paying for VIP?" asked Moya.

I nodded. The VIP service was a way of expediting the crossing between Jordan and Israel, a notoriously slow affair if done by normal means. The VIP service was an expensive queue jump though, costing $110 per person, but it would save at least an hour of waiting, which, for day trippers like me, meant an extra hour in Jerusalem. It also meant I could use the VIP Building.

Imagine velvet drapes and a butler waiting by the door. Imagine leather upholstery and cocktail waitresses serving champagne and champignons. Imagine glossy magazines and an area set aside for laptops and iPads. This is exactly what the Jordanian VIP Building was NOT like.

Moya led me into a building full of smoke, old chairs and a thin gaunt man handing out tiny glasses of tea. Moya pointed at a poky room at the far end, telling me I should go there with my passport. I nodded uncertainly and Moya took his leave, informing me he would be waiting upon my return from Israel later that evening. With Moya gone, I had to fend for myself.

4

I wandered to the little room and handed over my passport. A harried man took it and told me to sit in the room outside the office. I did so, choosing one of the empty seats arranged in a semicircle. I stared at the large chandelier dangling from the ceiling, and then at the three other Westerners already seated. They were part of the same group: one older man and two teenagers. They looked as confused as I did.

Five or six other people waited too, but they looked Middle Eastern, most probably Palestinians. On a wall-mounted TV screen, an Islamic scholar was preaching to the camera, while a newsreel of Arabic script scrolled past the bottom section.

"You want tea?" asked a man carrying around the tray.

I thanked him but declined. He moved to a man sitting a few seats away, who took a glass. All I wanted was to get my passport back so I could get on with the journey.

Twenty minutes passed and the man who had taken my passport appeared from his room. He barked a name in an accent so heavy that I couldn't understand him. He shouted it again, scanning the people waiting, but, when no one came forth, he yelled it at the top of his voice. "JAHSIN SMATT!"

I rushed up to him and, after he'd checked my photo against my face, he handed my passport over, passing out a few others at the same time. Another man led us outside to a minibus for our VIP journey to the Israeli border. Because of our status, our vehicle bypassed the lines of cars, trucks and buses queued up at the border. Some of them would be waiting hours, I hazarded. In the middle of no-man's land, we stopped at an army checkpoint. A solider armed with an automatic weapon checked the underside of the vehicle with a metal detector and mirror. After deeming us explosive free, he waved us through. Shortly afterwards, we began the short drive over the Allenby Bridge, crossing over the River Jordan. Next stop was the Israeli border. My stomach lurched at the thought.

5

Inside the Israeli border building, I went through a metal detector and then a young uniformed woman directed me towards an empty immigration booth. Everyone else in the minibus was directed to another VIP waiting area – a small room full of seats. Why the woman had singled me out, I couldn't tell, but it sent my nerves on edge.

Behind the booth sat an attractive Israeli woman in uniform aged about thirty. I smiled as best I could, said hello and handed her my passport. She smiled back, returned the greeting and then busied herself by studying my passport. She slowly checked every page. She paused at the stamps for Lebanon, Kuwait, Oman and the U.A.E., pausing further to study my Saudi Arabian visa, but stopped dead when she arrived at the page with my Qatar resident's permit.

"Qatar?" Her eyes flicked upward.

I nodded.

"Resident? So you work there?"

I nodded again, trying not to let my nerves show. I'd read that if they desired, Israeli border officials could detain and question a tourist for hours. With only one day in Jerusalem, I couldn't afford that happening to me. The security official asked how long I'd been working in Qatar.

"Just over three years."

The woman studied the resident's permit sticker that covered an entire page of my passport. "What is your job in Qatar?"

"Teacher."

"Arabic teacher?" she shot back, studying my face. One of her hands was hovering out of sight, perhaps near her stamping tool.

"No, no!" I answered, shaking my head. "English teacher. It's a British curriculum school. It's in Doha and it's—"

"What is your full name?" she interjected, throwing me off track immediately.

"Jason James Smart."

"Father's name?"

"James," I said.

"And grandfather's name?" She was studying my face.

I had to think. "James." I said. I laughed nervously. It sounded implausible but it was actually true. James was both my father's and grandfather's name, the same as my middle name. James, James, James.

"Do you know anyone in Israel?"

I shook my head.

"Where will you visit in Israel?"

"Just Jerusalem."

"Not Palestine?"

"No. Just Jerusalem."

"Where in Jerusalem?"

"The old town."

"Where in the old town?"

I shook my head and opened my mouth. No words came out. It didn't matter, though, because she was already asking the next question. "Which religion are you?"

I told the truth. "I was brought up a Christian, but I am not religious."

"Why not?"

I struggled to answer. The woman was studying my eyes now. "I don't know. I'm just not into religion."

"Why are you visiting Israel?"

My mind was spinning. The questions were coming thick and fast, perhaps as a way of tripping me up. The beautiful young woman behind the counter was a master of interrogation. I was unnerved. The woman stared at me, awaiting my answer.

"Just to visit," I stuttered. "I love visiting new places and I've always wanted to visit Jeru—"

"What was your Grandfather's name again?"

"Ah…James."

"You look nervous. Why is this so…?"

I didn't know how to respond to that. What was the right answer? My eyes flickered between the woman's gaze and her hidden hand.

"Relax; I'm not going to stamp your passport." She placed my passport on her scanner and then handed it to me. Then she passed me a little white card, which said: State of Israel – *Border Control*. My name and photo were on it (presumably lifted when the woman had scanned my passport). "Don't lose it," she said. "It will serve as your travel document in Israel."

I thanked her, feeling sweat running down my spine despite the air-conditioned room. "That's it? All done?"

"Of course. Welcome to Israel." she smiled sweetly. I thanked her and shuffled away.

6

Outside was a collection of minibuses, taxis and men waiting with name boards. Because I had already arranged my transport to Jerusalem, I had a man waiting just for me, a gentleman in his sixties with wild hair. A few minutes later, we were off, with me as the only passenger in a vehicle that could have easily held a dozen.

My first observation about Israel was that the highway was in better condition than its counterpart was across the border. The scenery was the same, though: dramatic beige hills scattered with scant vegetation. We passed a road sign saying that the Dead Sea was to the left, with the town of Jericho to the right: names that evoked strong Biblical images. We carried on straight ahead, bound for Jerusalem, capital of Israel, and proclaimed capital of Palestine, a city lodged between Arabia to the east, the Mediterranean to the left, and the Judean Mountains to the north.

I looked at the high ground we were passing, noting the occasional smattering of shack-like dwellings that clung to some of the plateaus. At first, I took them to be animal sheds, or perhaps long abandoned buildings, but then I saw people around some of the hovels. Outside one, a small boy was playing with a black plastic bin liner, using it as a kite to catch the wind. A few minutes later, when we passed another similar settlement, I asked the driver about them.

"Bedouin," he replied. He was a man of few words.

Rural Arab Bedouin settlements, I knew, were a thorn in the side for the Israeli government. Their argument was that the Bedouin had settled illegally and therefore were not eligible for government services such as water, electricity and sanitation. The sites I was passing looked in a bad way, with dwellings grouped together intermittently. None looked like they had any power beyond their own fires, and most looked medieval. But this was partly intentional – the people who lived there knew that if they ever built anything more permanent, then there was a chance the Israeli authorities would come and knock it down.

Forty minutes later, I knew we were approaching the city of Jerusalem because of the thickening traffic and shop fronts emblazoned with Hebrew. Similar to Arabic, Hebrew was a language read from right to left: like Arabic, I couldn't read any of it. As we hit the city itself, the buildings grew taller and the traffic even busier. But one thing that was immediately apparent was that Jerusalem looked affluent. Modern green trams plied the busy intersections and, on the horizon, a line of spindly cranes was helping to construct a new glitzy skyline.

The size of Jerusalem surprised me too. I'd always assumed Jerusalem to be small, more of a town, really. But it wasn't – it was enormous, home to over three quarters of a million people. In the centre of the city, my minibus pulled over at the side of a busy street. Across from me were a pair of white tourist coaches. Further along, a collection of blue and white Israeli flags were fluttering in the light breeze. "This is Jaffa Gate," my driver said.

I nodded and thanked the man. Jaffa Gate was where I'd arranged my drop-off to be. It marked the start of the old town.

"Please come back here at 6pm. I drive you back to border. Don't be late. Border might close early today."

I nodded, stepped out of the minibus and regarded Israel.

7

Jaffa Gate is one of eight entrances to Jerusalem's old city. As such, it was busy with tourists, hawkers, policemen and soldiers. From my quick calculation, the soldiers seemed to make up about a quarter of the population of the old town. I'd never seen so many soldiers hanging around a city, except for perhaps in Ashgabat,

Turkmenistan's capital. A platoon of young recruits was standing by the entrance, chatting among themselves, not bothering anyone, not even when I walked past them, staring. The original Jaffa Gate was actually on my left, a blocky entrance that had been out of action since a section of the city wall to its right had been knocked down in 1898. Today, the gap is wide enough to allow cars and streams of people through.

Through the entrance, shops selling souvenirs, men flogging huge pieces of round bread from mobile carts and a tourist information centre awaited me. Tour groups, families and groups of nuns were everywhere: it was the most tourist-heavy place I'd visited on my travels around the Middle East so far. Above me were some sturdy ramparts that surrounded the old city. The section I was looking at was near the Tower of David.

Inside the tower was a feast for history buffs. It was full of Roman arches, terrifying towers, bold statues and a series of maps, TV screens and even holograms that explained it all. I read that the Tower of David had once been King Herod the Great's palace and that during his reign, he had built three new towers, all named after people he knew. When Herod died, the Romans took over the fortress until a set of marauding rebels came and ransacked it, leaving it in ruins. And that was how it might have remained had it not been for Suleiman the Magnificent, a sixteenth century Ottoman sultan, who ordered a rebuild. He re-established Jerusalem as an important trading city, and it began to flourish once more. Their reign ended during the First World War, when British troops captured the city. The man in charge was called General Edmund Allenby, for whom the bridge between Jordan and Israel was named.

At the top of some steps, I found a platform that overlooked the complex. I was standing on the Phasael Tower, the only one that remained from Herod's reign. Below me, Roman ruins poked up between bushes and pathways. Near one bush was a collection of chairs, which a group of young female soldiers were lounging about on. Most were laughing and joking, seemingly waiting for something or someone. What it was, I didn't know, because I was already leaving my vantage point. It was time to explore the old city from ground level.

8

I found myself standing with a throng of people in front the Church of the Holy Sepulchre: the holiest place in all Christianity. Inside its hallowed walls was where Jesus was crucified and supposedly buried.

The large brown church was squeezed into a tight courtyard that was rapidly filling with people, a lot of whom were carrying palms. This explained why the old town was so busy, I realised – it was Palm Sunday: the Christian feast that marked the start of the Easter Holy week. As I joined the crush, a large tour group arrived, the guide holding a water bottle in the air to gather his charges around him. Another group were huddled around a guide holding a feather. The poor woman was shouting at the top of her voice so she could be heard over the ceaseless din of chatter and noise. I looked over at the darkened arched entrance of the church and wondered whether I should try to get in. I quickly decided against it, because, unless I wanted to fight with a line of nuns, and barge my way past a whole brigade of old age pensioners, I was in for a long wait. Besides, something was about to happen. I found a spare bit of wall and waited.

A guide in front of me pointed at something on the church. His tour group looked up and I did too. It was a short wooden ladder leaning against an upper storey archway. It looked like a window cleaner had abandoned it there, or perhaps an errant builder. I listened as the guide explained that no one knew who had left it there. "The strange thing is," the man said, "no one has moved it since it first appeared in the eighteenth century."

He explained things further. Some people claimed that the Armenian Orthodox Church should move the ladder, others claimed that the Catholic Church should move it. But four other Christian orders had a say in church matters too, and if anything was going to be moved, then permission was needed by all of them. And that was the problem: none of them could agree on anything – even the simple matter of moving a ladder.

As a result, in the 1960s, the Pope decreed that the ladder should remain in position until such a time that the various church factions could unite. Anyone who moved the ladder would have him to answer to. And from that day forward, this mundane piece of climbing apparatus became known as the Immovable Ladder.

A few policemen arrived in the square and began constructing a makeshift barrier by the entrance to the Church of the Holy Sepulchre. Somehow they managed to push the crowd back behind it and stopped anyone from walking along the corridor they had created. Just then, a tall man accompanied by his young daughter tried to access the corridor. A policeman blocked his path.

"Why?" the man asked.

"Just move away!" the policeman barked.

The man stood his ground, holding his little girl's hand tightly. "I'm happy to move, but not happy to be spoken to like this."

The police officer said nothing. The tall man shook his head and walked away.

The policeman was clearly stressed, and despite what had just happened, another group of people tried to squeeze past. He barked at them, and they all scattered like children. Then he set to work clearing a path down a set of steps that led away from the church.

I looked back at the church's darkened entrance; there seemed to be some sort of activity going on. A few people were huddled in the shadows, but then I realised that the action was not coming from the church, but from my left, coming down the recently cleared steps. A trio of fez-wearing men carrying ceremonial daggers on their belts were leading a procession of black-clad men down the narrow stone steps. Close behind them were some priests donning dramatic black hoods. One of them was carrying a bush. Behind this group was a single priest, the youngest man there. He carried a huge olive branch. It was the Palm Sunday procession, celebrating Jesus' return to Jerusalem. The procession walked past me, and then along the corridor towards the church entrance. With the crowd jostling for position, trying to get the best footage on their cameras and phones, we all stepped forward to watch them.

And then something odd happened. As soon as the men entered the Church of the Holy Sepulchre, a God-awful wailing began. The cacophony sounded like a cross between a screaming banshee and the war cry of a Native American about to go into battle. It was such a strange screech that I couldn't even tell whether a man or a woman was making it. As the wailing continued, and the crowd shuffled, I saw movement again by the entrance. The same procession that had entered a few minutes previously trooped back into the open. With another surge from the crowd, the men retraced their way back up the steps and disappeared around a corner at the top.

9

The old city was a rabbit warren. One alleyway led to ten others, and some of them stopped at maddening dead ends. The main thoroughfares were packed with shops filled with scores of people gawping and touching the wares on offer. Religious paraphernalia, jars of oil, mounds of spices, arrays of jewellery, T-shirts, flags, mobile phone covers and fabric bags emblazoned with I Love Jerusalem filled the sides of the stone alleyway. I tried to dodge my way through the crush, but with the two-way traffic, and the unpredictable motion of many pedestrians, this proved impossible.

Along one particularly bad section, a woman with a pram was causing no end of problems. She was ambling along the cobbles pushing her infant, taking up the centre of the route though the alley, blithely unaware of the chaos going on just behind her. I was caught up in the logjam, which suddenly got worse when the woman decided to stop at a candle stall. Everyone behind her banged into each other as our acceleration was abruptly halted. In the confusion, I somehow managed to step inside an open shop doorway to negotiate myself around her and her infernal pram. Congratulating myself on my manoeuvre, I stole a glance behind and saw that the woman had managed to block the entire alleyway. Behind her, the mob waited; in front of her, a mob was stuck, but she refused to budge. It was only when a man driving a cart full of water bottles beeped that she moved.

I emerged from the main alleyway, taking cover in a less busy one, cursing myself for coming to Jerusalem on Palm Sunday. The place was overrun, not just with tourists, but also with priests, nuns and people carrying crosses. There were plenty of Jewish men about too, easily identifiable by their black hats, beards and ringlets of hair. Jerusalem was a carnival of activity.

I needed to find my bearings and so sought out a soldier to ask him the way to the Wailing Wall. He pointed in some vague direction to my right, which turned out to be accurate. I emerged from the hot, noisy souq-like alleyway straight to a vantage point that overlooked not only the famous wall, but also the quite magnificent Dome of the Rock.

10

The distinctive golden dome of Jerusalem's most iconic landmark shimmered in the glare of the midday sun. The dome stood atop its equally distinctive main section: a part decorated with different shades of blue mosaic tiles. The 1300 year old Dome of the Rock is one of the oldest pieces of Islamic architecture.

As well as being the third holiest site in Islam, after Mecca and Medina (Muslims believe that the site of the Dome of the Rock is where Prophet Muhammad ascended into heaven), Jews hold the area in awe, mainly because, before the mosque's construction in the seventh century, Jesus had worshipped in a temple there. Indeed, Jews regard the Foundation Stone, which is inside the Temple of the

Rock, as the holiest of all sites in Judaism: supposedly where the world was created and where God's eyes are always looking. Because of these conflicts of interest, Temple Mount continues to be a contentious issue in Israel, with both the Israeli and Palestinian authorities claiming it as their own.

I couldn't take my eyes away from the dome. Twenty years previously, it would not have looked anywhere near as good. King Hussein of Jordan donated the gold in 1994. To cover the $8.3 million price tag, he had to sell one of his plush London homes. A sound caught my attention: it was a woman rattling a tin in my direction. I dropped a few shekels into it, heading downhill towards a large square. At the far end was the Western Wall, otherwise known as the Wailing Wall.

After the Dome of the Rock, the Western Wall is the most sacred place in Judaism, because it had once formed part of the original temple where Jesus prayed. The Romans destroyed the temple and banned Jews from going anywhere near the ruins. Then they banned them from Jerusalem as a whole. When the Christians took over in the fourth century, they allowed Jewish people back into Jerusalem, but only once a year so they could gather by the wall. This they did, sobbing at the destruction of their temple. Later it became a Jewish obligation to cry at the wall, especially since God was always watching them.

From footage I'd seen on TV, I'd expected the wall to be short, but it stretched along the edge of the square for almost two hundred feet (the same length of a Boeing 767), and then carried on for another third of a kilometre behind the buildings of the old town. It was higher than I had expected too – over sixty feet high – and there were two parts: a large section for men and a smaller part for women. Jews wearing skullcaps were praying right up against it or else silently reading from the Torah a short distance away.

Access to the wall seemed to be along one side of the square, to my left. As I wandered towards it, a man stopped me and pointed to a large container. It was full of skullcaps. I didn't know whether they were for Jewish people only and so decided to err on the side of caution and left them alone. The same man continued to watch me and when it was apparent I was not going to pick one up, he reached down and chose one for me, gesturing that I should put it on my head. I did so, finding it a snug fit. The man nodded and waved me to the wall.

There were about thirty men praying at the wall, and quite a few others sitting on white plastic chairs reading Holy Scripture. I stood watching them for a while, also noticing the white pieces of paper – written prayers – stuffed into the cracks of the ancient wall. I'd read that over one million prayer notes got stuffed into the Western Wall every year, a worrying statistic for the chief Rabbi of Jerusalem. Twice a year, the notes are cleared, bundled into bags and then buried in a cemetery on the Mount of Olives.

An arched entrance was to my left; believing it was an entrance to the Dome of the Rock complex, I went in. I was wrong; it was an enclosed section of the wall inside a cave of sorts. Men were praying fervently, this time in what looked like private booths. As far as I could tell, women were not allowed. The silence was eerie and the only smell was the aroma of parchment. Hundreds of books and Torah scrolls filled the cavern, stacked up or housed by the dozen on rocky mantelpieces. I left the men to their silent prayers, exited the cavern and tried to find an alternative way to see the Dome of the Rock.

11

There seemed no way to get anywhere near the Dome of the Rock complex. Every alleyway was blocked by police officers who all told me the same thing: I couldn't proceed any further. I looked in the guidebook and discovered that non-Muslims were only allowed to enter Temple Mount by one single route: along the side of the Wailing Wall. I retraced my steps, but another trio of policemen blocked the non-Muslim entrance too. I tried to saunter past them but they spotted me. "No entry," one man said simply.

"But I am a Christian."

"I said, no entry."

I sighed. "Is there anywhere else I can go to see the Dome of the Rock?"

The officer shook his head and returned to his colleagues. I had no option but to give up. Instead, I carried along another alley until I came out near a small car park full of waiting taxis. I lingered long enough for one of the drivers to wander over. He was a short, olive skinned man, aged about fifty, with short grey hair and a pronounced paunch. "You want to go to Mount of Olives?" he asked hopefully, stubbing his cigarette out. "It is the best view in Jerusalem. The sight of the Dome of the Rock is amazing. Only takes ten minutes."

I ignored the question. "Is Temple Mount closed today?" I asked.

"Yes. Because of Palm Sunday. Open tomorrow. Maybe you come back?"

So that was why all the entrances were blocked. Of all the days to visit Jerusalem, I'd picked the worst. So maybe a quick drive to the Mount of Olives would be good thing, I thought. I might be able to take some good photos, if nothing else, and so we quickly agreed upon a price for a journey there and back. As we walked towards the car, he told me his name was Riza and that he was an Israeli Muslim.

"Muslim?" I asked. For some reason I'd assumed he would be a Jew.

"You probably didn't guess because I don't have a moustache," he said. "But yes, I'm a Muslim." He told me that almost all Muslim taxi drivers in Israel have moustaches. "I had one too – but I got sick of the police stopping me at checkpoint wanting to see my papers. With a moustache, they knew I was a Muslim and so stopped me. But since I shaved it off two years ago, no more stopping at checkpoints. Easy for me and my passengers."

We climbed in the car and then followed a thin sliver of road, barely wide enough for one car, up a steep hill. The route took us past the Garden of Gethsemane and the Church of Mary Magdalene. The former was the where Jesus and His disciples had prayed on the eve of His crucifixion. Nowadays, it is a quiet grove of old olive trees. The church was on my left, and looked like it belonged in the Kremlin: white with seven golden onion domes. Riza braked sharply. A car was coming in the opposite direction and there was nowhere for us to go. Riza and the other driver seemed unconcerned, though, and after some deft manoeuvres, the other car slid past our wing mirror with barely a millimetre to spare. With a shift of gear, we were off again, passing a horde of pilgrims trooping up the hill. A minute later, we arrived at the top of the Mount of Olives, where a man and a camel were blocking the road.

12

The man was a portly tourist, who, in a moment of comedy, was trying to swing his fat legs across the camel's back. He couldn't quite do this and ended up kicking the seat instead. He tried again with the same result. I watched this spectacle from my prime spot in the taxi because the camel was sitting in the middle of the road. In the end, the camel master had to help the large man out, hoisting him by his backside with a barely concealed grimace. The camel didn't seem overly concerned by the burden it was about to carry and simply stood up. At the side of the road, the man's wife was trying to take a photo but couldn't because she was laughing so much.

The camel moved off, allowing us to find a parking space. Plenty of other tourists were at the top, most congregating by a vantage point that overlooked the skyline of Jerusalem. Riza was right – the view was great, a panorama of churches, synagogues and mosques of the old town, with a line of skyscrapers behind them. The Dome of the Rock was right in front of me.

I heard what sounded like a gunshot from far below. It had come from an area of closely packed residential buildings near the old town. Then I heard another shot, then another. Riza was standing beside me taking a drag from his cigarette. We both looked and saw smoke rising from around some buildings. Then there was another loud crack. "Gunshots?" I asked, wondering whether I ought to be taking cover.

Riza laughed. "No, fire crackers. The people down there are not happy that Dome of the Rock is closed today, so they demonstrate. Anyway, how about a trip to Bethlehem, my friend?"

"Bethlehem?"

"Of course. The border between Israel and the West Bank is open today, so there will be no long wait at the checkpoint. It will be an easy trip – maybe take one hour to get there. One hour to look around, and then one hour back. You will see where Jesus was born and you can take many photos. After three hours, I can drop you wherever you want: at your hotel, Jaffa Gate, wherever."

I pondered Riza's proposition. It tempted me. It tempted me a lot. Plus, his quoted price sounded reasonable too. I looked at my watch. I had plenty of time before I needed to be back at Jaffa Gate for the return journey to Amman. Besides, with Temple Mount off limits for the day, I had a block of time to fill. Going to Bethlehem would fill it nicely.

"Bethlehem's in the West Bank, isn't it?" I asked. The notion of crossing into Palestine sounded slightly scary, even if the border was open.

"Yes, but it's safe. In fact, Bethlehem is safer than Jerusalem! It has many tourist police to keep visitors safe." Riza laughed to himself. "They do not want any harm to come to people who might spend money there."

Riza, perhaps sensing that he had almost won me over, added some cream to the milk. "One more thing, have you have heard of the shepherds? The ones who saw the Baby Jesus?"

I nodded.

"I can show you where they lived."

I was sold. We were off to Palestine.

Top row: Detail on the Dome of the Rock; The Church of the Holy Sepulchre (note: underneath one of the upper arched windows is the Immovable Ladder)
Middle row: Young Israeli soldiers hanging around the entrance to Jaffa Gate; Robed priests doing the Palm Sunday Parade
Bottom row: Two traditionally dressed men walking through the old town of Jerusalem; The more modern part of Jerusalem; The Western Wall, otherwise known as the Wailing Wall

Chapter 15. Palestine and the Bible

FCO travel advice: The situation in the West Bank remains tense. You should take care when travelling anywhere in the West Bank. Travel in and out of the West Bank is not possible without passing through at least one Israeli military checkpoint.

It was just after two in the afternoon and I was going to Palestine. Riza carefully snaked his taxi back down the Mount of Olives, following the thin winding road we had ascended earlier. I noticed a grove of olive trees in the distance, but then the presence of nuns in the middle of the road took up my attention. About sixteen of them, mostly elderly, were glaring at us, wondering why we were in a car. Riza took the hard stares with barely a sigh, waited for them to squeeze to one side, and then moved past them. At the bottom of the hill, the traffic was thick and unending. The city's mass transit systems seemed unaffected, though. I watched as a sleek silver tram slid to a stop on its gleaming metal rails. A group of young Israelis jumped aboard, carrying their iPhones and tablets with them. Once again, the affluence of the city struck me. I mentioned this to Riza.

"Affluent for the government, maybe," he answered with a snort. "Not affluent for the people."

We came to another stop beside a restaurant. Across it was a mixture of four languages: Hebrew, English, Arabic and Cyrillic. The latter surprised me, but when I studied some of the businesses further along, Cyrillic splashed their establishments too.

"Let me tell you something about the Russians," said Riza. "They are coming here all the time. In Jerusalem, it is not so bad, but in Tel Aviv, the Russians are everywhere. There is a Russian Mafia there. If you want drugs, women, even weapons, there are places in Tel Aviv – the Russian quarter – where you can get them. The police turn a blind eye, of course, because they are paid off." Riza tutted.

As the outskirts of Jerusalem thinned, we began to pass through parched brown countryside dotted with stunted shrubs and trees. And then we came to one of the checkpoints that acted as the border between Israel and Palestine. Like Riza had promised, it was unmanned, and so we drove through without stopping. With barely any other vehicles on the stretch of highway with us, we entered Palestine.

2

"So now you are in another nation," said Riza, "except of course, you are not." He slowed down and stopped near a large red sign. The top section was in Hebrew, the middle in Arabic, but I read the bottom section in English. *This road leads to Area A under the Palestinian Authority. The Entrance for Israeli citizens is forbidden, dangerous to your lives and is against the Israel law.*

"Okay," I said, turning to face Riza. "That sounds serious."

"It is serious, but stupid, too. The main reason for this sign is that Israel does not want its people to visit the West Bank. They do not want Israelis going to places like Bethlehem because, if they do, they might spend money there. This will contribute to Palestine's economy."

I looked back at the large red sign, reading the final sentence again. "So are you breaking the law by driving me to Bethlehem?"

Riza searched for the right words. "As a Muslim taxi driver...I am okay. The warning is for Jewish citizens. If they want to visit Palestine, they must do it in secret. If anyone stops them, either the Israeli or Palestinian authorities, they will have to say they are tourists from another country. This usually works for them. On some occasions, I have taken Israeli Jews to see Bethlehem. At the checkpoints, they say they are from America."

To be honest, the whole Israel/Palestine/West Bank/Gaza thing confused me. I was ignorant of what the differences were between them. I knew that Palestine had once been a hot news topic during the 1970s and 80s when Yasser Arafat was leader of the Palestine Liberation Organization (PLO). I vaguely recalled that Palestinians were responsible for numerous bombings, hijackings and other terrorist attacks during this time. I also knew that, in their own eyes, they were not terrorists, but freedom fighters, battling to secure their Muslim homeland in the face of Israel incursion. And I knew that this embittered conflict was still a major issue today. Indeed, not long after my visit to Jerusalem, Israel would start bombarding Gaza with aerial attacks, and in return would receive rockets from Gaza. By the time a shaky ceasefire had been put in place, over two thousand people were dead. But my major confusion was not of politics, but of geography. Riza said we were entering the West Bank, which was Palestine, but why did they have different names. And wasn't Gaza also Palestine? Were there two Palestines?

"The West Bank is here," explained Riza, "and is part of Palestine. Gaza is another area of Palestine, to the south of here, near Egypt. It does not border the West Bank, but both Gaza and the West Bank are Palestine. Both are ruled by the Palestinian government."

We set off driving along a road in noticeably poorer condition than the road across the border. The cars plying it seemed more battered too, and when I looked closer, each had a number plate with green numbers and a large green letter P on the side. Hebrew lettering had disappeared, replaced by Arabic, and not just from the number plates: the shop signs, too. I was firmly back in the world of Islam.

3

Palestine relies largely upon international aid to survive. This money originates from the US, the EU and the rich Gulf States, and without it, Palestine would collapse, which is exactly what Israel wants. To make it as difficult as they can for Palestine, Israel does two things. Since 2007, it has blockaded the Gaza Strip, barring the movement of supplies in or out of Gaza. This effectively seals Gaza off from the outside world. The same thing happens in the West Bank, though not with a supply blockade: large walls and checkpoints, reminiscent of Berlin during the cold War, seal it off from the outside world. Inside these closed borders, the citizens of Gaza and the West Bank have to fend for themselves – which is why they depend on international aid. With it, they organise their own education, healthcare, power and water. Palestine is one of the most dependent economies in the world.

"Do you think Palestine will ever be independent?" I asked Riza. We were passing a building site that looked as if it was making slow progress. A single man was working on what looked like an office block. A lack of materials was probably the cause.

"No I don't think so. It's too…complicated. There are too many factors at play."

A settlement loomed ahead. Riza told me it was not Bethlehem but Beit Sahour, a small Palestinian settlement, home to around 12,000 people, located just north of Bethlehem. "We will stop here so I can show you something," he told me. We parked at the side of a dusty road lined with even dustier shops. A clapped-out car was parked by the shop with its Palestinian number plate barely hanging on. A couple of old gents came out of the shop to regard us. They stood and stared with their hands in their pockets.

I waved at them, and one of them waved back. Riza ignored them totally, locking his car doors. A large arched entrance heralded the entrance to a tree-lined walkway. Riza told me it led to a Roman Catholic chapel. "Come on," he said. "I'll show you the Shepherd's Cave where the Angel told the shepherds that Jesus was about to be born." Riza had turned from taxi driver to tour guide.

The chapel at the end of the path was small. It reminded me of churches I'd seen in Armenia, in that it was made from stone with a single dome in the middle. It was also empty. Inside, Riza pointed at a fresco showing the shepherds gazing at the Star of Bethlehem, the miracle that supposedly led them to where Jesus was born.

"So this is where it happened?" I asked. 'On this very spot?"

"No. This is just the church. Come with me; I'll show you."

At the rear of the chapel was a cave of sorts. Inside were a series of pews and a whole shelf of lit candles. Who had lit them was a mystery, because Riza and I were the only people there. The rough walls and low-level ceiling gave the cave an authentic Biblical feel.

We stood in the middle of the grotto. It was about the same size as a classroom. Riza spoke. "This is where the shepherds lived. Look at ceiling." It looked like soot was covering it. "It is from the fires the shepherds made. This cavern is over two thousand years old. Older than Christ."

I thought back to my primary school days when we'd learned about the Nativity. In one Christmas performance, I'd played a shepherd, or was it an inn-keeper? I couldn't recall, except that my hat had fallen over my eyes, scuppering any chance of a star performance.

"So the shepherds from the Bible, who saw Jesus, stayed here – in this actual cave?" I asked Riza, feeling the roof with my fingers. My tips came away black.

"Yes."

I couldn't quite believe it. The notion I was standing in such a significant place in Christian history, and one that every schoolchild in the United Kingdom of my era would know about, seemed so outlandish. I found it difficult to believe that the cave even existed. And if it did, where were the hordes of pilgrims clamouring to see it? The site where an Angel had visited the shepherds would surely be one of the prime religious sites in the world. Yet, here I was, standing all alone, with only a taxi driver for company.

"It's because of Palm Sunday," explained Riza. "Everyone is in Jerusalem today. Yesterday, there were crowds. Tomorrow there will be crowds."

I am not a religious person by any stretch of the imagination, but to be standing somewhere that featured so heavily in my childhood schooling seemed quite special. Later I would learn that archaeologists were not exactly sure where the Shepherds' Cave was located. Half a kilometre south of where I was standing was a rival site. There, the Greek Orthodox community had built a church.

"Finished?" asked Riza a few minutes later. I was staring at the candles. One of them had gone out and I was tempted to relight it. Instead, I nodded and followed Riza outside.

"Let's go to Bethlehem, then," he said.

5

Bethlehem didn't look particularly holy. As we traversed the excellently named Manger Street, it looked like any other city in the Middle East: Arabic storefronts, men sitting outside them sipping tea and smoking cigarettes, beige buildings and a few minarets – Bethlehem looked like the backstreets of Beirut or Amman.

The wall was different, though. The concrete monstrosity, twenty-six feet tall, topped with barbed wire and covered in graffiti (but only on the Palestinian side – the Israeli side was squeaky clean) encircled the West Bank for almost three hundred miles. Any Palestinian wanting to cross it had to do so at one of the Israeli military checkpoints.

Israelis call the wall the *Separation Fence*, a barrier against potential suicide bombers. They correctly point out that since the wall's construction, the number of suicide attacks in Israel has fallen dramatically. This may be true, but for innocent Palestinians living on the wrong side of the wall, it meant reduced freedom and, in many cases, loss of land. They called it the *Apartheid Wall*.

The section I was looking at was covered in graffiti. Above the scrawls, a CCTV camera surveyed Palestine from its lookout position. One section of graffiti was hard to make out: it looked like an elephantine man playing a trumpet, or maybe a fat robot sucking oil from a straw. Near it, someone had sprayed *Zionism is a disgrace to humanity* in red paint. Another section of wall had a thick black arrow painted on it. The arrow pointed to Banksy's Shop.

Banksy, the famous British graffiti artist, had visited the West Bank in 2005, adding some of his creations to choice sections of the concrete wall. One piece depicted two small boys playing with buckets and spades. Above the boys was a large crack in the wall. Through it, Banksy had painted some tropical palm trees, an azure ocean and a gorgeous blue sky, a scene at odds with the grey concrete it was sitting on. Banksy described the barrier that separated Israel from the West Bank as 'the ultimate holiday destination for graffiti writers'. As far as I could tell, none of the graffiti I was looking at was Banksy's work, which was a shame, because I'd liked to have seen it. Riza climbed out of his car and lit a cigarette. After a minute, he joined me at the wall. I pointed at the arrow. "Is the Banksy shop around here?"

"I think so, yes. It sells souvenirs and prints. You want to go?"

I shook my head. I didn't have time. "So on the other side of this wall is Israel?"

"Yes."

"How long has the wall been here?"

"Since 2003, but it is not finished yet. Every once in a while, the Israelis build some more. It is ugly, yes?" He dropped his cigarette on the pavement where it joined hundreds of other stubs. He extinguished with his foot.

I nodded. The wall was a horrendous thing to live beside, a monstrosity despite the splashes of colour from the graffiti. We climbed back into the car.

6

Riza drove us downtown to a district full of souvenir shops – most selling exactly the same thing: wooden carvings, hookah pipes, ceremonial daggers and a whole host of religious paraphernalia. We parked on a steep hill outside one of them.

Riza explained that because he was a Muslim, he was not allowed into the Church of the Nativity – the birthplace of Jesus Christ. "But

I know someone who can take you. I rang him earlier. And don't worry about paying him. I will sort it out from the fare."

A tall, bespectacled man, who had the look of a scholar, came bounding out of the souvenir shop. He opened the back door of the taxi and jumped inside. "Hello, Jason. My name is Fadi," he said. "I understand from my friend Riza, here that you do not have much time in Bethlehem. Is this so?"

I nodded.

"In that case, I will make the tour of the church brief."

Riza and Fadi conversed in Arabic. Then we drove up the hill to Manger Square, the heart of old Bethlehem. The Church of the Nativity, one of the oldest churches in the world, was at one end of the square, and unlike the Shepherd's Cave from earlier, the place was heaving. Hundreds of tourists were wandering towards it or else were milling about in the square with their guides. Visiting the site of Jesus' birth was clearly a tourist winner.

We parked at the far end of Manger Square, where I said goodbye to Riza for the time being, and stepped out of the taxi with Fadi as my new guide.

"The Church is administered by three branches of Christianity," he told me as we joined the crowds making their way to the church entrance. "The Greek Orthodox, Roman Catholic and Armenian Apostolic all have monks who live on site. Each branch is responsible for one part of the church."

Fadi told me that the groups were highly protective of their respective areas. In 2006, over a disagreement on who should dust some chandeliers, some monks ended up in hospital after they started brawling. In December 2011, during the great clean-up following the annual Christmas celebrations, rival monks starting attacking each other with brooms. Amid insults, screams and flying cleaning apparatus, the Battle of Bethlehem, as the press later dubbed it, escalated to the point where someone called the local Palestinian police. Thankfully, they managed to restore order before anyone was seriously injured.

"You know," added Fadi, "this silly rivalry between the monks is causing problems for the church. None of them can agree who should pay for repairs. So no repairs are done! The roof leaks like you wouldn't believe."

7

Like the Church of the Sepulchre in Jerusalem, the Church of the Nativity's rather mundane stone exterior belied its importance to Christianity. I entered by way of a tiny door known as the Door of Humility. Almost everyone before me had kissed the entrance as they stooped through the threshold.

Inside, people were huddled and grouped around guides, their conversations amplified by the high ceiling and stone floor. "The grotto where Jesus was born is below ground," Fadi said, guiding me with a practised hand through the masses. We stopped and he pointed to my right. "Do you see that?"

I nodded. It was a horrendous line of people. I guessed they were queuing to visit the grotto under the church. Inwardly I groaned.

"It will take perhaps two hours," said Fadi. "But you do not have time for that. Come with me."

I followed him, hoping he wasn't going to push me to the front of the queue – that would be embarrassing – but he led me to a place well away from the line, towards an open area underneath some high wooden rafters and massive chandeliers. Fifty or so people were milling around, taking photos and chatting.

"There are two entrances to the grotto," whispered Fadi, conspiratorially. "One way is at the front of that line; the other is over there. See that policeman? The one sitting down?"

I looked and nodded. "I see him."

"Go over and say this to him: 'Hello Ashraf, how do you do?'"

I stared at Fadi blankly.

"Go over to him and say: 'Hello Ashraf, how do you do?' Look him in the eyes and then shake his hand. You must do this soon."

I looked over. The policeman was standing up.

"Go now," urged Fadi. "Before it is too late!"

Without knowing what I was doing, I walked over to the policeman who was surveying the crowd around him with an experienced but bored eye. I stood in front of him and felt foolish. "Hello, Ashraf, how do you do?"

The policeman regarded me, then looked over my shoulder, presumably at Fadi, and then looked back at me. I reached out to shake his hand, which he accepted. He then told me to follow him. I did so, trailing him towards a side entrance to the grotto. Some steps led downwards.

"Go," the policeman whispered. "Quick."

As it turned out, it wasn't a side entrance: it was the exit for all the people who had queued up for hours. Some were making their way up the steps, giving me strange looks as they passed. I tried to ignore their stares, feeling immensely guilty, until I reached the bottom. In a tiny cave-like compartment, a mass of humanity was crouching, praying, crying, pushing, shoving or elbowing each other in order to touch or kiss the spot where Jesus was born. It was a scene of unbridled religious fervour.

As I adjusted to the scene, I saw there were two parts to the grotto, separated by a narrow corridor. I braved the masses to see the section on my right, the place where Mary had laid Jesus in his manger. I could hardly see anything because of all the hands touching the spot. I considered whether to crouch down like everyone else, but it didn't seem fair; after all, they had queued for hours.

Across the other side was an even bigger crush of people. The crowd was about ten people deep, all of them trying to converge on a single spot hidden under a tiny altar about the same size as a microwave oven. There was no way I was going to fight my way into that, especially with all the pensioners there. Instead, I turned around, wanting to escape the madness. I headed for the exit steps.

There stood Fadi. He must have followed me down. "You can't leave, Jason. You haven't seen the 14-sided silver star – the exact location of Christ's birth. Go see."

I gestured to the crowd, and then at the people waiting in the narrow, cramped aisle leading to it.

Fadi smiled. "Don't be polite; just push your way in."

To be honest, I wasn't that bothered about seeing the star up close. But for sake of Fadi, who obviously thought me more religious than I was, I joined the scrum and clawed my way forward, dropping, like everybody else, to my knees as I did so. And there it was: the place where Jesus was born, the birth of Christianity itself, a silver star surrounded by lanterns, clutching hands, tearful cheeks, flashing cameras and sighs of pure amazement.

8

It was almost time to leave Palestine. Fadi and I walked from Manger Square, down a hill towards the little shop we'd parked outside earlier. Riza was sitting outside sipping on a small cup of coffee, enjoying the warming sun and the slight breeze. Fadi told me to join Riza while he made me a cup of coffee. I did so, sitting in the white plastic chair next to the taxi driver.

Riza put his cup down. "Did you see where Jesus was born?"

I nodded. "So many people."

"Ah, but you didn't have to wait in the line like the other tourists, did you?"

Fadi came out with my coffee. I thanked him, not just for the drink, but for his assistance at the Church. Without him, I'd have never entered the grotto. Fadi smiled, shook my hand and returned inside the shop. The coffee was sickly sweet. Most of the coffee I'd had in the Middle East, apart from the lattes I'd bought in the Starbucks and Costas, had been just like it: black liquid with copious amounts of sugar.

"So you're glad you came to Bethlehem?" asked Riza.

"It's been great," I answered honestly. "I've loved every minute."

Both of us sat and watched the people of Palestine going about their daily business: men sitting outside their shops, women walking with children and taxi drivers prowling the streets. It was difficult to believe I was in a country that most of Europe and North America did not recognise as a state, a land that had caused conflict for decades and one that was almost closed off to the outside world. Everything seemed so perfectly normal.

"Why don't you move to the West Bank?" I asked Riza.

"Me? No. I would lose too much. If somebody said to me, you can move to the West Bank tomorrow, free of charge, I would say, no. Look, Jason, I have to think of my children. In Israel, we have security, education and healthcare. Here, I am not sure about those things. I'll tell you one thing, though, my friend: Palestinian Muslims do not like Israeli Muslims. They think we are traitors because we live under Jewish rule. They cannot understand why any Muslim would want to live like that. That is why I'm sitting near my taxi. It has Israeli plates and the Palestinians will not like that."

"Really? The Muslims here don't trust you?"

"Some don't. But I am safe because I know many people here."

Ten minutes later, we handed our empty cups to Fadi, climbed back into the taxi and scuttled across the border into Israel.

9

I made my rendezvous near Jaffa Gate with the same old man with the scraggly hair. Twenty minutes later, we were back at the Israeli border where I went through the reverse immigration progress, this time without my VIP status. It took much longer, but it saved me a pocketful of cash. At the Jordanian side, I was the last person off the bus, and found Moya sitting on a bench, smoking a cigarette.

"I thought you were stuck in Jerusalem," he said, standing up. "I was about to give up and go home."

I told him about the delay in finding a bus to take me through No Man's Land. "It took ages to come, and then we had to wait for the driver to have a cup of tea."

Moya nodded, as if this was normal, which it probably was.

As the streets of Amman grew dark, Moya dropped me off outside my hotel after a thoroughly enjoyable day across the border. I thanked him and handed him a tip.

"Enjoy the rest of your evening," he said. "What are you doing tomorrow?"

I decided to lie. "I'm flying back to Qatar." I didn't want to tell him I was going to Iraq.

"Really? So soon? Well, have a good trip."

I thanked him and watched him drive away. Twenty minutes later, I was packing my suitcase for another flight to another country in the Middle East. It was time to see Iraq.

Top left: Downtown Bethlehem; An ominous sign just after the Israeli checkpoint into Palestine
Middle row: Entrance to the chapel near the Shepherd's Cave; Inside the Church of the Nativity – the site where Jesus was born
Bottom row: Graffiti on the wall separating the West Bank from Israel; Me about to step through the Door of Humility, the tiny entrance to the Church of the Nativity

Chapter 16. Iraqi Kurdistan

FCO travel advice: We advise against all but essential travel to the whole of Iraq, except to the Kurdistan region, for which we have no travel restrictions.

I was sitting in the departure lounge of Amman Queen Alia International Airport looking at those around me. Most were businessmen, suited up and staring at laptops. A few seemed harassed by the announced flight delay, but most, clearly veterans of air travel, simply carried on with whatever they were doing. I looked up at the screen again and saw the word Erbil plastered across it. My stomach fluttered once more.

Of all the places I had visited over the years, Iraq was surely the most dangerous. It was a war zone, for God's sake, a place of suicide bombers, of roadside carnage and of men in robes who took delight in kidnapping foreigners. And yet I was about to board a plane and fly there. For fun.

Of course, I was not going to *that* Iraq. I was not flying to Baghdad or Basra: cities in perpetual turmoil. No, I was flying to Erbil, capital of the Kurdistan region of Iraq, a city that had marketed itself as the new Dubai, a place of investment, of rapid development and of stability. When I checked the British Foreign Office website earlier that morning, it stated that visits to Erbil were usually trouble-free, and, as such, the British government had not placed any travel restrictions on travelling to Kurdistan. (This status would change a few months after my visit. In order to stop the advance of Islamic State fighters, the US military conducted airstrikes around Erbil, making it an immediate no go area – advice which still remains current.)

After the one hour and twenty minute delay, we boarded the Royal Jordanian Airbus. So this was it, I thought. I *really* was going to Iraq. The flight was not full, but there were enough people on board to make me think that Erbil was not such a terrible place. It couldn't be if men with laptops and suits were going there.

As we took off, leaving Amman in our wake, I calmed down. There was nothing I could do about it now, anyway. I flicked to the moving map on the screen to look at the flight route. AMM was the starting point, the airport code for Amman, and the destination was BWG, which was odd, I thought, because I'd assumed that Erbil would have an airport code such as ERB or EBL. Thirty seconds later, the map switched to the names of cities and my stomach lurched. BWG was Baghdad! We were flying to Baghdad!

I looked at my fellow passengers, but none seemed concerned that we were flying to the Iraqi capital. I looked at the moving map again, staring at it with growing alarm as it cycled through the various maps until it returned to the one saying Baghdad. The flight path had a thick yellow line leading right to it. There was no mistake: we were on course for Baghdad.

For a moment I wondered whether we'd been hijacked, but then thought of a more credible reason. Perhaps we were stopping at Baghdad to pick up more passengers before continuing on to Erbil. I'd been on a flight once from Doha to Heathrow that had done something similar: it had landed in Bahrain to pick up a few extras.

When a member of the Jordanian cabin crew wandered past, I stopped her. "Excuse me; are we going to Baghdad or Erbil?"

"Erbil, sir."

I pointed at the map on the seat in front. "But this says we are going to Baghdad."

The young woman peered briefly at the screen. "Yes, Baghdad."

I looked at her quizzically, but she took this as her cue to leave. I returned my eyes to the moving map, none the wiser.

And then I grew a little bit excited. A transit through Baghdad might be interesting. My wife already thought I was half-mad for going to Erbil, but when she received a text from Baghdad, she would think I'd made the full conversion to lunacy. As we thundered above the parched orange land at thirty-four thousand feet, I stared at the little plane symbol edging ever closer to the capital of Iraq. It would be a fun diversion, as long as no one tried to shoot us down on approach.

And then, the aircraft suddenly banked to the right. After completing a forty-five degree turn, the autopilot levelled out again. Instead of Baghdad being ahead of us, it was a new airport code: EBL.

2

We began a bumpy descent towards Erbil International Airport due to high winds. I peered down at the same orange-brown land that had hardly changed since Amman, a landscape of bone-dry river plains and the occasional black highway. One hour and forty minutes after leaving Amman, the wheels of our airliner touched down on the runway after a particularly ferocious approach that tested the pilots' ability to land in such a strong crosswind. As we trundled towards the gate, the airport looked pleasingly modern.

My phone found a signal and then a text message popped up. *Welcome to Iraq*. Ten minutes later, I was following a group of businessmen inside the terminal building. *Welcome to Kurdistan*, a large sign read. There was no mention of Iraq anywhere.

Unlike Iraq, Kurdistan offered a simple fifteen-day tourist visa on arrival, which the man behind the desk quickly stamped into my passport. "Are you here on vacation?" he asked.

"Yes. I've always wanted to visit Erbil. I'm looking forward to seeing the sights."

The immigration officer nodded. "Kurdistan welcomes you. Enjoy your stay." I thanked him, collected my bags and was soon on my way.

The road from the airport looked modern and well constructed. Large white 4x4s zipped by my taxi, and in the distance, a series of high-rise construction sites filled the horizon, a sure sign that money was coming into the city,

"You American, my friend?" asked the taxi driver, a wiry individual with a bald head.

"No, British," I answered.

"Been here before?"

"No, this is my first time in Iraq."

The man scoffed. "This is not Iraq. This is Kurdistan, my friend. We are a separate country. Here in Erbil, it is safe to walk the streets, day and night. People can live normal lives. *Baghdad* is boom, boom, boom! Everywhere bombs. You are not in Iraq, my friend. Please remember that."

Not strictly true, but I did take his point. I'd heard that the people of Kurdistan were patriotic about their heritage, and well they ought to be; Kurdistan was prospering while all around was descending into ruin and chaos. With Syria to the west, Iran to the right, and the warzone of Iraq to the south, Kurdistan should have been a failing state. But it wasn't, mainly because of its oil reserves, its foreign investment and its security efforts around the border. Kurdistan also held free democratic elections, and even better than all that, kidnappers had not taken a single Western hostage in over a decade.

3

My hotel, the Erbil International, was in the centre of the city. Its rooms were expensive, but its lobby was plush and it had four restaurants. It also had an airport-style scanner inside the entrance to thwart any would-be bombers. My room looked dated, though, as did the swimming pool, which was devoid of water, but the view was good, highlighting a panorama of minarets, sand-coloured buildings, swaying palm trees and a large yellow, helium-filled balloon with the word *Korek* splashed across it. It was advertising a Kurdish mobile phone operator. Behind it were a few skyscrapers. Erbil was hardly Dubai, but it was still a world away from most people's perceptions of an Iraqi city. I rang my wife and told her I had arrived in Kurdistan without drama and then wandered outside to see the lay of the land.

The afternoon traffic was starting to build up: a collection of honking cars, old trucks and cream taxis. There were a notable number of flags rippling in the breeze, too: Kurdish flags with red, white and green stripes and a flaming sun in the centre. I passed something called the Vana Mall, which turned out to be a large carpet emporium. For some unfathomable reason, it had a large plastic statue of Popeye outside its entrance. Litter had collected around the sailor's bulbous shoes. I passed a veiled woman walking along the well-kept pavement, and wondered how she would react at seeing a Western man wandering her city. The answer was that she barely glanced at me. This cheered me, because the next day I'd be walking into the centre of the city where the crowds would be. Deciding that Erbil was safe enough, I returned to the hotel in high spirits.

A few hours later, I was sitting in one of the hotel restaurants. When a waiter wearing a jaunty red and black suit came over, I decided to order a beer. The man nodded, running a finger through his slicked back hair. It looked greasy enough to cook chips in. "Which beer?"

"Do you have Iraqi beer?"

The man scowled. "Iraq beer? We don't have beer from *Iraq!*" He almost spat out the last word.

"Sorry, I meant Kurdistan Beer."

"No Kurdistan or Iraq beer! Only Heineken and Amstel."

I ordered a can of Heineken and a shish taouk: marinated cubes of chicken on skewers. The beer came first and my food arrived five minutes later. I tucked in, eyeing the only other patron in the restaurant, a fat business man smoking a shisha pipe. Apart for us, the huge room was empty, except for the fifteen waiters hovering near the kitchen. The chicken was tasty, but there wasn't much of it, and there was a distinct lack of bread too – just a floppy piece of grease-stricken pita that I had no intention of eating. But there was a whole onion and fiery-looking chilli. I ate the chicken and found myself still ravenous. After I'd paid the bill, I headed upstairs to another restaurant on the second floor.

This time I ordered a can of Amstel and chicken tikka. When it arrived, it was the same as the shish taouk, right down to the onion and chilli. Still, I was hungry and the chicken was delicious, so I ate my second meal and then finally retired to my room, planning my sightseeing for the next day.

At eleven that night, some incessant and ridiculously noisy beeping shattered the silence. I pulled the curtains apart to see a convoy of cars on the street below me. Every vehicle had flags waving from their windows and sunroofs. I could also hear some yelling. So this is the Jihadist invasion, I thought: my first day in Erbil, and I was going to be kidnapped and held for ransom. Except, of course, it wasn't. Thirty seconds later, the sound of whatever celebration they were enjoying died down and peace returned to the streets of Erbil.

4

The next morning, I was ready to see the sights. I meticulously planned my route to the citadel, Erbil's most famous attraction, by noting its location on Google Maps and by staring out of my window to see the lie of the land. According to Google Maps, the journey should take 21 minutes.

Before venturing outside, I stopped at the hotel money-changing desk to swap a hundred US dollars for 110,000 Iraqi Dinar. With the wad safely ensconced inside my wallet, I left the hotel. The breeziness from the previous evening had gone, replaced by the default weather in the Middle East: heat and humidity. That was the problem with Arabia, I felt – the temperature. It was inescapable: a never ending presence from above. Even standing in the shade could only partially alleviate it.

I passed a line of kebab and carpet shops; there was also the occasional juice stall. On my right was the traffic. Cars accelerated only to brake after only a few hundred metres, wasting energy and fuel in equal measure. I saw one car beep at a veiled woman crossing the road. She ignored it and carried on to the other side.

I checked my watch. I was eighteen minutes into my walk, which meant the citadel should be up ahead. But it wasn't. I passed a series of car repair shops, all of them full of cheap Chinese tools and equipment, and then I reached a busy open air market.

A man pushing a cartful of watermelons was causing a blockage along the main drag of the market. He didn't care one bit. Everyone behind him would just have to wait. Piles of fruit and vegetables were everywhere: cucumbers, tomatoes, oranges, garlic and sometimes arrays of strange cheeses. The citizens of Erbil crowded the produce. Young, old, stooped and fleet footed, everyone wanted to haggle over the goods. I stopped to take a photo of one fruit stand but was distracted when a nearby vendor shouted across to me. Now he had my attention, he picked up a plum from his stall and lobbed it in the direction of a man standing a little bit further along. The shot was a good one: it bounced off the man's head. The man looked drunk, or perhaps not at full mental capacity: either way, he didn't notice the plum thrower, which was a good job as he was doubled up laughing. I left the market and crossed the road.

5

Across the road was Souk al-Ghazal, another open-air market, this one dedicated to livestock, mainly birds, goats and rabbits. Men sipping tea from tiny cups were sitting around the stalls, chatting and waiting for customers. I took the scene in, spying a man picking up a rabbit by its ears and dangling it in front of a potential buyer. The new man prodded the creature and then shook his head. The stall owner man nodded and replaced the rabbit it its hutch.

I looked at some long-legged and scrawny chickens roaming free in a large open air enclosure. They pecked the dust while a group of men studied them. The biggest section of the market was a central zone dedicated to cooing and chest-puffing pigeons. There were hundreds of them, all in cages, sitting proudly while men crowded around sizing up the best specimens for purchase. One man had already bought one. He carried it carefully by its curled-up wings until he placed it into a cardboard box. I wondered whether the pigeons were for food or for racing, so I decided to ask a man standing near me. He was carrying a large cage with maybe half a dozen pigeons inside. He couldn't understand me but the teenage boy with him could. He turned out to be the man's son.

"Not for the food," the boy told me in broken English. "My father keep the bird for the fun."

"Does he fly the pigeons?"

The boy looked blankly at me so I flapped my arms. Both looked at me like I was some sort of idiot. The boy spoke. "Yes, the birds go in sky. My father have thirty pigeon, and now...more."

I thanked them and they walked away. Later I discovered that the art of pigeon fancying was a big deal in Erbil, and indeed across Iraq as a whole. It started in the 1920s when the British took over Iraq and local men began to keep pigeons like the British men did. Saddam Hussein put a dampener on things, not because his regime had anything against pigeons, but because the trading of pigeons became almost impossible with the border closed to international trade. After Hussein's downfall, pigeon fancying took off once more, with birds arriving from Iran, Turkey and even some parts of Europe. Some of them swapped hands for thousands of dollars. In the tea houses of downtown Erbil, Kurdish men gathered after sundown to exchange tips about caring for their pigeons.

At last, I spied a road sign written in English. It told me that the citadel was to my right, and so I left the livestock market and walked past more car repair shops and lines of men drinking tea. Sipping on a hot drink seemed the biggest pastime for men of a certain age in

Erbil. And then, forty minutes after leaving my hotel, I saw the citadel in front of me: a huge pink-brown fortress built on top of a hill. Almost blocking it from view was a parade of shops. One was called Wild Tiger, a purveyor of cheap jewellery. Another sold Morad Tea, and a third sold only inflatable crocodiles. I wiped the sweat from my brow and looked for a route up the hill.

6

Erbil, if viewed from above, is a circular city, and in the centre, on a round hill about one hundred feet high, sits the citadel. Due to its elevated position, people have lived in the citadel complex for thousands of years. Pottery fragments found there have dated the earliest settlements to five centuries before the birth of Christ. This means that Erbil is another city claiming to have the oldest continuously inhabited community in the world, the third one I'd visited in the Middle East so far.

Erbil's claim is rather dubious. Before the 1960s, a few thousand people did live in the houses inside the citadel walls. There were schools, mosques and shops to service them, but then, when a whole raft of houses were cleared to make way for a new road, fewer than nine hundred people remained. Then, in 2007, all of them were evicted (receiving a healthy relocation allowance to ease their pain) except for one single family. That one home was, the authorities felt, enough to secure the citadel's 7000 years of unbroken habitat.

A busy ring road ran along the edge of the citadel, thick with traffic and poorly-parked cars. I followed it trying to find a way up the hill, but instead found myself in a hectic central square full of fountains, wooden benches, ornate street lamps and a brick clock tower favoured by pigeons. Scores of old men were enjoying deep, gesture-filled conversations on many of the benches while young couples ambled around near the fountains. Behind them all, through some stone archways, was a selection of juice and tea stalls. Further back from the square was a blue, orange and white striped dome belonging to an old mosque. It looked like an oversized tea cosy. As I stood watching the scene, I found it hard to believe that I was standing in Iraq. Sane people didn't go on holiday to Iraq, the same as they didn't sit on a sun lounger in Somalia or slap on some sun cream in Afghanistan. And yet here I was, standing in Iraq's third largest city, watching its citizens enjoying the sun, and I had never felt safer.

I finally found a steep stone pathway leading up to the entrance of the citadel. A party of teenage schoolgirls was coming down in the opposite direction, causing noise and mayhem in their wake. Unlike the schoolgirls I'd encountered in Jordan, a lot of whom had said hello, these girls avoided all eye contact. Besides, they were too busy snapping photos of each other on their phones to bother with me. Their male teacher glanced at me, though, and we nodded as we passed each other. At the top of the path, I came to a large sign. It stated that, due to important structural work, many of the citadel buildings were closed to the public.

Damn, I thought. I've come all this way for the final hurdle to thwart me. But the schoolgirls had been in, so I reasoned that there must be something to see. I walked past the sign to see for myself.

7

On the other side of the arched entranceway was a stretch of road in dire need of repair. Potholes, cracks and trenches gave it a look of abandonment. Either side of the road didn't look much better either – almost all of the buildings were taped off with blue plastic to discourage investigation. Most had no glass or doors. One of them had a lonely pair of stepladders leaning against its wall. The citadel was a building site and it didn't look particularly old, either. I'd expected the citadel to be medieval, perhaps like the fortress in Byblos or Jerusalem, but it looked more like a deserted 1960s village.

One building was open, though – a carpet museum. With sights so threadbare in the citadel, I decided to go in. As expected, it was full to the brim with carpets. Most were on the walls but others were dangling from wooden poles, or on the floor. Black, orange and red patterns covered the majority of them. There was also some weaving tools and a few mannequins dressed up in traditional Kurdish costumes. I had a quick look at it all, thanked the man in charge, who nodded, and then headed back outside. I decided to look at the giant flag.

Like all enormous flags, the Kurdish flag on the end of the pole looked like it was moving in slow motion. I stood staring for a while until I heard voices. From around a corner came two men with tools. They stopped by a manhole cover and prised it open. I decided to investigate.

"Hi," I said to the men. They were both peering down the hole where a sound of gushing water was echoing. "Do you speak English?"

Both men looked up and one of them nodded. I asked him about the work going on, and he explained that, because of poor water drainage, together with a lack of general upkeep on the citadel, it was now in need of major repair. "When it rains," the other man told me, "water rushes over the sides of the citadel and erodes the stone work. Large sections have slipped away. It is very dangerous."

I thanked the men and left them to whatever they were doing. After wandering around the corner the men had come from, a group of six security guards stopped me. The one in charge told me it was too dangerous to continue any further. I decided there and then that I'd had enough of the citadel and headed back down into the main part of the city.

8

There are no touts or fast food restaurants in Erbil. No open-topped buses or pricy souvenir shops blight the city. On the other hand, there is no easy way of finding something quick and easy to eat for lunch. It was either a kebab house filled with shisha-smoking men or a falafel house crammed with shisha-smoking men. Feeling hungry, I decided to catch a taxi back to the hotel and eat there, but this was easier said than done. The first three taxi drivers couldn't understand where I wanted to go: none spoke English. The fourth looked at me blankly, and the fifth shook his head and drove off before I'd even finished explaining.

Resigning myself to walking, I decided to ask one more and was delighted when he told me he could speak a little English. He was about thirty, with short black hair, and claimed to know where my hotel was. I climbed in the passenger seat, and almost immediately he switched his radio on. It was tuned to a channel devoted to insanely irritating dance music. The taxi driver turned it up to full blast.

"You like?" the man asked, bobbing his head in time to the beat.

"It's great," I lied, trying to block out the infernal racket. At least we were moving and I was finally out of the sun. As we joined the scrum of traffic on the ring road around the citadel, the taxi driver changed the channel. The music was worse, but he seemed to like it more.

We zipped into a lane parallel to ours that was already taken. A beep came, then another. My driver waved it away. "They need to relax."

Despite his taste in music, I decided I liked the taxi driver. He certainly knew how to keep calm. And I liked him even better when he admitted he had no idea where my hotel was. "But no problem, I find!"

And somehow he did. When he dropped me off, he offered his services as a driver for the next day, if I wanted. When I inquired what he could show me, he reeled off a list of things, saying that he would drive me to them all. After negotiating a price, I accepted, and arranged for him to pick me up at nine the following morning.

The driver's name was Karwan, and, as promised, he picked me up the next morning. As we drove past the hotel's security booth, I asked him how he had learned English so well.

"I worked in Sweden for few years," he told me. "In factory. I lost job after a few months but stayed for a while longer with my cousin. That's where I learn the English: the people in Stockholm did not speak Arabic, and Swedish was too hard for me. I learn a little English – everyone happy! No problem!"

Karwan decided to show me Minare Park first. He pulled into a small car park and stopped next to a large white archway decorated with a black metallic bird of prey. Judging by the people going through, the park was a popular shortcut to somewhere else because most of them were carrying bags of shopping. I climbed out and Karwan did too, but instead of accompanying me, he found a patch of grass and flopped down on it. "I sleep for forty winks!"

I wandered through the entrance, just behind a woman in a purple headdress. As I suspected, she was not in the park to appreciate the shrubs, the butterflies or the beautiful flowers, she was taking a route through the park to get to the street on the other side.

Above my head was a cable car circuit. Each car was empty and still, dangling from a thick grey wire. They looked like they were out of action. I then noticed a young Kurdish couple standing near a scale model of Erbil citadel. I walked over to it, nodding my head at them as I passed. They smiled and moved to let me see the model. It made the citadel look impressive: all domed archways, thick-cut windows and imposing walls. I hoped the current renovation work would restore it to this former glory and not turn it into some sort of Disney Land attraction. The young couple asked me to take a photo of them, managing to get their message across via the medium of mime. I did so, receiving a babble of Arabic in return, the only word of which I understood was *shukran*, the Arabic word for thank you. I left them and wandered to a tall brown tower that looked like a

Victorian-era chimney. In fact, it was the Sheik Chooli Minaret, the only part of a grand thirteenth-century mosque to survive the passage of time. I looked at my watch. I'd been in the park for over half an hour, so I returned though the arch to find Karwan asleep on the grass. When I coughed, he jumped up. "Did you enjoy the park?"

I told him I had.

"You like the ladies?"

My mind couldn't compute the link between the questions and my face must have showed this, because Karwan grinned. "Kurdish ladies are beautiful, do you not think so?"

I nodded, unsure of what he meant by the question. "Very beautiful."

"When I was younger, I met many women in this park. It is still a popular place for young couples. Let me tell you something, Jason. There are three things I like in this world: women, beer and sport. And some days I like all three. Tell me, do you like beer?"

"Yes."

"I love it. I drink seven, eight, maybe nine cans of beer in one night."

That seemed a lot. "You have nine cans every night?"

"No," laughed Karwan. "Sometimes I have fish."

"Fish?"

"Yes, of course."

The conversation was taking on a surreal flavour and so I decided to shut up.

10

"Now we go to mosque," said Karwan, almost shouting over the din from the radio. "You will see that it is very beautiful. Maybe the most beautiful mosque in Kurdistan."

We were travelling along a busy four-lane highway that might have had a fifth lane if not for the haphazardly parked cars at the side of the road. Above us, yellow bunting hung, suspended from lampposts. Karwan explained it was to do with the election.

"What election?"

"For the new president."

I asked him about the politicians in Kurdistan.

"They are mostly good. They have to be, otherwise Kurdistan will go bad. That is why the elections are important. Most days I read a newspaper to see what they have to say and what they will do for my country. My wife, she watches the news on TV."

I was surprised to hear he had a wife. I'd assumed him single with all his talk of beer and women. I was also surprised to hear that he had an interest in politics.

Five minutes later, Karwan asked if I minded a slight detour.

"For what?"

"I need to buy a bottle of Jack Daniel's."

"They sell it here?" I asked.

"Yes. No problem. I show you. You want a bottle?"

I declined, but was interested to see where he was going to buy his alcohol from, because I'd not seen any liquor shops anywhere in Erbil. Karwan left the main highway and turned towards a towering building called the Divan Erbil Hotel: a luxurious skyscraper that looked like it belonged in Dubai or Abu Dhabi. He found a space in their car park.

"They sell it in there?" I asked.

"No, over there." He pointed at an adjoining building. It wasn't advertising the fact it sold alcohol, which I supposed was how it worked in Iraq. Before we went in, though, I wanted to see inside the Divan Erbil Hotel. Karwan looked at me oddly, but nodded. I followed him through the grand entrance.

Opulent grandeur would be a good description of the hotel lobby. Expansive marble flooring, a pointed crystal chandelier, a grand piano and multitudes of soft furnishings were everywhere for the eye to savour. Karwan and I walked past the bellboys, where I picked up a hotel brochure. It told me that one of the Divan's plush restaurants specialised in Japanese food. There was also a well-equipped gym and huge swimming pool. If I wanted to, I could sip cocktails in the Saray Lounge.

"Is it expensive to stay here?" I asked Karwan, who seemed less enamoured of the lobby. In fact, he looked bored.

"Very expensive, my friend. Double your hotel."

It was hard to believe that such a lavish hotel could exist in Iraq.

"It is a business hotel, though," explained Karwan. "The Divan is close to the airport, so a good location for business people. They come here, do the deals, then fly away. Their company pays the bill and so hotel can charge what it likes."

We headed across the road to the fabled liquor store. Inside, it was tasteful and understated, and it reminded me of the booze souq in Doha. Karwan was obviously a veteran of the store because he knew exactly where to go for his bottle of Jack Daniel's. He also picked up a six-pack of beer.

"Are you going to drink all that tonight?" I jested.

"No," answered Karwan. "Save for weekend."

We climbed back in the taxi for the journey to the mosque.

11

"So how safe is Kurdistan?" I asked Karwan. We were back on the highway, with his alcohol safely stowed in the boot.

"Very safe. No problem here."

"So not like Baghdad, then?"

Karwan reached towards the dashboard and turned off the radio. "Look, Erbil is nothing like Baghdad. It is not safe there. I would not go to Baghdad if you paid me. You are not thinking of going to Baghdad, are you?"

I avoided the question. "So why is Erbil so safe?"

"Because we are not Iraq or Syria. Our borders are safe and the suicide bombers cannot get through."

Not long after my visit, Islamic State breached the border that Karwan thought so safe. They got within twenty miles of Erbil, proving just how fragile the peace was in the Middle East. Instead of tourists and businessmen filling the hotel rooms of the city, it was refugees. As the men in black robes advanced, the US sent in the warplanes. Without these airstrikes, Erbil might well have fallen.

Karwan did some lane switching, laughed when someone beeped and then did a madcap manoeuvre that saw our taxi swinging across three lanes so he could mount a kerb and park his car beside Erbil's grandest place of worship – the Jalil Khayat Mosque.

As I climbed out, Karwan decided to remain in his taxi. "I go to sleep. Very tired today – been working since 11pm last night."

I looked at my watch. It was almost lunchtime. "You've been working through the night?"

Karwan nodded. "Usually I go to sleep at nine in morning. But today, I keep working – just for you, my friend."

He'd been behind the wheel for over twelve hours. No wonder he looked so knackered. It was a wonder we hadn't crashed.

The mosque's design reminded me of the Blue Mosque in Istanbul, except, instead of being hundreds of years old, it was less than a decade old. Another difference was that the Jalil Khayat Mosque exterior was brimming in aquamarine. Shiny blue tiles covered its domes, and, along one side, Arabic lettering laid out in beautiful shades of turquoise covered the walls. If any mosque deserved to be called the Blue Mosque, then surely this was it.

Beyond the highway that ran alongside the mosque was a modern, five-storey building coated in shiny blue glass. It sold upmarket household goods. Next to it was Erbil's biggest shopping centre, the grandly named Royal Mall, which, as well as shops, boasted restaurants, a cinema and even a bowling hall. I turned back to the mosque, snapped off a photo and then returned to Karwan. He awoke with a start, looking bleary eyed. I took pity on him, claiming I was tired too. Twenty minutes later, he dropped me off at my hotel and I wished him well.

"You too, my friend. Erbil welcomes you next time."

12

That evening, my last in Erbil, I stood in the hotel elevator and pressed the button for the top floor. I wasn't supposed to go to the top because it was out of bounds, but no one tried to stop me because I was the only person in the lift. The top floor of the Erbil International Hotel had once been a posh restaurant and nightclub, but not anymore.

I exited the elevator and found myself in a building site. Crumbling concrete columns, rusting steel girders, dangling cables and discarded tools made it look like a bomb had gone off inside the restaurant, which was precisely why the management of the hotel didn't want anyone to see it. A bomb hadn't caused the carnage, though; it was merely stalled renovation work. But I wasn't there to see the construction site; I was there to see the view.

Stepping across loose rubble, I emerged from the concrete husk into an open air section, which, when the hotel had been the Sheraton, had been the outdoor seating and cocktail sipping area. I sidestepped an old piece of rope and avoided the shards of broken glass until I reached the intact barrier at the far edge. Next to me stood a pair of flagpoles, one with the Kurdish flag, the other with the Iraqi flag. I took up position next to them and stared at the view.

Erbil was massive. It stretched out in every direction, the urbanisation only ceasing at some distant mountains. I could see the citadel and its lofty flagpole; beyond it, some skeletal skyscrapers were under construction. Most of Erbil was low-level, though, with only the minarets poking above the mass of dwellings, stores, offices, hotels and advertising hoardings. But Erbil was not a pretty city, at least not from a bird's viewpoint. It looked grimy, brown and almost chaotic. However, as the sun started to go down, it doused the rough edges in shadows, shrouded the clogged-up traffic and left a certain twilight beauty.

When it was almost dark, I realised that if I didn't retrace my steps soon, I might be left stranded on the top floor. I threaded my way back through the tools and broken glass to the elevator. After a brief moment of panic when I found the doors closed, I was relieved when it binged open. When I reached my room, I started to pack in preparation for the final stop of my tour of the Middle East. The next day, I was flying back to the U.A.E. to visit two Emirates I'd never been to before. I'd promised myself a pint of Guinness in Ajman with a friend of mine to celebrate the end of my trip. Once I'd finished packing, I looked out of the window at Erbil. I had survived Iraq without any drama whatsoever.

Top row: Central square in downtown Erbil; The flags of Iraq (on the left) and Iraqi-Kurdistan
Middle row: Erbil Citadel sitting on a hill; busy market in downtown Erbil
Bottom row: Divan Erbil Hotel; Old men enjoying hearty conversation in the central square; Sheik Chooli Minaret, the only part remaining of a thirteenth century mosque;

Chapter 17. Ending in Ajman

My flight was scheduled to depart Erbil at 7.25am, which meant I had to be at the airport by 5.30am, which in turn meant rousing myself at the ungodly hour of quarter to five in the morning, a time of day seldom seen by normal people. I have never been a morning person, and this shock to the system meant my eyes were bloodshot, my brain slow and my mood keenly sour. Dragging my suitcase behind me, I took the elevator and then found myself in an eerily silent hotel lobby.

There was not a soul in attendance. The metal detector security thing was unmanned, the check-in desk was devoid of people and the chair reserved for the woman who seemed to do nothing, apart from stare into a computer screen, was empty. Faced with this situation, I did something I'd never done before: I banged on the silver metal bell on the check-in desk. The solid resonating sound echoed around the cavernous interior, jolting me from my half-slumber, but waking no one else. I banged on the bell again, three times in quick succession. This time, a youth appeared from a side office. He looked in worse shape than I did. His crumpled black suit suggested he'd been asleep for a while.

Nevertheless, he efficiently checked me out and then banged on the bell himself to summon my airport transfer driver. When this had no effect, he lumbered to a side room and banged on the door. From it, a horrendously tired man emerged. Bloody hell, I thought, had there been some sort of party the previous night?

I followed the driver out to the car and the only thing he asked was to find out which airline I was flying with.

"Air Arabia," I said.

The man nodded, remaining silent for the rest of the journey.

Air Arabia is a low-cost airline based in the United Arab Emirates. Its base is Sharjah Airport, the onetime stopping point for Imperial Airways, who flew high-fare paying travellers between the UK and Australia. Back in the 1930s, the journey took almost a month, stopping in France, Italy, Greece, Egypt, Iraq, Kuwait, Bahrain, Sharjah, Pakistan, India, Burma, Thailand and Malaysia, all in a rickety Handley Page biplane, a type of aircraft prone to serious mishaps. But for the highbrow passengers who could afford the trip, the journey promised adventure, high-end travel and literally the trip of a lifetime.

Erbil airport processed me quickly and efficiently, and I was soon waiting in the departure lounge. After a quick bite to eat, it was time to board. As aircraft left the stand, over the intercom sounded the Islamic call to prayer: a reverb-laden recording of a haunting male melody. Two and a half hours later, we were making our approach into Sharjah Airport and I gazed downwards, wondering what those trailblazing Imperial Airways passengers would think now. The azure of the Arabian Gulf would have looked familiar, but everything else would be different. Gone were the Bedouin settlements, the sand dunes and the camel trains; instead, there was a mass of development stretching along the entire coast. Through the haze, the skyscrapers of downtown Dubai shimmered on the horizon. And then, following one of the smoothest approaches I'd ever experienced, we were on the runway in the final country of my Arabian adventure.

2

"Have you been to the United Arab Emirates before?" asked the security official at passport control of Sharjah Airport. He was flicking through my passport, so I reasoned he knew the answer already due to the number of U.A.E. stamps already in there.

"Yes. Many times."

The man continued looking through every page. After reaching the end, he flicked back through in reverse, and then, seemingly bored with that, turned to the front section with all my details. "What is your name?"

"Jason Smart."

The Arab shook his head. "Jason James it says here." He pronounced it *Jass-on Jams*.

"That is my middle name. Jason *James* Smart."

"Yes, yes." The man stared at his computer screen. "Mister Jason, where you come from?"

I told him I'd just arrived from Erbil, which brought a raised eyebrow, but no comment. Just when I was thinking I was going to have a problem with entering Sharjah, the man in the spotlessly white thawb stamped my passport and handed it back. "Welcome to the U.A.E.," he smiled.

Outside, walking under yet another Arabian sun, I headed for one of the orange-topped taxis. "Ajman Kempinski," I said to the driver. For my final night, I'd decided to upgrade to the best hotel in town, a fitting way to end my trip.

3

The Kempinski hotel was in Ajman, the smallest of the United Arab Emirates. It was only twenty minutes from the airport and was so small that Sharjah surrounded it. Skyscrapers, shopping malls, well-ordered traffic (by Middle Eastern standards) and groups of low-paid expats toiling in the sun brought me squarely back to the Gulf with a bang. Beneath the glass and steel structures were long lines of small shops with names such as King of Tea, Oasis Bakery, Gulf Typing and the intriguing S&M Saloon.

Beauty Saloons were common across the Gulf States, the simple misspelling so commonplace that I hardly noticed it anymore. Typing shops were just as common. Inside these poky establishments, groups of Indian men, well versed in Arabic script, pored over ancient typewriters, or, if they were lucky, old laptops. Their job was to type out the documents needed for driving licences, medical cards and, most importantly, ID cards. For all the supposed modernity of places like Qatar, Bahrain and the Emirates, the old systems still reigned supreme. When Angela and I had first applied for our Qatari driving licences, we had to go through a protracted rigmarole involving a typing shop. After presenting ourselves to an official in Doha's traffic department, we were told that we had to present documents in Arabic to prove who we were. When we told him we didn't have any, he told us to go and get them. This meant finding a backstreet typist shop (a cottage industry if ever there was one) so we could pay an Indian gentleman to type everything for us. With this done, we returned and got the official to stamp it. Then we wondered what to do next.

An enterprising Pakistani man, witnessing our ineptitude, offered himself as a guide through the quagmire – for a small fee, of course. He put us in the correct queue where the Captain, the police official in charge, sanctioned our newly acquired forms with another stamp. Not quite done yet, the Pakistani man led us to another small room.

Inside the room was an Arab man sitting at a computer. On the wall opposite him was a large white screen. At the far end were a couple of plastic chairs. It was the eye-testing room.

I went first while Angela sat in one of the chairs. The guide sat in the other. The man in charge asked me to stand behind a line and then told me to stare at the white screen. He pressed something on his computer and a series of numbers and letters appeared, exactly the same type of thing seen in opticians around the world. I read the first, second and third lines in quick succession, and was just about to start on the fourth when the Arab man told me to stop. "You have passed. Everything correct."

Angela's turn was next. We switched places and, because her unaided eyesight was pathetically poor, she reached for the glasses in her handbag.

"No spectacles," said the man in charge.

"Why?" asked Angela, worried immediately.

"Because your photo has no glasses." He waved the application form at us. Angela's passport photo was stapled to the top corner. She wasn't wearing glasses. "You must do eye test like this."

Angela glanced at me and looked ashen. If she failed the eye test, which was highly likely, it would mean another trip to a photo booth, to take a snap of Angela in her glasses, then a return to this godforsaken traffic department. That would take up another half-day.

"Ready?" asked the Arab man.

Angela nodded uncertainly and the man flashed up his letters. 'A' was at the top, and only a blind person wouldn't be able to read it.

"A," said Angela.

The second line had the letters, 'Z', 'C' and the number '3'. The man asked her to read them.

Angela squinted, clearly having difficulty. "2, C and B?"

I inwardly sighed, but the man said nothing and so Angela went onto the third line. She got them all wrong. It was disastrous and embarrassing to watch. When she read the next line and got all of them wrong again, I sat in despair.

"You have passed," the Arab man said. Angela looked dumbfounded. Next to me, the Pakistani man was beaming. I couldn't believe it. No wonder there were so many road accidents in Qatar if half-blind people were allowed behind the wheel. Shortly afterwards, we were both issued with Qatari driving licenses.

Back in Ajman, I checked into the Kempinski, dropped my bags in my room and was soon in another taxi, this time heading back to Sharjah City, the U.A.E.'s third largest metropolitan area. It was time for a bit of sightseeing.

4

The Eye of the Emirates is the tallest Ferris wheel in the Middle East, and was therefore a good landmark to give the taxi driver. It was a pity I wouldn't be able to enjoy the view from the top myself; I simply didn't have the time. My visit to Sharjah was going to be hellishly brief, with only enough time to zip around the main sites before catching a taxi back to Ajman where I was going to meet up with my friend.

The Ferris wheel was near a narrow stretch of water called the Qasba Canal. Tall skyscrapers, tropical palms, a Starbucks and a Nando's restaurant lined both sides of the waterway. After grabbing a latte – more to escape the heat than to get a caffeine fix – I strode up one side of the canal until the heat became too much. My plan had been to walk to Sharjah Museum, but I decided to abandon that idea and find a taxi instead. I climbed some steps and found myself on a main road. I stood on the pavement, looking for a taxi, but after a few minutes realised there weren't any and so started walking. The heat was terrible and soon I was sweating like a man on the edge of cardiac arrest. I took a large gulp of my water, and then another, until there was none left. I had been outside for less than twenty minutes and was already in danger of collapse yet I had no option but to carry on walking.

The phone in my pocket vibrated and I pulled it out. "How ya doing, pal?" said the voice on the other end. It belonged to John, my pal who worked as an engineering consultant in Ajman. I knew him from Qatar, where he'd lived in the same compound as Angela and me. He asked where I was.

"Wandering the streets of Sharjah," I answered. "I'm sweating like an idiot. There are no taxis."

"Really. That's unusual. Well, I'm ringing to say I'll meet you at the Holiday Beach Club at five. So when you've finished with Sharjah, jump in a taxi and tell the driver to take you to the Ajman Holiday Beach club. He'll know where it is. I'm looking forward to showing you the sights of Ajman. All three of them. Anyway, have to go. See you later."

I replaced my phone and surveyed Sharjah for taxis. Only a cavalcade of Land Cruisers, Hummers and Lexus 4x4s sped by. And then I spied a small grocery store. When I entered the tiny emporium, the Indian proprietor looked up, his bored expression quickly replaced by a look of genuine concern. I ignored him and shambled towards the fridge, grabbing three bottles of water. At the counter, I could hardly think straight. "Do you know where I can get a taxi around here?" I croaked, fishing out a ten dirham note.

"You need taxi, sir?"

I nodded and wiped the moisture from my eyes. My hand came away slick. My lips tasted of salt.

"I phone one for you. Taxi come here. This okay?"

I nodded again, grateful for the assistance, but more interested in the water, which I was already gulping. The man picked up a phone and talked to someone, presumably a taxi company.

"Where you go?"

"Sharjah Museum." I drained the bottle and started on another.

The man finished his phone call. "Maybe you should go back to your hotel for a rest, sir."

I nodded and put the second empty bottle on the counter. "Maybe I will."

But I had no intention of doing any such thing. The water was working its magic and, a minute later, when the taxi pulled up, I thanked the man for his kindness and left.

5

The Al Hisn Sharjah Museum, former residence of the ruling family of Sharjah, was not open. I lamented the number of times this had this happened to me on this trip. First the fort in Qatar, then Temple Rock in Jerusalem, followed by Kuwait Towers and the Citadel of Erbil. Everything was closed.

I walked up to a large tower, the only remaining part of the original fort, and looked up. It was tall and reassuringly fort-like, with tiny slit windows and jagged crenulations. Four decades previously, in an act of gross stupidity, the brother of the Sultan had decided to demolish the fortress in order to erase all memories of the previous Sultan. As the bulldozers and heavy machinery moved in to do their work, his brother, in Egypt at the time, heard the news and rushed back to Sharjah. He arrived too late to stop most of the destruction and only managed to save the tower at which I was staring.

I walked to the corniche, a coastal pathway full of palms, museums and galleries. On the other side of the water was the Sharjah Law Court, a huge sandstone palace topped with a massive bulbous dome. In front of it, a wooden dhow was puffing out blasts of acrid smoke as it jostled for position along the jetty.

At the end of the corniche was the Radisson hotel. When I reached it, I was overheating again, and so decided to go inside. Besides, I was knackered. After so many days of constant sightseeing and traipsing around airports, all I wanted to do was have a rest. I found a table, ordered some drinks and did nothing for the next two hours. At a quarter to five, I jumped in a taxi so I could meet John in Ajman.

6

"Great to see you, mate!" beamed John, pumping my hand. He was waiting in front of a whitewashed sign for the Holiday Beach Club. Beyond it lay a collection of similarly white buildings. The place looked dead. "You found this place okay?"

I nodded. "The taxi driver knew exactly where it was."

"I bet he did." John had a wry smirk on his face. "And I'll show you why, later tonight. Come on, let's take a walk along the corniche. I'll point out where I live and then we can see a few of the sights." We set off walking northwards.

Ajman looked no different from Sharjah. It had the same stretch of highway running along the same stretch of Arabian Gulf. It had a similar line of sparkly skyscrapers, one of which John pointed out as his home.

"You live there?" It looked like the tallest building along the corniche.

"I know. It looks impressive, doesn't it? The views are great. If Diana's not about, I can ogle the Russian beach babes."

We walked along the sea front until we came to a large hotel that looked like an Arabian Palace due to its sand-coloured exterior. Appropriately enough, it was called the Ajman Palace: one of the three main upscale hotels in Ajman. John told me it was a dry hotel, meaning it didn't serve any alcohol.

"So alcohol's hard to come by in Ajman?" I asked. I was getting hot again, but nowhere near as bad as I'd been earlier. The long break in the Radisson had paid good dividends, as had the dip in temperature since midday.

"You must be joking. You can get it everywhere! This part of the city we're in is the Ajman Free Zone, which means that companies are exempt from paying taxes and fees to the government. It's supposed to promote economic growth. But it also means that alcohol is available. There's even a hole in the wall; I'll show you it later. It's not like that one in Qatar where you have to show your ID. Here you can buy what you like, when you like, and however much you like."

"So is it literally a hole in the wall? You, know, hidden from the authorities?"

John laughed. "It's across the road from the Ajman Ruler's Court, so what do you think? It's a proper air-conditioned shop with aisles of beer, wine and spirits. But there is a small hatch around the back where the Indian workers can buy individual cans of lager. It's all they can afford. When it gets dark, they hang around on the beaches swigging their beers, enjoying the sea breeze. Fair play to them."

The next hotel along was the Ajman Beach Hotel, a rather downbeat, white apartment block. "It's a brothel disguised as a hotel," John informed me. "It's where cheapskate Russians stay for a bit of rest and recuperation with the Filipino prostitutes. To keep order, the hotel has hired a whole load of hard-looking bouncers from Nigeria. On the plus side, it does serve the cheapest beer in Ajman."

"How do you know? Been in?"

"As if Diana would let me loose in there. Do you know what's funny though? The hotel's tag line is 'Leisure with Pleasure'! You couldn't make it up. I laughed my arse off when I found that out."

Next door was the more salubrious Saray Beach Hotel, which, John told me, was also popular with Russian tourists, though more affluent ones. I asked why so many Russians were coming to Ajman. Dubai seemed the more obvious choice.

"Hotels are cheaper for one thing, and usually less busy. Plus, if the traffic's okay, you can be in downtown Dubai in forty-five minutes. So it makes sense to a lot of them, especially when they find out that the hotels are actually rather nice."

We walked through the grand entrance of the Saray straight into a gorgeous outdoor area at the rear: a holiday brochure scene of palm trees, blue lapping water and sun loungers, which spoiled the scene somehow because fat middle-aged Russians were lazing about in them.

One hefty male sunbather sported a humongous bronzed belly; his girth was squeezed into a tiny pair of black Speedos. Out on the beach, John and I watched Olga from Vladivostok, an obese lady with massively drooping breasts, paddling in the water. She caught my gaze and looked like she was about to charge, and so I turned in the other direction, noticing another large lady, this one snoring on a sun bed. I turned to John. "So are these the superbabes you spy on from your apartment?"

"Yes, Jason, these are exactly who I mean."

We wandered over to the beach bar and ordered a couple of cooling lagers. When they arrived, I asked John how he found living in Ajman compared to Qatar.

John took a large gulp of his drink and so did I. Drinking a cool beer on a beach in the Middle East had to be one of the best things in the world. "There's no comparison. It's a much freer life here. We have none of the bureaucracy you have in Qatar – well not much, anyway – and travel is much easier; Dubai's on the doorstep and so is Oman. The traffic is nowhere near as bad, and here's something else – Emiratis are much nicer than Qataris are. They seem more...cultured."

We both watched an obese Russian couple waddle over to the pool. They climbed in, submerging themselves under the water, their heads popping up like hippos in a river.

"Do you know what I've noticed about the Russians?" John said. "On the public beaches, the ones close to our apartment, they sunbathe until late afternoon. That's their limit. Then, when they're gone, the Indians and Pakistanis come down, men, women and sometimes their kids. They stay until sunset; then it's time for the Egyptians and Palestinians to come and have barbecues. When they pack their bags – usually late at night – it's the turn of the Emiratis who park their Land Cruisers and clap, bang drums and drink endless amounts of coffee from paper cups. The next morning, the beach is covered."

John looked at his watch. "Right then, Jason. I have to go and pick the kids up from swimming. But we'll meet back here at seven. Then I'll take you to the den of inequity and hedonism otherwise known as the Ajman Beach Club."

I watched him leave, drained the last of my drink and walked next door to the Kempinski so I could grab something to eat.

7

John grinned. A few hours had passed and it was now dark. The scene outside the Ajman Beach Club had changed from eerily silent to hectic activity. "I told you this place was a den of sin."

The Ajman Beach Club was busy with crowds of people and lines of cars waiting to get in. Everybody in Ajman, it seemed, wanted a piece of the action at the Beach Club. But then I realised I was wrong; not everyone wanted to visit the Ajman Beach Club: only men.

John and I opened the door of a small nightclub called Thirumayam. The single room inside Thirumayam was about the same size as a small UK pub. It was dark and blaring with Indian music. A set of chairs and tables faced the raised stage at the front, where five young Indian women, in full saris, were sitting on a bench. Another young woman, similarly attired, was dancing. It was hardly a titillating show, but the audience on the cheap seats were enthralled, every one of them an Indian man. With their wives and girlfriends thousands of miles away, and with no prospect of seeing them for a while, these women offered a tempting proposition.

"Are they prostitutes?" I whispered to John.

He nodded. "I think so. Every now and again one of them will disappear with one of the men."

We stepped outside, closing the door behind us. All around were similar nightclubs, each offering a different slant on international prostitution. Shebele specialised in African women, Baywatch specialised in Filipinos and another catered for Pakistanis. We left the nightclubs and relocated to a bar at the far side of the complex. It served fish and chips and pints of Guinness. Unsurprisingly, it was popular with Ajman's Western ex-pat population. John and I found a table and sat down. I still couldn't believe what I'd just seen.

"Later this evening," said John, "the Land Cruisers will start queuing up: Emiratis waiting for their turn with the prostitutes."

"And the authorities allow it?"

"They'll have a purge every now and again. But it's a bit half-arsed, if you know what I mean. I think they'd rather brush it under the carpet, or just ignore it, rather than deal with the real issue: human trafficking. A lot of these girls have come here under false pretences. They thought they were getting work as housemaids or domestic cleaners. And then they end up here. That's the really sad story here."

After a few more drinks, it was time for John and me to say goodbye. It had been great catching up with him, and gaining a little insight into life inside the smallest of the seven Emirates. We wished each other well and headed our separate ways.

8

So that was it. My journey around the Middle East had ended. From the beauty and bullets of Beirut to the leech vendors of Istanbul, from the glamour of Doha's skyline to the historical temples of Jordan, I had enjoyed a wealth of sights and sounds across Arabia. I had swum in the Dead Sea, seen dolphins in Oman, almost bought a gold bar in Abu Dhabi and experienced the warmth of the Kurdish people in Iraq. I'd proved that the Middle East is a region to be embraced and enjoyed, not to be feared. Not once in my travels had I seen a hint of malice, a glint of an unfriendly stare or any sign of Islamic extremism. No, all I'd seen were smiles from people genuinely proud of their heritage.

The one regret of my travels was not visiting Yemen. Not that I didn't try. At one point, I even booked some flights and a hotel, but after a spate of kidnappings and a round of deadly car bombs, I cancelled and flew to Kuwait instead. But even so, the draw of Yemen, and especially its old world capital, Sana'a, pulls me. Hopefully one day I shall get there, and also to Iran, a country shrouded in relative mystery but renowned as having some of the most hospitable and welcoming people on Earth. The one thing I am thankful for is that my wife and I managed to get to Syria before the madness of civil war erupted.

Inside the Ajman Kempinski, I wandered onto my hotel balcony, watching the line of twinkling lights moving across the black ocean: container ships transporting building materials around the Gulf. Below me, in the elegantly titled Zani-Bar, the sound of Russian tourists enjoying a final nightcap was loud enough to carry over the din of the waves. I stood for a few more moments, savouring the ocean smell of Arabia. It was time to go home.

Top row: Ajman Corniche; The golden dome of the Sharjah Archaeological Museum
Middle row: A cannon sits proudly outside Sharjah Museum; One of the nightclubs of Ajman Beach Club; Sharjah Ferris wheel
Bottom row: A mosque in Sharjah; The gorgeous beach of the Ajman Kempinski

If you have enjoyed this book by Jason Smart, then perhaps you will also like his other books, which are all available from Amazon.

The Red Quest

Flashpacking through Africa

The Balkan Odyssey

Temples, Tuk-tuks and Fried Fish Lips

Panama City to Rio de Janeiro

Bite Size Travel in North America

Crowds, Colour, Chaos

Rapid Fire Europe

Meeting the Middle East

Take Your Wings and Fly

Visit his website www.theredquest.com for more details.

Printed in Great Britain
by Amazon